PENGUIN HANDBOOKS

EYEOPENERS!

Beverly Kobrin earned an undergraduate degree in Music Education from the New England Conservatory of Music in 1957, a master's degree with a major in Education from Stanford University in 1972, and a doctorate in Elementary Curriculum and Instruction from Brigham Young University in 1978. She has supervised music in the elementary grades in Mount Lebanon, Pennsylvania, and taught general music in junior high school in Quincy, Massachusetts. Dr. Kobrin has taught the fourth, fifth, and sixth grades as well as gifted children from first through eighth grades in Mountain View, California. While continuing to teach, she has, since 1980, simultaneously published *The Kobrin Letter,* the only periodical to review and recommend children's nonfiction literature exclusively.

Dr. Kobrin also conducts workshops on the use of children's nonfiction books at home and in the classroom. By June 1988, she had addressed 12,158 parents, teachers, librarians, and others at 193 sessions in 115 cities in the United States and Canada. (She keeps a computerized list.)

Beverly Kobrin has a nonfiction-reading, 28-year-old son, and she lives in Palo Alto, California, with her pugnacious cat Monte and her very, very patient husband.

BEVERLY KOBRIN

EYEOPENERS!

How to Choose and Use Children's Books About Real People, Places, and Things

Photographs by RICHARD STEINHEIMER
and SHIRLEY BURMAN

PENGUIN BOOKS

PENGUIN BOOKS
Published by the Penguin Group
Viking Penguin Inc., 40 West 23rd Street,
New York, New York 10010, U.S.A.
Penguin Books Ltd, 27 Wrights Lane,
London W8 5TZ, England
Penguin Books Australia Ltd, Ringwood,
Victoria, Australia
Penguin Books Canada Ltd, 2801 John Street,
Markham, Ontario, Canada L3R 1B4
Penguin Books (N.Z.) Ltd, 182–190 Wairau Road,
Auckland 10, New Zealand

Penguin Books Ltd, Registered Offices:
Harmondsworth, Middlesex, England

First published in simultaneous hardcover and paperback editions by
Viking Penguin Inc., 1988
Published simultaneously in Canada

1 3 5 7 9 10 8 6 4 2

Grateful acknowledgment is made for permission to reprint "Slow Reader" from
Please, Mrs. Butler by Allan Ahlberg (Viking Kestrel, 1983). Copyright ©
Allan Ahlberg, 1983. By permission of Penguin Books Ltd.

Library of Congress Cataloging in Publication Data
Kobrin, Beverly.
Eyeopeners! : how to choose and use children's
books about real people, places, and things.
1. Children's literature—History and criticism.
I. Title.
PN1009.A1K597 1988   809'.89282   88–40115
ISBN 0–670–82073–3
0–14–046830–7 (pbk.)

Printed in the United States of America by
R. R. Donnelley & Sons Company, Harrisonburg, Virginia
Set in ITC Garamond Light

To my sister, Betty Cooley,

my son, David,

and my husband and coauthor, Don,
who lets me take all the credit—
and, of course, the responsibility for
any Eyeopening errors and omissions.

Contents

Acknowledgments

With an undergraduate degree in music and a doctoral dissertation on the use of the hand-held calculator, it may seem strange that I am now the author of a book on how to choose and use children's nonfiction literature. My circuitous route was shaped and my life enriched by many talented people whose paths I've crossed.

While my gratitude extends to scores of people, I'd like to acknowledge these individuals for their help and their inspiration: my mother, Pearl Mason, who read to me and taught me how to read; my father, Morris Mason, who taught me how to work; Dorothy Grenbeaux, my now-retired principal, under whose wise guidance students and teachers learned and grew as individuals; Barbara Armstrong and Beth McLean, teaching colleagues whose creativity fired mine; Jim Jacobs, whose class in children's literature changed my life; Andrea Stryer, with whom I co-taught my first children's nonfiction literature course; Jan Lieberman, whose friendship, creativity, and boundless enthusiasm for the best in children's literature buoys me; Steve Herb and the other gifted librarians and teachers who patiently tolerated my repeated requests for details about their books-to-kids connections.

Bill Morris and the late Bill Backer among the many marketing pros at publishers, who warmly welcomed me to the trade and generously provide thousands of books for me to consider; Ralph Libby, Roger Bonilla, Elnor Paul, indeed all the Palo Alto reference librarians who field my endless questions; Katie Obringer and her staff at the Palo Alto Children's Library and their counterparts in Mountain View, who graciously share their collections and ideas; Former District Librarian Judy Laird, the staff and children of Sacramento's San Juan School District for their cooperation with this book's photographs; Shirley Burman and Dick Steinheimer, who took the photos; the authors and illustrators of children's books that enthrall me as an adult as much as they did when I was a child.

Deborah Brodie, my persistent, patient, and ever-positive editor, who gave me the welcome opportunity, at age fifty-three, to once again alter my course by becoming an author.

Introduction

Although I had spent my adolescence and most of my adulthood in Springfield, Massachusetts, where Beverly Kobrin spent her childhood, we had never met until a November evening in 1982 when she cornered me in a Washington, D.C., book and coffee shop. Through tea she admonished me for not paying enough attention to nonfiction books for children, through dinner she listed the books that were too good to be missed by anyone, and through dessert she stated what she planned to do about such neglect and need.

More than four hours after we began the conversation, I waved goodbye to her at the subway track and thought to myself, I'm so glad she's on our side. All of us who cherish the world of reading and children can gratefully exclaim, "What a friend we have in Beverly Kobrin!"

And then on my walk to my hotel that evening, I pondered the points she'd made about children's growth through nonfiction. Sure, *Call of the Wild* had been my first true love in reading, but that same year (1953) I'd been given a book called *The Golden Treasury of Natural History,* which still sits on my bookshelf—thumbprinted and worn into a second binding by two generations of Treleases. No history or science textbook came even close to rivaling it in my mind. We read it, traced its pictures, reported from it, and daydreamed over it.

I thought about my family's encyclopedia volumes, those pages tracing the human anatomy that somehow never lost their fascination for us, the pages of wildlife, flora, military armor—pictures that I'd pored over endlessly in search of answers to those mysterious childhood questions: Who am I? Why am I?

I remembered my brother and I waiting impatiently each Thursday for the mailman to deliver the week's issue of *Sports Illustrated.* Groping our way through adolescence, we were seeking heroes who weren't dead yet, who were still sweating and punching and kicking and running. And between devouring the magazine's pages and pasting its covers on our walls, we read a lot. By the time I read J. P. Marquand, John Dos Passos, William Faulkner, and John Steinbeck in college, I'd already read their nonfiction in *Sports Illustrated.*

And the more we read, the better we got at it; and the better we got at it, the more we liked it. So pretty soon we were reading not just the articles but the ads and the letters to the editor. And before long, we were reading sports biographies and basketball strategy books from the library.

Walking up Connecticut Avenue from the subway, I wondered what made it all so indelible, even after all these years. It certainly mattered that all of it was elective and unforced. We were free to roam and graze, encouraged but not regimented, surrounded by magazines, newspapers, and books, nurtured by parents who were readers. I tried to remember if there were any reading-level warnings on the books and magazines to sound alarms that we were, heaven forbid, reading beyond our grade level. Thankfully there were none. Also, it was real. Books and writing about people and places and things you could touch and see appealed to us greatly.

And then there was the way all of it was written. At the time, I didn't know *why* recreational reading was more interesting than textbooks; I just knew it was. Today I know why; indeed anyone with experience in education can tell you why: Textbooks are written by either committees or an author who has to please a committee of editors, who in turn must please a curriculum committee, which must please a school board (another committee).

So textbook writing and publishing decisions are made on the basis of the lowest common denominator—the fewest number of committee members or special interest groups who will be offended by a pabulum text. The end result is a book without a personality and voice, a textbook without texture. And for this reason, no one grows up having a favorite textbook. (You never hear someone say, "I'll always remember my sixth-grade science book, *Meadows and Streams.*")

By the time I walked into my hotel, I clearly saw Beverly's point of view, a message about nonfiction writing that had been staring me in the face since childhood. All I'd needed was someone to open my eyes. Children are naturally curious about everything. Give them access to good nonfiction books, books with hearts by people with voices, and they'll read them up ravenously. And the more they read, the more they know.

For nearly fifteen years before the Commission on Reading (in *Becoming a Nation of Readers*) was calling for fewer textbooks and more *real* books in classrooms, Beverly Kobrin had been doing it the right way in her classrooms. Years before we'd heard about the information explosion brought by computers, she and her students had been detonating with books. And all along she was taking notes and keeping lists of which books made the biggest impression—of which you, the reader of *Eyeopeners!,* are now the beneficiary.

In closing, let me share one other thing I learned on that fall evening: Dr. Beverly Kobrin would make a terrible politician. She's not into unrealistic promises or theories; no glad-handing from this woman. Instead, she's into hands-on solutions to everyday reading problems. She has practical, real-life things parents, teachers, librarians, and even grandparents can do to keep children's natural curiosity from draining to empty. Instead of closing your eyes, she'll open them to books and ideas that in turn will open the world to child and student.

And unlike some politicians, she's not into long introductions. So I'd better get out of the way.

—Jim Trelease, author of
The Read-Aloud Handbook

EYEOPENERS!

1

What's in This Handbook?

Are you a parent, a grandparent, a teacher, a librarian, a friend of one, about to become one, or any combination thereof? If so, this book is a bundle of ideas just for you—a passel of persuasive prose about the pros of children's nonfiction books.

The more than 500 nonfiction books I review and discuss will interest just about everybody. These eye-openers are a delight to look at, a pleasure to read, and a source of fascinating information on subjects that hold children and other readers spellbound. Get some and see for yourself.

Nonfiction books published for the general public are called trade books. A trade book is "not a textbook, not a technical treatise, but the sort of thing that could (and the publisher hopes will) interest everybody," as *Webster's Third New International Dictionary* explains. If you thought that "nonfiction books" mean textbooks or turgid, data-filled tomes, you are in for a wonderful surprise.

AMONG THE VERY BEST

The attractive nonfiction books I recommend present factual material in imaginative, enriching, exciting ways. I've culled them from the best of those published in the United States, Canada, and Great Britain. All were in print and available in the U.S. at the start of 1988.

I believe nonfiction trade books are an essential element in the education of all children. I explain why in Chapter 2 and describe how I came to integrate them into my classroom teaching in Chapter 3.

In Chapter 4, you'll read how you can use nonfiction books to encourage reading and enhance a child's innate need to know. I've offered tips to help you link books to childrens' everyday experiences.

If you are a teacher, those tips can become Non-Book-Reports (see Chapter 8), assignments that use books as stepping stones to more reading or activities. Since you may play many roles—parent or grandparent and teacher or librarian—simultaneously, I hope you'll look through all the chapters written especially for you.

YOUR CHILDREN'S LINK TO LITERATURE

Although I espouse nonfiction, I do not believe it better or more valuable than fiction. They are literary coequals. In Chapter 4, "Give your Kids TLC—the Total Literature Connection," I explain that children deserve the best of *all* literature.

I've recommended more than 500 books in the Guide. You are entitled to know how I selected them from the thousand or so review copies that publishers send me each year. On page 56, just before the reviews themselves, you'll find the beginning of "How to Judge a Book by Its Cover—and Nine Other Clues." In that chapter, I tell you what I look for in children's nonfiction—and found in the books I've recommended.

Please remember that my recommendations are a guide—not gospel. Ultimately, it is *your* attitude and the enthusiasm of *your* recommendation that most influence your youngsters' willingness to read.

I've arranged my recommendations in the Guide, pages 70–277, by topics—more than 60 of them. This is browsing territory—for good books and good ideas. Look up a topic that fascinates your youngsters and you'll find a group of books on the subject.

FIND IT FAST!

If you, or a student hunting information for a research project, need books on a particular topic, turn at once to the Quick-Link Index on page 281. You will be led to appropriate books regardless of their titles: *What's for Lunch?,* for example, when you search for books on seashore life! I've explained how to use the Quick-Link Index on page 278.

A conventional, alphabetical listing of the titles, authors, and illustrators of the books I have mentioned follows the Quick-Link Index.

Now, reach into the book bundle and pull out some ideas!

Good reading,

2

WHY NONFICTION?

Why a book devoted to children's nonfiction books?

Good question! Let me count the whys:

1. CHILDREN ARE FASCINATED BY THE REAL WORLD

As infants, they reach out and touch—everyone and everything. They explore, taking things out of whatever they're in and putting them into whatever they're out of. As soon as children speak, they're a fountain of questions. I often thought my son, David, was born with a silver question mark in his mouth. He was a steady stream of whos, whats, wheres, whens, and whys. As author Anne Weiss once said, "Kids are born hungry to learn. That's why the word *why* was invented!"[1]

Eye-opening nonfiction books, books about real people, places, and things, begin to satisfy that curiosity. The best nonfiction answers questions and inspires even more.

2. CHILDREN AREN'T GETTING ENOUGH
NONFICTION BOOKS TO READ

The adults in kids' lives simply aren't as familiar with nonfiction as they are with fiction. Many hear the negative-sounding term *nonfiction*, think *ugly*, and lose interest. (Imagine naming a daughter "nonSally"!) Author Jane Yolen says the word *nonfiction* sounds as if it had been in a contest with fiction—and lost.[2]

Some people equate nonfiction with the dull, boring textbooks they had to read in school. Truth is, good nonfiction is everything most textbooks are not; it is well written, well illustrated, and well designed by first-rate authors, illustrators, editors, and art directors. You'll find more than 500 titles in the Guide—just to get you started!

Also, many people, including parents, professional educators, and booksellers, believe "recreational" reading means only make-believe. A 1987 Gallup survey reveals that, while adults buy equal numbers of fiction and nonfiction books for themselves, that's not so for children's books; they buy "predominantly fiction (70%), with nonfiction titles representing only 29% of purchases."[3]

Children *do* love a good story, but they are fascinated by facts, a fact too often ignored. Time and again in bookstores, I hear clerks say, "What you want is a good story..." and watch as they direct gift-seeking buyers to the shelves of fiction. But when *I* redirect them (I rarely control myself), more often than not they buy a nonfiction book.

Teachers and librarians at my workshops describe children's literature courses they've taken that had little or no time set aside for nonfiction. They speak of colleagues who won't let children write book reports on nonfiction and librarians who booktalk only fiction. These are symptoms of the neglect of nonfiction.

Nonfiction has been "literature non grata" when it comes to book awards, too. Of the 125 listed in *Awards and Prizes,* published by the Children's Book Council,[4] nonfiction is eligible for a mere 27. Humph! But perhaps Russell Freedman's well-deserved 1988 Newbery Medal will now open eyes to the fine art of fiction's counterpart.

3. NO ONE ELSE HAS WRITTEN A BOOK LIKE THIS

Though there have been many articles about the value of children's nonfiction in professional journals, I know of only two other books that have addressed the subject:[5] both are excellent, scholarly, and persuasive reference works. Neither, however, set out to recommend specific up-to-date titles and to suggest ways they help children learn at home and in school. Both, unfortunately, are also out of print. I've created this guide to provide you with a practical reference book, so you can find useful ideas at a glance.

4. NONFICTION HAS BEEN THE UGLY DUCKLING FAR TOO LONG

Ladies and gentlemen: May I present ... the swan.

3

How I Began...

"Mrs. Kobrin! Mrs. Kobrin! You know that book I read? My dad and I went out after dark to look for the North Star like it said and..."

"Mrs. Kobrin! Mrs. Kobrin! They ate the whole thing! I picked one of the recipes from that cookbook and made it for my family last night. Mom says..."

"Mrs. Kobrin! Mrs. Kobrin!..."

I didn't always have kids bursting into my classroom, erupting with excitement about books, homework, or what we'd read in class. I used to be greeted by rather stoical children prepared for another day (yawn!) with paper, pencil, and texts.

On a warm fall day in 1969, I'd walked into Whisman Elementary School in Mountain View, California, enthusiastic about inspiring kids to read and learn. I began teaching the fourth grade the way I had been taught to teach: use textbooks and workbooks. For everything. Ad infinitum.

After a few weeks on the job, I found that textbook-per-topic teaching unrealistically separated each area of the curriculum into periods regulated by the clock: Reading Time, Math Time, Social Studies Time,

Science Time. Related workbook assignments conditioned my children to strive for "right" answers, rather than to think creatively. And the whole process meant hour after hour of Correcting Time for me! What had seemed practical in college theory proved impractical in classroom practice.

My students were learning that each subject began with a capital letter, came at a certain time of day, and always had questions that were marked *right* or *wrong*. They were not learning about how closely subjects are related, or that what we did in the classroom has relevance to their lives away from school. *I* was instructing and correcting. *We* were not exploring and challenging. I was bored and so were my kids.

So I abandoned the routine. Little by little, I replaced textbooks with trade books. I surrounded my students with an ever-changing assortment I'd perused and picked especially for them. My classroom bulged with books borrowed from nearby public libraries. Books about motorcycles, mummies, dinosaurs, Disneyland, and Big Foot. Baseball, popcorn, pirates, space ships, and whatever else they expressed interest in.

The effect was electric.

Enthusiasm replaced ennui. My children demanded more reading time. They simply couldn't wait to open the books I'd brought. And once opened, they were read—by those who requested them and others who caught their excitement. Nothing is as effective as kids' personal endorsements in a classroom. Every time one child said, "Wow! Mrs. Kobrin, look at this!" or "That was baaaad!" (read: "not to be missed"), everyone else wanted the book. The room buzzed with energy and book talk.

I did away with workbooks. Each week my youngsters reported on at least one of the books they read. I read every one, then created Non-Book-Reports, assignments designed to use each book as a stepping stone to other books and subject areas. Assignments that involved the youngsters' families, whenever possible. (You'll find my ideas on Non-Book-Reports in Chapter 8.)

By 1977, I had been teaching by the book—library book, that is— for almost a decade. During the summer, while at Brigham Young University completing requirements for my doctorate, I registered for Children's Literature #628.

The first morning of class, Dr. James Jacobs, Associate Professor of

Elementary Education, asked us to sign up for a small group project. We were to select one category from his list (fantasy, folktales, historical fiction, and the like) and, at the end of the term, "sell" our choice to the class as a whole.

I was fourth from last when the sign-up sheet reached me. Every topic was spoken for but one. Surprised, I raised my hand. "Dr. Jacobs, no one has chosen nonfiction..."

Before I could finish the sentence, my classmates, experienced teachers all, reacted as though I'd nicked a nerve. "Nonfiction? It's so BORING!"

I was amazed. Nonfiction was the backbone of my teaching. We couldn't have been thinking about the same thing. When I asked why they'd reacted so strongly, I learned, sadly, that they equated nonfiction with textbooks.

Even then, there were few activities I enjoyed more than talking about teaching with good books—particularly nonfiction. I signed my name under nonfiction and persuaded the three still-undeclared teachers to join me. Seven weeks later, our eye-opening presentation received a standing ovation from our classmates. They were sold on nonfiction.

That presentation is where this book began.

I returned to California after my summer at BYU. In 1979, in addition to teaching in elementary school, I began teaching university extension classes, speaking at reading and library association conferences, and conducting workshops for teachers, librarians, and parents. Each presentation had a single focus: how to use children's nonfiction literature in school and at home.

In September of 1980, I began publishing *The Kobrin Letter,* still the only periodical devoted exclusively to the review and recommendation of worthwhile children's nonfiction.

Since then, I've been selling the virtues of nonfiction to every parent, teacher, and librarian I can reach. And the books continue to receive standing ovations. When I review the anonymous evaluations after each workshop, I read...

"I see nonfiction now as a way to stretch the imagination, not just for information. It's a whole new world."

"I've always been a fiction-pusher, but I'm thinking of changing my stripes."

"I feel that I won't be able to sleep tonight. I don't know of any bookstore open this late. I know what I'm going to be doing this weekend."

"I will use nonfiction more often than just to teach facts. There are many ideas that grow from one book—the book is just the beginning."

Readers, I hope this book of eye-openers will be *your* beginning.

4

Give Your Kids TLC—
the Total Literature Connection

In the September 1980 issue of *The Kobrin Letter*—Volume 1, Number 1—I described myself as "a parent, a teacher, and a zealous advocate of children's nonfiction literature." I still am. But that doesn't mean I believe nonfiction to be more important than fiction. On the contrary, children need both.

My goal is to persuade everyone who links children and books to give equal time to nonfiction and fiction. I call that linkage TLC—the Total Literature Connection.

READING IS MORE IMPORTANT THAN CLASSIFYING

The division into fiction and nonfiction is often clearer to adults than to children. Youngsters who have experienced emotions described in a story "know" the story is true. After all, the same thing happened to them! And kids who look at a drawing of an okapi, a short-necked creature related to a giraffe, sometimes consider it make-believe. After all, they've never "seen" it.

Often it's difficult to draw a sharp line between fiction and nonfiction. In this nonfiction guide, you'll find reviews of David Macaulay's *Cathedral*, Aliki's *Medieval Feast*, and Robert McClung's *Rajpur, Last of the Bengal Tigers*. Each character or object is the author's creation, the fruit of skillful research. There is no anthropomorphism—the tiger Rajpur doesn't speak or exhibit human emotions, nor are any of the narratives embellished with dialogue. These fine books are about fictitious people, places, and things, but they accurately depict their lifelike subjects.

Whether you label them fiction or nonfiction is unimportant. Don't let the terms close your eyes to the power and worth of both. Supply your youngsters with good literature.

I've devoted 90 + percent of this book to nonfiction to redress an historical imbalance. But this is a guide—not gospel. Balance the books in this handbook with recommendations in other guides. Think *good literature*. There are more than 500 volumes of it right here.

READ NONFICTION ALOUD, TOO

The Read-Aloud Handbook[6] has probably done more to encourage parents to read aloud to children than any other book. It is making an important contribution to the raising of children. After reading Jim Trelease's book, however, you might infer that only fiction is suitable for reading aloud. Nothing could be further from the truth. You *can* read nonfiction aloud to children. I know!

Nonfiction books made my students and me cry over Christa Mc-Auliffe's death, become angry over hunger in America, find ourselves helpless in the face of California condors' impending extinction, feel on top of the world because we'd solved a tough puzzle, marvel at the belly of a rattler magnified 9,000 times, and fall in love with pandas. You do not have to read make-believe to entrance children. By their very nature, they are information sponges. They want to know about the real world.

By the way, you don't have to read aloud whole books. Much nonfiction is particularly suited to reading in bits and pieces. Feel free to pick and choose from many books, and to mix and match excerpts from nonfiction with fiction as you make the read-aloud TLC. When I read *Incident at Hawk's Hill* to sixth-graders, for example, I insert excerpts from books about badgers. I've matched *Charlotte's Web* with *A Spider Might* and *Joel: Growing Up a Farm Man* and *The Wild, Wild Cookbook* with *Sign of the Beaver*. You will find ideas for other TLC choices when you scan the Tips in the Guide.

TRUST THE KIDS

Children will read, if you surround them with books about subjects that capture their fancies. You'll attract them with books that take them to the scene, behind the scene, or to any other place they cannot ordinarily go. You'll enthrall them with books that reveal what lies beneath their skin, nestles in the niches of the planet, or soars through other solar systems. You'll captivate kids with views of what was, what is, and what might be—in fiction and in the real world.

In medicine, TLC means tender, loving care. That's what you're giving your children as you make the Total Literature Connection.

5

For Parents Especially

It's up to you, you know. You're in charge. Teachers and librarians can do only so much in the little time available. Most of the job of linking kids and books must be done before and after school, on weekends and vacations—during the approximately 80 percent of a child's waking hours spent outside the schoolroom.

How can you link kids to books?

First of all, remember that kids are copycats. If *you* set aside time for books and reading, odds are your children will. If you don't, chances are they won't.

Second, memorize four letters—*R, E, A, D*. They'll help remind you of some ways you can raise the odds that your child will link up with books.

R: *Read*—alone, together, silently, or out loud. YOU are the most influential Reader in your family.

E: Establish an *Environment* that Encourages reading

A: Aid and Abet reading by your Actions: Adjust YOUR *Attitude* if necessary.

D: *DO IT*. NOW! WITH NONFICTION.

R = READ

Take a tip from teachers. Sustained Silent Reading (SSR) isn't reserved for schoolrooms. SSR is the activity teachers use to help children acquire the habit and discover the pleasure of being alone with something good to read. I call it SQUIRT for Sustained Quiet UnInterrupted Reading Time.

As my son was growing up, I set aside a short reading-to-myself time each day while he was up and about. I was out of bounds, but David could set his reading chair or spread out on the rug next to me to look through his own books. As long as there was "No Talking." Pretty soon, *my* reading-to-myself time became *our* reading-to-myself time.

At first, we were alone together for a very short time, so that David could become accustomed to the rules. As his attention span increased, so did reading time. But I kept it just beneath his limit. We never went beyond fifteen minutes. The duration was unimportant; its repetition—and ease—essential.

Read with Your Children

I wanted to establish a custom. We read to ourselves every day and, as I had hoped, it became a habit. As much a habit as my reading aloud, another daily event. Our days were never complete unless we shared both times. He doesn't remember that he pulled his chair up to mine with "Reading time, Mom." I do. He doesn't remember—but he still reads.

Set aside alone-together sessions with your youngsters. Make certain they have many books to peruse and that they understand that no talking is the rule. Keep the first experience short to guarantee success. Stop before their span of attention ends, so that they look forward to tomorrow's session when they can be "grown up" and "read" quietly. Remember, you want to establish a habit of enjoying a private time with a book.

Read newspapers, magazines, cookbooks, small appliance manuals. Even phone books. In many areas, they are a handy quick reference for community and emergency services, lifesaving techniques, and time zones. We are surrounded by practical nonfiction that is both fascinating and enlightening.

The phone book brought my son countless hours of pleasure as soon as he was able to identify his name. He loved to see it in print and no matter how often we went to the library, he'd head for the telephone book collection to see where else in the world he could find a Kobrin.

As they get older, let your children join the ranks of family read-alouders. While his dad was recovering from recurring bouts of illness, David read aloud from the *Guinness Book of World Records.* Together, they pursued trivia (before the game was invented) from the assorted almanacs and books of lists in his collection—nonfiction was and still is his favorite reading. Long automobile rides were dramatically shortened as all of us (except the driver) took turns reading aloud.

Use every opportunity. Share cookbooks in the kitchen. Before a trip, have children read about the destination; as you travel, let them read maps. Read movie reviews together. Have your child keep a weather log, getting information daily from the newspaper.

Once he began to read, David read to my husband, Don, or me while we prepared dinner. He'd go over recipes aloud to make certain we didn't forget anything. At the end of the day, he became the "real, live TV newsman" and read aloud cartoons and brief squibs to us from the newspapers, as well as articles he found interesting. He'd read to us from the junk mail to see if it contained anything we needed.

Choice Nonfiction for Children

Read nonfiction aloud to your youngsters from the time they can look at pictures with you. Their eyes will open wide when you *Take Another Look* together. Consider *Holes,* meet *Farm Animals,* guess *What Happens Next?,* discover *Animal Runners,* visit *Zoos,* learn about *26 Letters and 99 Cents,* compare *All Kinds of Feet.*

As your children grow older, read about *Bananas,* learn that *Chickens Aren't the Only Ones,* discover *How Sports Came to Be.* Share *Lots of Rot* the next time food spoils; *Kids Camping from Aaaaiii! to Zip!* before you leave on a family excursion; *The Louisville Slugger* after the next baseball game; *How Do Ants Know When You're Having a Picnic?,* you know when; *What Was the Wicked Witch's Real Name?* if cheering up's needed; *Why Does My Nose Run?* when there's a cold in the house; and any of the others in this handbook, whenever.

Read Adult Books, Too

And don't limit yourself to children's literature. Read adult nonfiction aloud. It doesn't matter if youngsters don't understand all your words, what matters is that you speak new ones. They'll pick up the general meaning of the unfamiliar word from the familiar ones that surround it. That's how their vocabulary increases. When youngsters are young, you buy clothes a little too big so that they can grow into them. The same should be true for books. The more language children hear, the more they will use; the more fluently they speak, the easier reading becomes.

Among my husband's favorite read-alouds were Gerald Durrell's books for adults (*Bafut Beagles,* to name one) describing the zoologist's animal-gathering trips for zoos. After Don read about the exotic animals Dr. Durrell had to care for, he and David would look in our encyclopedia and/or go to the library to find out more about the creatures.

When children start to choose their own books, *never* admonish them with "That book's too easy (or hard) for you. Put it back and take one that's harder (or easier)." Books that are "right" for children are the ones they want to read—or look at—now!

No one chastises us for flirting with books that are too easy or too hard. As adults we can take pleasure in beautifully illustrated books designed for toddlers and read nonfiction children's books as an introduction to unfamiliar subjects. We browse through weighty tomes, taste the language, look at the photographs and illustrations, and perhaps read the captions in books far too technical for us to understand. And we relax on occasion with an indulgence of romances, mysteries, fantasies, mass-market blockbusters, and other fast-read publications that provide a breezy change of pace.

Allow children the same freedom. A book is its own reward. That reward is unique to each reader. Kids cannot learn which books are "right" for them until they—on their own—have discovered which ones aren't.

Keep Kids Thinking Critically

If children are to be critical readers and thinkers, it's essential that they learn to check and double-check what they've read in one place with what's written in another. Teach your children not to believe everything that's said. If they read something or hear something on TV that they distrust, encourage them to react. Show them how to look up facts, how to check several sources, how to challenge a position with one of their own. Using the information gained, encourage them to write to people they agree with—or do not. They can begin by writing to the manufacturers of toys that don't live up to their advertisements. Or, as the children in Colorado Springs, Colorado, did, cause the *Wall Street Journal* to reconsider suing their *Small Street Journal*.

Bedtime Is One of the Best Times

And, of course, remember books at bedtime. Few moments with children are as warm, loving, and long-remembered as those between tucking in and the last sweet-dreams kiss. Many adults say their strongest childhood memories are of a bedtime reading ritual. I remember my mother reading to me as vividly as if I'd fallen asleep last night to the sound of her voice. Share counting books, alphabet books, books about trains and dinosaurs, sharks and space flights, knights and motorcycles. Use wordless picture books, newspapers, magazines, comic books, and books of lists and world records. In whole or part. One book or many. Once or over and over and over again. Fact or fiction. Both.

E = ENVIRONMENT

Reading rooms and reference desks aren't only for libraries.

In your own home, you can provide a comfortable place to read. It doesn't have to be a whole room. Any nook or cranny with a comfortable chair—even pillows on the floor—will do. Make sure there's good lighting. Make certain there are special places to keep books neatly: on bookshelves or tabletops reserved for books-being-read.

Provide your youngsters with special places for their personal collections as soon as you begin buying books for them. Books do NOT belong in a toy box any more than your favorite records belong in a tool box. Make or purchase decorative bookmarks and bookplates. Treat books as honored guests.

Make a reading hat, jacket, apron, or special pin you and your toddlers can wear at reading time. Provide paper and crayons and encourage your children to draw pictures of what you are reading to them.

Build a home reference center. Start with the reference works you may already have: the dictionary, atlas, almanac, and phone book. Add books on subjects of interest to your children; sports, camping, space travel, movie stars, heavenly stars, fact books, and books of lists.

A = ATTITUDE

No matter how frequently you *say* that books and reading are important, you must *act* as though they are, or your children will not believe you. Remember that kids are copycats. They follow the leader. You.

Give books as gifts to your friends. Children's books. Don and I recently gave an artist friend Leonard Everett Fisher's *Alphabet Art* and *Number Art* (both Four Winds) as house gifts. He was delighted. We gave another friend's daughter *The Oxford Junior Companion to Music* (Oxford) for her first piano recital and marked a neighbor's Bar Mitzvah with *The Young Reader's Encyclopedia of Jewish History* (Viking Kestrel). Give books as presents to your children; to the new baby; to the new baby's sibling to celebrate the family addition; as an Afikoman prize during the Passover Seder or as stocking stuffers for Christmas; as end-of-the-school-year, moving-up-to-a-new-grade gifts; and for that extra special no-special-occasion, just-because-you're-you gift.

Suggest children give books to their friends on birthdays, when they are convalescing, moving away, or any other gift-worthy occasion. On your children's birthdays, donate money for books to the school library in their names. Volunteer to read aloud in your children's classrooms, at children's hospitals, or at senior citizen centers. Send grandparents with failing eyesight gifts of large-print books. Frequent Friends of the Library sales for bargains you can add to your own library—or your school's.

Read as a family. Set aside ten minutes every night for family alone-together time. Read the newspaper, a cookbook, the comics, *TV Guide*—whatever you read, do it together. Set aside a day a month (make it a habit) to demonstrate the fine art of browsing by visiting a library or bookstore as a family. Make part of your vacation budget a new book the whole family will enjoy. Pick it out together.

Friends of mine started a family read-two-books-a-month club. With family support, the youngsters in my classroom had little difficulty reading a book a week—about three dozen in a school year. That gave them a pretty good start in a country where an estimated 27 million adults do not read even one book a year. Your family could begin with a twelve-a-year pledge. And once you start, I'll bet you can't read just one book a month!

With the librarian's approval, donate books you no longer want to libraries, so others can enjoy them. As your children grow older, suggest they do the same. Ask the librarian to apply bookplates listing them as the donors or make your own bookplates with your children. They can't give whole libraries as Alfred Carnegie did, but it's a start.

D = DO IT NOW!

A few years ago, a parent/psychologist at one of my Washington State workshops told me that any activity done twenty-one consecutive days becomes a habit. (She was on day nine of reinforcing her New Year's resolutions!) If you and your children start today and read books together every day for a month, you will begin a habit that is likely to endure. And you will establish the positive attitude toward books and reading that will help your youngsters become better readers and thinkers.

But don't think your job is done once your child enters school. Parents too frequently tell me, "My child's in school now. The teacher can take over." That doesn't work. If your interest appears to diminish, your children will believe that "Mom and Dad don't think reading is important anymore." Teachers must have your support—in words and action.

Encourage Reading at School

While you're encouraging your children to read at home, find out what is happening at your school. Ask the principal how reading is encouraged there. Are library books granted equal time with textbooks? Are there daily schoolwide Sustained Silent Reading (SSR) and read-aloud times? Does the principal join in? Does your school board provide trained librarians, or is the very important task of selecting and presenting books to children left to untrained volunteers and inadequately trained paraprofessionals?

Have members from the community-at-large been asked to volunteer to read to the class? Throughout the school year, I invited adults from my students' neighborhood to visit our classroom: a mail carrier, a gas station owner, and a butcher were three. I asked each one to come just before read-aloud time. In that way, after we'd learned about our guests and their jobs, each could read an excerpt from whatever book was currently on my read-aloud agenda. Readers and listeners seemed to enjoy that part most of all.

How does the budget for the library compare with that for athletic equipment? Are the books in the library as up to date as the sports gear? At one of my workshops in the Northwest, a librarian told me her budget was facing a drastic cut. On the assumption that the community would more readily contribute bats and balls than books, she suggested the principal reduce funds for athletic equipment instead. He did. And, luckily, the community contributed. The local Lions Club provided the needed athletic gear and neither books nor ball games suffered.

Read your newspaper book review column. If children's books aren't included, write a letter to the editor or call and ask that they be reviewed.

Support Your Local Librarians

Make going to the public library a weekly event, at the very least. Introduce your child(ren) to the librarian. A dedicated children's librarian can have profound influence on an inquisitive young mind. By guiding book selection from a child's early years through the time that child makes his or her own choices, the librarian can raise and sustain interest in good books. A quick check of your municipal records will confirm that librarians' rewards are not received in the form of high salaries. Their satisfaction is derived from the pleasure of their patrons—your children and you.

Librarians love to be asked. Questions are their bread and butter. Ask your children's librarians for recommendations, suggest books for acquisition, discuss your reaction to books and invite your children to do so. When your library has story hours or seasonal reading programs, encourage your children to participate. And by all means, help keep the books circulating.

Support your school librarians, too. School is the best place for children to learn what librarians offer, what their specialized training and knowledge of the literature can add to learning. Parents can support

librarians by insisting they be retained and by asking school admin-
istrators to seek grant funds to augment library budgets. Your support
is critical: in my state, California, there was a 36 percent net decline
of librarians based at elementary school sites in the five years between
1981–82 and 1985–86.[7] Shameful!

Volunteers and/or aides can, of course, keep books in circulation
when budget cuts eliminate librarians. But when librarians disappear
and their replacements are in charge of passing out books one day
and ice cream the next, the message is clear: a librarian is no more
than a book distributor and it takes no special skill or training to be
one. During one of his morning commentaries on San Francisco's
public radio station KQED, Norm Howard said that librarians are the
protectors of the symbols of our heritage. That's a more appropriate
image for children to retain.

If the fabric of knowledge is woven of books, skilled librarians are
among the master weavers. Employ them!

Support Your Local Bookstore

The large, ubiquitous bookstore chains will survive without your children's book business, but your local bookstore with a good children's
department may not. And if your neighborhood is blessed with a shop
dealing exclusively with books for youngsters, that store cannot survive
without local support.

Employees of a chain (many of whom are working on a temporary
basis) may have an interest in children's books, but the chances are
they'll be familiar only with the most publicized titles. You'll find that
the proprietor and staff of a children's bookstore will know about or
will have read most of the stock; they know the literature and can
suggest books that are "right."

It helps, of course, if the people at the store know your children,
and that's easy to arrange: bring them along when you visit the store
or drop the older ones off to browse and let them make their own
purchases with gift or allowance money.

You Are the Most Important Resource

Your youngsters' principal route to reading is—you. Children learn by
observation. If you respect good books, have them around, frequent

their habitats, demand their use in school and, most importantly, read them yourself, then you are well on your way to developing children who read. And when those books are nonfiction, your readers will become critical thinkers as well.

With nonfiction titles from this guide, suggestions from your youngsters' teachers, and ideas from librarians and your bookshop proprietor, you can give the gifts that use no batteries and require no assembly. Eye-opening gifts that can be shared, savored, and cherished by generations of children.

6

For Grandparents Especially

I am not yet a grandparent. My grandchild isn't even a glint in my unmarried son's eye. But I'm ready. In my garage, I have accumulated (so far) nine forty-pound boxes of "grandchild books." Whenever I think of sharing them—some are the very ones I once read aloud to David—I smile. The serene smile I see on faces of friends as they speak about their grandchildren.

One such Cheshire grin inspired this "For Grandparents Especially" section. It radiated from my friend Addie Macovski's face as she described her exhausting but exhilarating day at the zoo with grandson Joshie. She was excitedly anticipating the next day, when the two of them would look through books with pictures of the animals they'd just seen. This was the first time I'd considered the deep bond between grandparents and their children's children or the special link books can provide in closing the two-generation gap.

I can't share personal anecdotes, but I've had little difficulty collecting books-and-grandchildren stories from others. Not one grandparent was too busy or in the least bit hesitant to share experiences with me anytime I asked—or before!

My neighbor Marti Wadensweiler, for example, told me about her four-year-old granddaughter's Book Bureau. Whenever Marisa visits, she heads straight for the bottom drawer, where "her" books are kept. No matter how many new ones Marti adds, Marisa always pulls out the same old favorite to be read "Now, gran'ma."

Author Milton Meltzer's grandson, Benjie, with parents who are "voracious readers," has all of the books Grandpa Milton and his wife saved from their childhood, as well as the ones Benjie's mom and her sister saved from theirs. I forgot to ask whether or not grandfather read aloud to grandson yet—Benjie was already five weeks old when I spoke to Milton.

Patricia Reilly Giff, also an author, reads to her grandson. Since infancy, James Patrick has been soothed by the sound of his grandmother's voice "reading" from memory picture books she's written and true stories she recalls about his great-great-grandmother and great-great-grand-father and their home in Ireland. When I mentioned the boxes in my garage, Pat told me she has a shelf in her study reserved for James Patrick's books and that present or future grandparents she meets across the country also have those "special" shelves.

The passage of parenthood's pressing responsibilities, it seems, provides grandparents the pleasure and luxury to Relax, Enjoy, Appreciate, and Dream with the youngest members of their family. Put them all together and they spell *R E A D*.

R = RELAX

Odds are, both parents of small children work today. Though they may reserve time to read to and with their youngsters, there is seldom enough of it. Grandparents, even those who work themselves, represent a reservoir of time unpressured by family-raising responsibilities. That's behind them. They can relax with book in hand and child on lap or snuggled close.

You may well be, in fact you probably are, the best audience your grandchildren have. When a book you share triggers a thought or a question, take the time to listen and take the question seriously. Children are information sponges; they'll absorb what you impart. Talk is important to children; the more youngsters talk, the easier reading becomes. If it's been a while since you've thought about parenting, you might like to read the chapter "For Parents Especially" to refresh your memory about books, reading, and little ones.

E = ENJOY

Enjoy introducing your grandchild to books you remember from your children's youth. Fill one "For *(grandchild's name)* Especially" drawer with those special volumes. I'm told that they and the memories they evoke are even richer when shared with grandchildren. They keep family stories alive and well and living in the hearts of another generation. They strengthen the bridge across a two-generation gap.

Enjoy the new books that have been published for children of all ages since your children's youth. You will be pleasantly surprised at their quality and variety. Set aside another drawer or shelf especially for them.

When on shopping trips or traveling—on business or pleasure—use spare time to browse through libraries and bookstores with new or used books. Search through thrift shops. At home, dig through trunks in the attic and cellar, if you have them, and boxes in the garage or closets if you don't, for family albums, old letters, postcards, report cards, newspapers, and other memorabilia.

As you plan vacations, read travel books with your grandchild so she or he will know where you will be going and what you expect to see. Send postcards from the places you read about together. When you return from your trip, you can compare what you saw with what the travel book said you would see. The two of you can make your own travel book out of the cards, as a souvenir. And don't forget to include among your gifts at least one children's book from a place you visited.

A = APPRECIATE

Appreciate your grandchild's interests. I'm told that's much easier to do with grandchildren than children. You need not agree with their likes and dislikes, but listen to them. Be a sounding board. Use your time together to help growing youngsters recognize their strengths and strengthen their weaknesses. Encourage when you can and expand horizons with books that support and challenge—in the relaxed aura of your presence.

A musician friend often speaks of her grandparents with fervid appreciation as she recalls the ear they lent and the support they gave as she was growing up. They took her to concerts, gave her recordings, and, most important, she maintains, bought her books for her own library so that she could find answers to questions when she wanted them. She still owns the now-outdated *International Cyclopedia of Music and Musicians* and the *Harvard Dictionary of Music* they sent. And she glows when she recalls how they surprised her with the multivolume *Grove Dictionary of Music* on the day she graduated from college.

Books can help you "be there" whether you are in the same room or thousands of miles away.

D = DREAM

Dream with your grandchildren: about your past and their future. They're linked. Patricia Reilly Giff said she plans to tell her grandson about his heritage—that he is alive because his great-great-grandfather lived opposite a field in which potatoes grew during the famine in Ireland from which so many others died.

You may not recall stories of generations past, but you can bring *your* generation alive and "start" a family history. On visits to the library with your school-age grandchildren, ask the reference librarian for newspapers and magazines published during your youth. Look through them together. Talk about the cars you rode, the movies you saw, the TV programs you watched, the world events that affected you. See if any of the books you read as a child are still in print. Read them together, if they are. Recall the games you played, the songs you sang, the friends you had, the similarities and differences between your childhood, your child's, and your grandchild's.

Ask your grandchild to write down your memories. In the *Foxfire*[8] tradition, work together on a book that will become a treasured family keepsake of the past.

The images you evoke will take hold. When older, your grandchildren will harvest recollections of your talks and read with interest what you wrote together. Your book about the real people, places, and things in their heritage will nourish the memories you shared. Those are the recollections they will pass on to their children. In their own special nonfiction book.

Relax! Enjoy! Appreciate! and Dream. With grandchildren and good books.

7

For Teachers Especially

Think of your students as locomotives. They have the power to go anywhere, but they'll go only where you lay the track. And that small fraction of the day when you're in charge—about 20 percent of their waking hours—is track-laying time. That's when you must forge an attitude toward reading and learning that will set their course for the rest of the time—actually, for the rest of their lives.

How can you "lay track"? First of all, remember that what you do is what you teach. Your actions deliver the message, not your words. If you integrate books—nonfiction and fiction—throughout your curriculum, odds are your students will learn that reading is a natural, necessary, and neat part of everyday life. Not just for Reading Time in school.

Then, memorize four letters—*R, E, A, D*. They'll help you remember some of the ways you can raise the odds that children will remain information hungry and in love with books:

R: *Read* children's literature. You are the most influential Reader in the classroom.

E: Establish an *Environment* that Enhances children's self-*Esteem* while it Encourages reading.

A: Aid and Abet reading by your Actions. Adjust your Attitude and your *Agenda* if necessary.

D: *DO IT.* NOW! WITH NONFICTION.

R = READ

Have you read any children's books lately? That may seem like a silly question, yet I often find myself addressing teachers, intent upon encouraging their students to read, who tell me "I know I should be more familiar with the books my kids read, but I just don't have the time."

Keeping current with the best children's books, especially nonfiction, is an essential part of being an effective teacher. Here's a quick and easy way you can add to your repertoire. I call it . . .

Beverly's Brief Book Break

Once a month, ask your librarian to provide books (one per teacher, including the principal) for your faculty meeting: new books or older ones she knows may be unfamiliar. Set aside two minutes for Sustained Silent Ready (SSR) during which everyone 1) scans a book and 2) thinks of one idea for using it creatively in the classroom. Just two minutes; no more. Use a stopwatch.

When the time's up, form groups of three. Allow each person two minutes (use the stopwatch again) to share with the others in the trio the teaching idea and its inspiration.

Is it possible to "see" enough in two minutes to learn about a book and think of a way to use it in the classroom? Absolutely! And it's fun.

If you do this once a month for the nine months of a school year, at three books per session, you will have discovered 27 new eyeopening books, exchanged as many teaching hints with your colleagues, and (perhaps best of all) enlivened your faculty meetings.

I use this strategy in my workshops to introduce the people in my audience to half-a-dozen new books in about ten minutes. Those of you who also teach children's literature courses can adapt it to your classes. After your prospective teachers or librarians have shared something they noticed about the book and a way they might use it with a child, have them also link at least two nonfiction books to each book of fiction and vice versa. This practice will help them think in terms of a Total Literature Connection (see Chapter 4) and appreciate how easy it is to connect fiction and nonfiction. It is essential that they provide their youngsters with both.

E = ENVIRONMENT AND ESTEEM

Libraries Aren't Only for Librarians

If you want children to read books, put them within easy reach: keep your classroom library well stocked. When I taught full time, I surrounded my students with book bargains I'd acquired at Friends of the Library sales, thrift shops, and garage sales, as well as publishers' promotional bonuses and giveaways and books borrowed from the public library. I kept them on the windowsills, floor-to-ceiling bookshelves my husband built, and every horizontal surface not otherwise covered. My kids couldn't say, "I don't have anything to read."

Transform every available surface into billboards that publicize books and reading. Set aside at least one bulletin board for books-read pinups. In the fall, for example, have youngsters write the title and author of every book they've finished on a two-inch paper-pumpkin pinup they've designed and cut out. By the end of October, you'll have a bulletin board filled with pumpkins. Clear the board so your youngsters can take the pumpkins home to show parents what they've accomplished, and start a new collection, of book-marked snowflakes and sleds. Or raindrops and umbrellas, if you live in a part of the country where winter brings rain instead of snow.

Have your children make advertisements for the books they've read and put them in your windows. Ask your librarian if you can borrow any extra posters acquired at reading/library association conferences. Put them on the ceiling when you run out of wall space. Suggest that your school subscribe to the Children's Book Council's *Features*[9] to learn about and order the beautiful posters, bookmarks, and book-related materials it offers, as well as free and inexpensive materials available from publishers. Make bookmarks during art periods.

Set aside special areas that invite readers. Stitch or tape together colorful rug remnants for a reading rug kids can spread out on during silent reading periods. Pile it high with stuffed old pillowcase covers children have brought in and tie-dyed. Visit a large appliance-store and ask for empty dishwasher or refrigerator boxes your kids can turn into miniature reading-room retreats during earned free time.

Nonfiction Raises Self-Esteem

SLOW READER

I–am–in–the–slow
rea–ders–group–my–broth
er–is–in–the–foot
ball–team–my–sis–ter
is–a–ser–ver–my
lit–tle–broth–er–was
a–wise–man–in–the
in–fants–christ–mas–play
I–am–in–the–slow
read–ers–group–that–is
all–I–am–in–I
hate–it.

—*Allan Ahlberg*[10]

Would you feel comfortable if every book you used let your colleagues know how your reading ability ranked against theirs?

Neither do children.

You don't read only those books on your "reading level." Why should children? Yet that's what we force them to do when we rely upon graded texts.

Children don't feel stigmatized when we give them books for readers of all ages, books that are attractive, engrossing, and challenging: adult photoessays or artfully illustrated information books, wordless picture and "first" books.

They may not be able to read all of the text in the adult books, but children will certainly learn from the pictures. The photos or art in a wordless book (see page 266) may inform as eloquently as any words. And if a good book for older children has no pictures, you can read an excerpt aloud or share something fascinating that you learned when reading it. Pique their curiosity, and they'll want more.

Children ordinarily in the bottom reading group will discover that they can learn from "hard" books: motivated by the illustrations and the subject itself, they'll work to make sense of the text. (I've yet to find a middle-grade reader too "low" to read the *Guinness Book of World Records!*) Children in the top reading groups will discover that they can learn from simple books. Carefully distilled texts and illustrations provide effective, confidence-building introductions to a subject for readers of all ages.

A = AGENDA

No matter how frequently you *say* that books and reading are important, you must *act* as though they are, or your children will not believe you. Remember that kids are impressionable; they take home gut feelings about books and learning. You determine that feeling. Make reading a noticeable part of your agenda. Be sure your children see you read. One of the most appropriate times would be during Sustained Silent Reading (SSR) periods. When I taught in the classroom full time, I renamed our SSR...

SQUIRT

SQUIRT stands for Sustained Quiet UnInterrupted Reading Time.

If SSR isn't yet in your lesson plans, jot it down. SSR helps children acquire the habit and discover the pleasure of being alone with something good to read. It also gives you a daily opportunity to catch up on children's books, in addition to the Brief Break during periodic faculty meetings.

I always began the school year with a daily ten-minute SQUIRT and gradually increased it until, by June, my youngsters were wrapped up in reading silently every day for twenty-five minutes. Me too. It's tempting to want to use that time to correct papers or finish other chores, but if you don't read during SSR time, a children's book or one of your own, children will assume that SQUIRT (or whatever you name it) is just another keep-the-kids-quiet-and-in-their-seats-while-I-get-more-important-work-done technique.

After you've tried SSR in your own classroom, spread the word. Perhaps you can influence your whole school or district to drop everything for a book. The English Department of Wilcox High School in Santa Clara, California, did. In 1986, they adopted a thirty-minute school-wide silent reading period and it spread throughout their district. By November of 1987, everyone from custodian to principal in the two high schools, the two middle schools, the two elementary schools, and an increasing number of classes in twelve other elementary schools was reading for twenty to thirty minutes every day!

During SSR, there is no communication except that between author and reader. One phone line in each school is kept open and only emergency calls are handled, a policy that is communicated to parents.

In one middle school alone, book circulation in the first three months of the school year increased 82 percent from 2,935 volumes in 1986 to 5,347 in 1987. Meanwhile enrollment had dropped one-third—from about 1,200 to 800 students! A larger, upgraded collection accounted for some of the remarkable rise in circulation, but district librarian Shirley Blaker attributes much of it to the SSR program. If you visit the schools, you'll find teachers and students walking around with books under their arms. There's no doubt that students on these campuses are getting the Reading Is Important message from faculty and administration.

The Read-Aloud Ritual

Make reading aloud another daily activity. I read aloud to my students each day. Fiction and nonfiction. Picture books and photoessays, poetry, joke, and riddle books. Children's books and adult books. I read aloud from magazines and newspaper articles and share noteworthy art, photographs, or prose from adult books I've enjoyed. It doesn't matter whether or not youngsters understand all of the words you speak; what matters is that they hear fluent, literate language. The more language children hear, the more they will use; the more fluently they speak, the easier reading becomes.

When you read aloud, try to read expressively, because when it's their turn, children will pattern their style after yours. On occasion, let children volunteer to practice an upcoming section. The self-esteem of poor readers in my room rose a noticeable notch or two after they'd practiced and read a portion fluently. Ask youngsters to read excerpts that might be difficult for you. I need assistance during particularly sad parts: David Kherdian's Boston Globe–Horn Book Award acceptance speech for *The Road from Home,*[11] for example. I start to read it aloud whenever I recommend the book to middle-school students. No matter how often I try, however, I cannot finish the description of Mr. Kherdian's mother reacting to his book. I must ask a student to finish for me.

Credit Books, Not Pages

When you ask youngsters to select books, please don't make them count the pages. Librarians wherever I speak tell me that teachers frequently impose minimum page counts. That is, a child cannot receive "credit" for reading a book unless it is at least 100 pages long. As if the length of a book were a measure of its quality!

Take biographies, for instance. With a 100-page minimum for credit, children would be discouraged from reading Jean Fritz's 94-page *Make Way for Sam Houston,* Milton Meltzer's 57-page *Dorothea Lange* from Viking's and Puffin's excellent "Women of Our Time" series, or Barbara Mitchell's 63-page *Shoes for Everyone* from Carolrhoda's equally notable "Creative Minds" series. The worth of books such as these is unrelated to length.

Help your children understand that good things *can* come in small packages. Teach them how to recognize quality without imposing false standards. Use analogies: tell them Leonardo da Vinci's *Mona Lisa* is only 21 by 30 inches; tell them *I* am 4 feet, 10 inches tall!

Give the Books' Creators Credit, Too

As you teach your students to identify good writing, also open their eyes to the splendid contributions made by the talented artists and photographers whose work they encounter. These professionals have often written and collaborated on many books for children. Suggest youngsters locate other volumes that contain illustrations and photos by one or more of them. What is distinctive about their styles? Do they always approach the subject the same way? How do their techniques vary from book to book?

When children have found a book particularly satisfying, it's not unusual to have them write to its author. Youngsters enjoy doing it and authors enjoy receiving thoughtful letters in appreciation of their work. The next time you share a book with distinctive artwork, let your youngsters express their thanks to the artists and photographers for a job well down.

Another word about letters to authors and others: do not make letter writing a routine event with a perfunctory "Thank you, I liked your book. May I have your autograph?" or "Please draw me a picture." At an American Library Association Authors' Breakfast, I overheard a group of writers bemoan the sacks of dittoed or mimeographed, scarcely legible, impersonal form letters they sometimes receive from teachers.

Teach young people that a letter should represent a sincere effort to communicate. Teach them to be specific, to introduce themselves, and to write what pleased them most, or least, or raised questions. Chances are, they'll receive a personal reply, particularly from non-fiction authors, who don't hear from as many children as do the writers of popular children's fiction. Next to a smiling face, a sincere, involved letter from a young admirer is one of the nicest thank-yous an author or illustrator can get.

Mail letters to authors or illustrators in care of the publisher. You'll find the name and addresses of publishers in *Books in Print* (Bowker).

D = DO IT NOW! WITH NONFICTION

Why nonfiction?

Nonfiction Books Make Children Want to Read

Will you read an enticingly written book with first-rate illustrations about a subject you find fascinating? So will children.

You can create more effective assignments for introducing, reinforcing, and reviewing skills with books students want to read. If one child likes sharks, another motocross racing, and yet another space exploration, gather together books about sharks, motocross bikes, and space exploration.

This strategy works, even for "difficult children." Every year for the past five, a teacher in a small town outside of Anchorage, Alaska, has written to me about projects she's created around topics and books recommended in *The Kobrin Letter*. After the completion of a particularly successful unit, during which youngsters could pick any topic to research, she wrote,

One boy (whose paper from his last school said "To whom it may concern: This boy is incorrigible") picked dinosaurs. I had ordered almost all the books on your list, so he had plenty to choose from. He began the month not able to read or write, took volumes home for his parents to read to him, and by the end of the month could read at least the more elementary ones, and even wrote a one-page report.

I had a similar experience one year with a belligerent eighth-grader. When I learned he had pet rats, I rounded up a few good rat books. The day I took them to school I became ill, so I stopped by his home-room to explain I'd had to cancel class but wanted to give him the books I'd brought especially for him. This usually antagonistic young man looked at the books, paused a moment, and bent over (he was a head taller than I) to put his arm around me. He hugged me gently, and said he was sorry I was sick and hoped I'd feel better soon. He straightened up, reentered the room, and quietly slid himself into his seat and the books into his desk.

The next time we met, he said that he and his mom had read and reread the books and could he please keep them for a few more days. He caused no more disturbances. Don't underestimate the power of books!

Nonfiction Books Help Kids Learn How to Learn

Do you believe everything you read?

Neither should children.

You don't base your decisions upon an isolated bit of information; why should they? Yet that's what we teach them when we hand them one text and one workbook for each subject. A single source of reference conditions children to assume all the "answers" can be found in one book. If we want them to become critical thinkers, we must teach children how to learn. That means checking and cross-checking what they read.

Set aside the textbook/workbook routine with its right-or-wrong answer activities. Surround your children with many books on the same subject. My rule is At Least Three, whenever possible, on whatever subject, when my students gather together books for reports. I want them to read critically, and chances are three books will present different views of the same subject.

When studying astronomy, for example, children must understand that the books they read are out of date as they come off press. That what we "know" about our solar system changes almost daily, in part because of space probes such as Voyager 2.

As they do their research, my students and I talk about what one book reports that the other doesn't. We compare photographs and illustrations. Occasionally, we find typographical errors or authors who don't agree. We play the Who's Older? game: Who's older, the reader or the book? (That's a sneaky way to teach kids to look for a book's copyright date and the age of its information.)

Dates of copyright, authors' qualifications, acknowledgments, and accompanying bibliographies take on added importance when children refer to many books on a single subject. They begin to appreciate that how much the information is worth depends upon its source and age.

Foment Revolution—a Teacher/Librarian Conspiracy (TLC)

Until now, some teachers have assigned homework without notifying librarians. Whole classrooms, even grade levels, have descended upon libraries with requests for the same references. Librarians have been caught by surprise, often without resources to complete kids' assignments.

TLC advocates that teachers consult with librarians in advance of lesson plans. Librarians share their knowledge of the collection and help teachers capitalize on what's available or what can reasonably be ordered. They estimate the time necessary to pull books together and to request, receive, and catalogue new ones. Forewarned, they work more effectively with young researchers.

TLC recognizes that all students need not have identical assignments. Teachers and librarians collaborate on a menu of homework options, employing a wide variety of resources that might otherwise sit unused on the shelf.

Since collections always change, assignments change, too. TLC keeps homework fresh and interesting, both to students and teachers. And librarians gain more satisfaction as they plan how their collections are shaped and used.

Viva la revolución!

Develop Parent Track-Layers

Take every opportunity to keep parents informed about what you do! Encourage parents to help you spike down that track. Provide recommended reading lists for gift suggestions and vacation reading so that parents can link children and books at home. Share ideas from the chapter "For Parents Especially."

Before your students leave school, review the day's activities with them: remind them that they've vicariously experienced the flight of a bat, for example, or have finished another chapter or two in a good book; encourage them to share what they've done with their families.

If "What did you do in school today, dear?" elicits "Nothing, the teacher just read to us," it's easy to understand why twenty minutes of reading aloud can seem like a waste of time. But if the answer is "Wow, the teacher read to us and I began to feel like a bat ... my fingers seemed to grow ... did you know the bat's wings are his hands? ... and ..." then the twenty minutes becomes time well spent.

As a teacher, you are aware that reading aloud to children is not just a time filler—that it stimulates visualization and exercises imagination; that sustained silent reading gives children practice in concentration and in reading for the sheer pleasure it brings. But it's not enough that you know. You must also make sure parents—and their children— understand as well. To the folks at home, youngsters are both your medium and your message. Make it loud and clear.

DARE Children to READ!

Keep in mind that *R, E, A, D* is an anagram that also spells *DARE*. Surround your children with nonfiction books and give them challenges they can't resist.

Teacher Elaine Griffin, in Chiniak, Alaska, did that in September of 1987. Two months later she told me that she, her students, and their parents couldn't be more enthusiastic about the results. She permits her fifth- through eighth-graders to read *any* book in the school library—regardless of the reading level. They select a book (most often nonfiction, she said), design a related project, and present their finished work to the class. They have no other homework.

Her students have become so excited about their self-motivated assignments, many spend the whole weekend immersed in projects—

often with as-interested parents. With her dad's guidance, for example, one girl spent sixteen hours over the weekend carving two wooden masks! Another student chose *Auks, Rocks and Dinosaurs* and built a model pterosaur. Yet another, having chosen the Alaska fish and game regulation book, made dioramas. She illustrated what is legal and what is not for each of the state's five regulations on gill netting.

In my fourth- to sixth-grade classroom, we've used the telephone book for any number of activities: To name characters, youngsters have been inspired by the longest, the shortest, the funniest, or the dreariest names. Names that were colors, things, or places. (It's a wonderfully sneaky way to get children to practice using alphabetical lists!) They've discovered people with identical names, or names of relatives, friends, and famous people.

My students have located emergency numbers and role-played the emergency so that they'd know what to do when one occurred. We've computed the cost of long-distance calls (sneaky math and map reading, since we also locate specific cities in atlases); figured out the closest repair service for broken appliances (which meant that we had to use city maps as well); and solved all sorts of problems they contrived from the wealth of information in that book of numbers.

Nonfiction Books Are Good for Teachers, Too

Nonfiction books keep us as enthusiastic, excited, and involved in learning as they do our students. We learn little and are challenged less using texts and workbooks that are, no matter how their titles or publishers change, virtually the same each year—someone else's plans for Everychild. In all my years of teaching, I have yet to meet Everychild.

With carefully selected nonfiction, you needn't struggle to make students interested in what you teach; they already are. Relevant books keep kids and, just as importantly, *you* learning. Instead of burdening children with texts that bore you year after year (how many times can you teach a subject with the same texts and workbooks and avoid burnout?), you'll read new books, the ones your kids read. You will be constantly challenged to find those books, devise new lessons, and teach whatever skills are necessary.

You will learn and grow along with your students.

Nothing is as versatile as nonfiction to match a child's interest and needs. Whether you are teaching math, science, or history; whether children are gifted, average, or struggling; whether they are young children or young adults, you can find books they will want to read.

By providing the right books at the right time, you can lay the tracks and direct your youngsters toward a self-motivated, lifelong interest in reading and learning. For pleasure and information.

All aboard!

8

The Non-Book-Report

WHY DO I CALL THIS A NON-BOOK-REPORT?

Because just plain Book Report brings to mind those everyone-does-the-same-thing, no-nonfiction-allowed-unless-it's-a-biography, describe-the-setting-who-are-the-main-characters-what-is-the-plot, paper-and-pencil assignments that children anticipate with as much pleasure as adults contemplate root canal work.

Non-Book-Reports are assignments children thoroughly enjoy. Everyone does something different, all books are allowed, and the reports are not necessarily written.

Rather than be constrained by one format, why not make the assignment a creative experience—for both teacher and student? Teachers who have adopted creative book report strategies to involve kids with books (I didn't originate the idea, I just named it) find that they greatly improve attitudes toward reading and learning. Children don't want to stop.

You'll notice that the Non-Book-Report form is almost a blank page. I developed this open-ended form after a few years in the classroom. It has proved to be the simplest, most effective way my kids and I stay interested in books, reading, and learning.

THE NON-BOOK-REPORT

Name_____

Date_____

Title_____

Author_____

Illustrator_____

Publisher_____

Date of copyright_____

Project_____

_____

_____

_____

_____

_____

HOW NON-BOOK-REPORTS WORK

1. Upon completion of any book they choose, my students pick up one of these forms and fill in the blank spaces after name, date, title, author, illustrator, publisher, and date of copyright.

2. They slip the form into the book and put both on top of the piano in my classroom. (The only horizontal surface not otherwise occupied!)

3. I take book and form home, read the book, and write on the form directions for a "project." I try to link what I read with what I know about the child's interest and academic strengths and weaknesses.

4. Back in the classroom, I return the book to the child, who completes the project, slips it or a note saying it is finished into the book, and returns it to the piano top.

5. I arrange a conference time and the two of us check out the work together.

Occasionally I assign different children similar projects, but usually each child has a different one. The last few years I taught full time, my youngsters were responsible for one book and one project a week. By June, almost every student had fulfilled that requirement and most of my youngsters had far exceeded it—some reading between seventy-five and more than a hundred books during the nine months. And many of them had created their own projects, more challenging than any I might have originated.

THE SUCCESS SECRET

Step 3 holds the secret to the success of this strategy: I read every book my students read. If we don't read the books we promote, our students will look upon our words as just another version of "Take this, kid, it's good for you (but I wouldn't touch it with a ten-foot pole)"!

I read every book. And yes, that meant reading or refreshing my memory on thirty to thirty-five books a week. Wait! Before you slam shut this book and exclaim that you don't by any stretch of the imagination have time to read thirty-five books a week, please understand that I didn't start that way.

When I began this system, my students were responsible for one book a month. Any teacher can read thirty-plus elementary-grade-level books a month. The next year, I raised the requirement to one book every three weeks and it wasn't until two years later, when I was familiar enough with the literature, and comfortable enough with the system that I set the one-book-a-week rule. By then I had to read only a few new books a month.

My youngsters thrive on the challenges I set them. I might ask a youngster with reading difficulties, for example, to pick a few paragraphs or pages (depending upon the size of the book) and practice until she or he can read them aloud to me, fluently. I've asked children to read aloud to me or the class, memorize poetry, build dioramas, locate on a map the places mentioned in the book, prepare a recipe for their family (cookbooks are popular), write to an author, or make up their own assignments.

They've interviewed parents or other relatives on book-related topics, polled the school for opinions, made a life-size image of an animal or a person, conducted experiments, made a five-minute audio cassette about the book (my school didn't have a video camera), visited another classroom and "sold" them on the book or demonstrated or taught them something they had learned from it. As often as not I have used each book as a stepping stone to another one.

NO FAKE! IT'S NONFICTION!

Use the Non-Book-Report form as a guide—a beginning, not an end. It is merely my strategy to develop, rather than diminish, the joy of reading; to use each book as the first words rather than the last; to help children appreciate that one book or activity can open the door to many others—all worthwhile.

As I've traveled the country sharing the Non-Book-Report form, creative teachers have taken the idea and run with it! Cindy Blackburn, a fifth-grade teacher in Worthington, Ohio, for example, set up a learning center entitled No Fake, It's Nonfiction. For each book in the center, she's devised a group of activities and written them on 3 × 5" cards. When youngsters have read the book, they can choose the options on any of the cards to earn credit for it.

Elaine Griffin in Chiniak, Alaska, combines the Non-Book-Report and Beverly's Brief Book Break. Every day for the first few weeks of school, her youngsters take the Break and brainstorm projects for each of the books they skim. Week three, Elaine institutes the pick-any-book-you-want-to-read-and-create-your-own-project assignment.

On Friday, her youngsters select a book. Over the weekend they determine how they are going to spend three hours with it. For example, they might decide they need one and a half hours to read it and one and a half hours to complete a project. As I described on page 39, the students and their families couldn't be more excited about reading. Elaine says that most students spend more than three hours on most assignments; many students are done by Monday and all of them are eager for Friday to come around so they can demonstrate what they've done and pick another book!

INITIATE YOUR OWN READING RENAISSANCE

Adopt the Non-Book-Report habit. It develops the enjoyment of reading. Now that you've finished this chapter, turn to the Guide (page 70) and scan the Tips. You'll find that they're frequently adaptable to books other than the one they accompany. Try them or their variations with your children. Before you realize it, you'll find yourself delighted by a room filled with Non-Book-Reporters.

9

For Librarians Especially

The books you buy, the titles you tout, and the environment you establish make the Total Literature Connection viable. You are our number one resource—the key link in the kids-to-books chain. Make that link the strongest of all. Forge it out of a balanced blend of fiction and nonfiction.

BOOKTALK THE BEST OF BOTH WORLDS

To young children, everything is real: mud and the Muppets, manatees and monsters, magic and magnets. With maturity comes an understanding of the difference between real and make-believe. And that's fine. The terms are unimportant. What is critical is that you open children's eyes to good literature. Popular, contemporary, classic. Prose, poetry, plays. Fact and fiction.

Unfortunately, Melville Dewey used a fact/fiction dichotomy as the basis for his decimal system, and this orderly method of shelving books split literature down the middle. That rift can be mended, though.

Hazel Rochman, former seventh- to twelfth-grade librarian for the University of Chicago's Laboratory Schools, explains how she interweaves fiction and nonfiction in *Tales of Love and Terror: Booktalking the Classics, Old and New* (American Library Association). She finds a single thread, a unifying theme common to a wide range of books to "lure readers to a wider variety . . . than they would find on their own."

With animals as the theme, Ms. Rochman has linked Allan Eckert's *Incident at Hawk's Hill* (Little) to James Herriot's *All Creatures Great and Small* (St. Martin's); she's joined *All Creatures Great and Small* to Roald Dahl's *Boy* (Farrar and Puffin), connecting the two as biographies; and she's tied *Boy* to Katherine Paterson's *The Great Gilly Hopkins* (Crowell) through humor. Throughout her work, she effectively demonstrates that one book can lead to many others. Regardless of the classification.

In a program for fourth- to sixth-grade children visiting the White Oak Library in Silver Spring, Maryland, Naomi Morse, Head Children's Librarian, connected youngsters to an Australian tale, retold and illustated by Joanna Troughton, *What Made Tiddalik Laugh* (Blackie). She linked the tale to Caroline Arnold's *Koala* (Morrow) and other books about marsupials and introduced the youngsters to the swagman, billabong, and other uniquely Australian terms as they sang "Waltzing Mathilda." Ms. Morse read Emmy Payne's *Katy No-Pocket* (Houghton), tucked it into her swag, and concluded with a movie about koalas.

DO WE DEWEY?

Jan Lieberman, Lecturer in Children's Literature at San Jose State University's Division of Library and Information Science, admonishes students to highlight books Dewey's system might bury on the shelves. "Display! Booktalk! Promote as imaginatively as you can!" she responds to students' query "Do we Dewey or do we display?"

The question arises yearly as prospective librarians discover books like Kathryn Lasky's and Maxwell B. Knight's *A Baby for Max* (Scribner's), Wendy Tokuda's and Richard Hall's *Humphrey, the Lost Whale* (Heian), Betty Leslie-Melville's *Daisy Rothschild* (Doubleday), and Francine Patterson's *Koko's Kitten* (Scholastic). All might languish because of poor circulation unless featured in special programs or otherwise placed in plain sight.

LINK LITERATURE TO LIFE

Librarians in Santa Clara, California, included Max in their program "You Must Have Been a Beautiful Baby," along with stories and pictures of themselves when little. They also told the stories their mothers told them about their youth, linking the reminiscences to Riki Levinson's *Watch the Stars Come Out* (Dutton), Russell Freedman's *Immigrant Kids* (Dutton), and Dayal Kaur Khalsa's *Tales of a Gambling Grandma* (Clarkson Potter), among others.

Although Humphrey, Daisy, and Koko will no·doubt be shelved among their own kind, they are not generic whale, giraffe, and gorilla, respectively, but unique individuals whose stories, like Lassie's or Misty's, will touch readers' hearts. Present them with as much feeling and frequency.

PROMOTE WITH PANACHE

As you select tales that you hope will entice listeners to become readers, remember that the truth can be as spellbinding as fiction. And that the beauty of storytelling nonfiction lies in its ability to sell itself—it can be so visual. Take *Steve Caney's Invention Book* (Workman). Imagine how youngsters will clamor for it after you roller-skate to the front of the room, earmuffs on head, Band-Aid on hand, to tell the stories behind the three inventions. You could even sip soda through a straw as you paraphrase its creation! Or, having wheeled out the volumes you are about to booktalk in a shopping cart borrowed (with permission) from a nearby supermarket, you describe its origin. Until the inventor tricked them, shoppers wouldn't touch Mr. Goldman's contraption, as you will discover in Don Wulffson's *Invention of Ordinary Things* (Lothrop).

Think action. Invite interaction. Displays need be neither flat nor static. If windy weather's due, pull out Tom Moran's *Kite Flying Is for Me* (Lerner) and other kite-making books and focus a fan on a high-flyer you've suspended from the ceiling or loosely pinned to a bulletin board. Arrange hair lotion, dishwasher detergent, paste, and other *Gobs of Goo* (Lippincott) in beakers and flasks along with Vicki Cobb's book; fill hands-on displays with magnets, materials they do and don't attract, and related books; spotlight Seymour Simon's *The Paper Airplane Book*

(Viking and Puffin) and sponsor a paper airplane contest; load a casette player with taped whale songs and surround it and a pair of earphones with whale books.

Call attention to those drab but worthwhile books. Take a tip from Helene Treat, co-owner of the Red Balloon Bookstore in San Antonio, Texas, and set aside a section prominently marked "Bad Cover, Good Book."

Imaginative displays can even save nonfiction. Dr. Stephen Herb, Coordinator of Children's Services for the Dauphin County, Pennsylvania, Library System, once rescued 70 percent of the about-to-be-discarded biographies in one library's collection. He posted a humorous letter from the books to library patrons. "Dear Patrons," it began. "We have only three weeks to live unless you borrow us. . . ." Most of the books circulated and remained on the shelves another year.

KEEP COLLECTIONS CURRENT

There are classics in fiction that will live forever, but the nonfiction you set out for children must reflect today's world. Texts that state astronauts may someday reach the moon; drawings that depict apatosaurus with a short, snub-nosed head; or atlases that identify Rhodesia and Southwest Africa on the African continent serve only to confuse and mislead. Pull them out.

Occasionally I hear, "I won't have anything left on the subject, if I throw out the old books!" Better fewer books than bad books! Mary D. Lankford, Director of Library and Media Services for the Irving Independent School District in Texas, concurs. She and her colleagues develop a "hit list" to help their librarians keep shelves free of dated or obsolete books. And the district strongly supports the strategy. It increases librarians' budgets one dollar for each book weeded!

Shocking statistics published in 1987 by the State of California "indicated that 80 to 85 percent of nonfiction books in [San Mateo, California] school libraries were copyrighted at least 10 years ago. Forty percent . . . were copyrighted at least 20 years ago."[12] In private conversations with librarians from other California counties, I've learned such statistics are typical. That "make-do" attitude toward books and learning delivers the wrong message to children. Don't let your state sink to the state of my state.

On the other hand, California is leading the drive for more literature in the classroom. In 1986, the California Reading Initiative was launched, calculated to develop lifelong, positive attitudes toward reading and writing. If educators resist the temptation to turn trade books into textbooks, this teaching trend might rehabilitate my state.

CALL IN NEIGHBORS

Ask community members with specialized skills to help satisfy and stimulate curiosity. Ellin Klor, formerly a librarian in the Palo Alto, California, Children's Library, invited scientist Dr. Stephen Terry to assist in "Ask Herr Professor Science." During the thirty-minute period, children performed experiments from such books as *Gee Wiz!*, *Bet You Can*, and *Bet You Can't*. Herr Professor Terry explained the underlying scientific principles and set them more challenges.

Librarian Donna Parks invited a beekeeper, his queen, and her entourage to the Washington County Free Library in Hagerstown, Maryland. Children sat enraptured by the glass-enclosed colony, as they learned about bees and their peripatetic pollinating. This keeper's colony was "hired" by growers as far south as Florida to fertilize flowers. Ms. Parks's meet-the-people program ran for three years and included an automobile racer from a local track and a potter who made simple pottery with youngsters. Almost all the men and women she asked were delighted at the thought of describing their professions or hobbies to youngsters. She found that most businesses will allow their employees an extended lunch hour or an hour's time off to visit the library. So be imaginative. Be bold. Ask.

MAKE KIDS CURIOUSER AND CURIOUSER

Program scavenger hunts to help children discover libraries' hidden treasures. Karen Bricker, Senior Librarian in the Mountain View, California, Public Library, designed Librology, a challenge her young patrons can't resist. Students from third grade through middle school accumulate points when they answer questions about topics as far afield as their ancestors' native land to storybook characters' names. Children earn a highly coveted "I am a Librologist" badge for their efforts. The focus changes each year and Ms. Bricker told me that many youngsters have become so skilled after years of playing, they would easily qualify as library pages.

RECOGNIZE YOUR REFERENCES

Create a Student Bureau of Investigation on your school campus. Kids join the SBI by tracking down information. Convert corners into Look It Up niches, home base for year-round scavenger-hunt activities, or highlight a different reference work—atlas, biographical dictionary, almanac—every two weeks to help youngsters feel comfortable searching for the information they contain.

Marge Ulrich, Library Media Specialist at K. R. Smith School in Evergreen School District, San Jose, California, posts an "Answer Me This" calendar in her library. Kids dig through thesauri, dictionaries, encyclopedias, magazines—whatever it takes to find the answers to Ms. Ulrich's daily questions. Right-answerers drop their names in a box and at the end of the month are eligible for a book prize.

As a former children's and young adult librarian in Chicago, Roger Sutton found that the public library's informal atmosphere afforded him many opportunities to connect kids to books. If kids are talking about gangs, sharks, sex, or Puerto Rico, Mr. Sutton starts with nonfiction, because it relates clearly to what they're interested in. "Nonfiction is often the best way to start a conversation about books with nonreaders, reluctant readers, or kids who are just hanging around in the library," he told me. "These kids often need the clear assurance that a book is *about* something and they particularly like it when the book is about the something you've just asked them to stop talking so loudly about!"

PROMOTE YOUNG AUTHORS

When you help children celebrate the books *they* write, illustrate, and publish, you demonstrate in a most impressive way that books are worth celebrating. You also enlarge youngsters' knowledge of literature's scope and provide insight into the literary process. And you give them an outlet for creativity and a meaningful way to use the language arts.

Ann A. Flowers, Childrens' Librarian for the Wayland, Massachusetts, Public Library, holds a Young Authors' Tea for the children whose books are "published" at her library. Any third- through fifth-grader may submit an original minimum-of-100-words manuscript on a family trip, pet adventure, tall tale, or any other subject. The amateur authors confer with a librarian or Friend of the Library, a minimal amount of editing takes place, their words are computer-formulated to allow room for illustrations and page folds, and the "book" emerges from the printer as a leaflet ready for illustrations.

Ms. Flowers and her staff catalogue and add each autographed edition to the library's permanent collection, where they are in continual circulation. Walk through the special Young Authors section and you'll hear children exclaim, "Oh, I know the kid who wrote this!" as they tuck the book under an arm. They take it home and read it—because it's written by a friend.

FAIR THEE WELL

Since 1977, the Reading Council, School Librarians Association, and Office of Education in my county, Santa Clara, California, have promoted and sponsored a Young Authors' Fair. In April, authors, illustrators, and publishers in kindergarten through ninth grade display, at a central location, the books they began in the fall. There, their families, teachers, librarians, and the general public admire them and each child receives a certificate: a certificate of recognition—fairs are not competitions.

BUILD BOOK BRIDGES

In Dauphin County, Pennsylvania, young authors join older ones. Dr. Herb told me of a four-session, seven-week intergenerational project his librarians implemented. They linked nine-year-olds to the residents of a nursing home. Inspired by James Stevenson's *When I Was Nine* (Greenwillow), both groups completed autobiographical booklets— oldsters writing of their past, youngsters of their present. The children read Norma Farber's *How Does It Feel to Be Old?* (Creative Arts) and other books on aging and made valentines for their partners. They heard Charlotte Zolotow's *My Grandson Lew* (Harper and Trophy) and Mordicai Gerstein's *The Mountains of Tibet* (Harper) and discussed dying, to prepare them if one of their project-pals became critically ill or died during the seven weeks. For their last session the younger generation met the older one at the nursing home, presented the gifts they'd made, enjoyed a scavenger-hunt introduction to the home, and together they listened to a storyteller.

MAKE BOOK FAIRS FAIR TO BOOKS

If you are asked to help organize a book fair, please be sure that its purpose is to raise literary consciousness and not merely to raise funds. There's no doubt that book fairs raise money; I've seen it done many times. Local book dealers and distributors cooperate because they profit, too. They fall into two classes, however: those that are in it primarily for profit; and those who really care about the quality of the books they offer children. Both will help your short-term cash needs; only the latter can aid the long-term mental growth of your children.

The excitement of a book fair and the involvement of parents or other volunteers provide you a rare opportunity to "sell' the very best books available, so please keep the quality standard high. It goes without saying (she says) that nonfiction books should be prominently displayed.

What does one *do* with the money raised at a book fair? One invests it in the library, of course. If the playground needs a new swing, let someone organize a swing fair. But to use book fair profits for anything *but* books, why, it's simply not fair.

ALL FOR ONE AND ONE FOR ALL

Whether you're a school or public librarian, you can adapt the strategies that I've collected here, or those I've recommended to parents, grandparents, and teachers in other sections, including the Teacher/Librarian

Conspiracy on page 38. Youngsters' enthusiasm and excitement about good literature—fiction and nonfiction—depend upon your ability to promote it to them and those who reach them.

Jo Carr prefaces her insightful book *Beyond Fact* (American Library Association) with "A child is not a vase to be filled but a fire to be lit." Let's light that fire together!

10

How to Judge a Book by Its Cover– and Nine Other Clues

Shortly after I began publishing *The Kobrin Letter,* my newsletter on children's nonfiction, I visited the British publisher Peter Usborne in London. My students adored his books (they were then, and still are, among the first borrowed and last returned) and I wanted to see how they came to be. During the course of our conversation, I mentioned that I taught classes on children's nonfiction literature and that criteria for their selection was a topic we discussed.

At the word *criteria,* Mr. Usborne smiled and asked, "What do you consider the most important criterion in the selection of good childrens' nonfiction?"

"Accuracy," I said without pause. "The information must be accurate."

He nodded politely, said that accuracy was certainly important "...and..."

"Currency, of course," I went on quickly. "You must make certain that the information is as up to date as possible." Again he nodded—"...and..."

"The author's credentials ... the quality of the artwork ... the appropriateness of the material and language ... ," I went on. With each new standard, he nodded politely and said, "... and ..."

I reached the bottom of my list, blushing with embarrassment. Obviously, I hadn't answered a simple question to his satisfaction. In frustration I asked, "What, then, do you consider the number one criterion?"

"All of the points you make are true enough," he said as he leaned forward. "But none of them matter, *if the child won't take the book off the shelf.* Most important, the book must be attractive."

Of course!

FIRST IMPRESSIONS COUNT

We admonish children, "You mustn't judge a book by its cover." But more often than not, the cover determines which book *we* judge. (When was the last time you peeked between ho-hum covers?) We reach for books wrapped in intriguing jackets. If a book remains unopened, what's inside is irrelevant.

I receive more than 1,000 books from publishers each year. Some have attractive covers and little else to offer. Some have unimaginative covers around nonfiction gems. I can't allow myself to be influenced by the cover alone, but children are not so constrained. They're turned off by drab-looking books—even good ones, so attractiveness must have high priority.

WHAT MAKES A BOOK GOOD?

The first thing I do with a book is scan it. If it appears to match my expectations, I'll start to read it. As I scan and read, I mentally check all the factors I think are important.

Before I list the ten criteria I use to evaluate a children's nonfiction book, however, I should point out that their order has little significance.

Also, the book does not have to excel in every detail. It's a little like judging a house: the location counts, the price, the general layout, the kitchen, the bathroom, and the distance from school. Each factor is individually important, but it is their combination which determines if this is the house you'll occupy. If the price is right, the school is close, and you love the design, you might take it even though the kitchen needs work.

Ditto with a book. I look for books that meet my criteria. Occasionally a particularly fine book scores well in all aspects. That's rare and much appreciated. But an excellent book that does not reflect the very latest research, for example, may have sufficient redeeming features to earn a place on my shelves if strengths outweigh weaknesses.

One book might have dramatic, informative photographs but a merely serviceable text. Another might contain writing that grabs you from the first sentence buried in graceless design or accompanied by inferior illustrations. Each book becomes a useful reference when supplemented with others to balance its deficits. I require that my students use a minimum of three reference books when doing research.

SKIM AND SCAN

How do I evaluate a book? First I skim the pages and wait to be hooked. I glance at pictures, read captions, and scan the text. If there are no illustrations, I begin reading to see how far I can get before my mind wanders. Sometimes, I can't put the book down! Most often, I catch the flavor, then put the book aside to finish later on. As I skim and scan, I mentally check against my criteria and imagine how I would use the book with children. If I can use a book, in whole, in part, or in conjunction with another book, to enlighten and excite a child, I recommend it.

And I don't always agree with other reviewers. There are classic works, for example, I've never taken to. In fiction, *Winnie the Pooh* and *The Hobbit* are two. My son grew up without hearing them from me. And in nonfiction there are books that simply do not touch me. I've read them and felt nothing, though others had given them laudatory reviews.

SETTING THE HOOK

Sounds like my approach is largely subjective, doesn't it? It is. What I most want from a book, as from a house, is to become excited about it, to be hooked. A good book involves me emotionally, I must show it to someone. Right away. (My poor husband!) If it doesn't grab *me,* I can't "sell" it to anyone else.

Writing that pulls the reader along transmits an excitement for learning. Barbara Tuchman has said that you should feel the author's "pulse" on the page.[13] That pulse converts indifference to involvement—even when you don't understand what you read.

There's nothing proprietary about evaluating books. You can do it as easily as I. But it does help to have a list of characteristics to check the book against. Here is my list:

TEN TESTS FOR NONFICTION

1. ATTRACTIVENESS
2. ACCURACY
3. AUTHORITY
4. APPROPRIATENESS
5. RHETORIC
6. STEREOTYPES
7. TONE
8. CAUTIONS
9. FORMAT
10. BOOK DESIGN

1. Attractiveness

My motto is "Say NO to ugly books." When I ask librarians to boycott their publishers, I frequently hear "But they're the only ones who have books on——." My reply is: "Better no book than an ugly one. Send youngsters to the public library to look through a magazine or newspaper for information." When we support ugly-book publishers, we're telling them, "We'll take whatever you give us." Don't! We do children a disservice by referring them to books that make reading and research a dreary task. This is particularly true of reluctant readers and writers, who need all the enticement we can provide.

In an intermediate- or junior-high-level book, for example, the pictures may be static or the text unimaginative. The book may be prosaically designed, with typeface and layout creating page after page of gray. I've learned that students who write reports from such books merely transfer information from printed page to notebooks to typed papers to wastebaskets. With great indifference and little learning in the process.

Books for junior high and older students often seem to lack the élan of books for younger readers. Does information have to be presented with less flair as readers grow older? I think not. For example, the wonderful photographs on the front and back of the jacket around Arlene Hirschfelder's *Happily May I Walk* (Scribner's) make you want to pick up the book. When you skim the pages you notice distinctive chapter numbers and titles; variety in photograph size, borders, and placement; crisp contrast between black and white—there are no blankets of gray on text-only pages, because the type size, leading (space between the lines), and margin widths are so adroitly balanced.

Milton Meltzer's *The Landscape of Memory* (Viking) is without illustrations. Yet, again there are no type-dense, gray pages to dull readers' interest. Cover illustration, book size, paper color, typeface, and bordered chapter headings contribute to the pleasing design. Both books beckon to readers.

I do *start* every ugly book I get. And when I discover one that is exceptionally well written, I finish the book and recommend it. Fine writing outweighs poor design. But in the long run, Peter Usborne is right. The quality of the contents is moot if the book stays closed. And ugly books stay closed.

2. Accuracy

Do both the writing and illustrations reflect the facts as they are known at the time of publication? Is the author qualified? If his or her background is not noted or known, do the acknowledgments or bibliography reflect careful research?

Bats Are Not as Big as Bears

To establish relative size, David Peters drew a man and woman near every group of animals in *Giants of Land, Sea and Air* (Knopf). Piero Ventura drew *Great Painters* (Putnam) in proportion to the size of the photographic reproductions of their paintings. Children who put a hand on the pages of Kenneth Lilly's drawings in *Large As Life: Daytime Animals* and *Large As Life: Nighttime Animals* (both Knopf) or Joyce Audy dos Santos's *Giants of Smaller Worlds* (Dodd) know exactly how they match up to the creatures—all three books contain life-size drawings. And there is no question as to how small is small in Lisa Grillone's and Joseph Genarro's *Small Worlds Close Up* (Crown). The coauthors noted the degree of magnification for each photograph.

Illustrations must give accurate impressions of size. Without a recognizable point of reference, pictures of isolated objects or animals can mislead readers. When amoebas, ants, and anacondas appear to be of equal girth in adjacent close-ups, adults may appreciate that they were drawn to different scales or photographed at different magnifications; children will be confused. Check contents carefully for clues.

Check Credentials

How can you be certain whether or not every book you read is accurate or current? You can't. Information is increasing so quickly that it is unrealistic to suppose anyone—parent, reviewer, or professional educator—can make a knowledgeable assessment of either accuracy or currency for every book.

What can you quickly and reasonably do to choose a book that won't misinform? Begin with the book itself. I frequently ask youngsters about information contained in the acknowledgments (How do you know that the author knows what he's writing about?), the bibliography (Where did the author go for information? Were her sources up to date?), or the book jacket (What can you tell me about the author?). It is as important for children to consider by whom and how a nonfiction book was written as it is to read it. Critical thinking involves consideration of the source of information as well as the information itself.

3. Authority

If the above information isn't available, ask your librarian for help. If she's unfamiliar with the book you've chosen, its author, or other books on the same subject, she'll check reviewers' comments. If your book is on a scientific subject, for example, she might turn to *Science Books & Films* or *Appraisal: Children's Science Books.* In *Appraisal,* she'd find two reviews of each book: one by a specialist on the book's topic and the other by a librarian. If the book is of general nonfiction nature, because the librarian, too, does not rely on a single source, she might refer to *The Horn Book, Bulletin of the Center for Children's Books, School Library Journal,* or the American Library Association's *Booklist.* And, of course, she'd also turn to *The Kobrin Letter,* where, if recommended, she'd find the book grouped among related titles—reviewed from my perspective as a classroom teacher.

Among your relatives, colleagues, or acquaintances might be an authority you can check with—someone who has knowledge of the subject in question. This person need not be an authority on children. That's where you come in. Use your judgment.

Get a Little Help from a Friend

My neighbor Julie Jerome is a teacher aide with a math background. I asked her to comment on a pop-up book about time. Though the facts were correct, she said, the pop-ups were sufficiently confusing to diminish the effectiveness of the book. She pointed out that pop-ups in other books I'd shown her added something; here they were gimmicky. I didn't recommend the book.

After I read the acknowledgments, there was no doubt in my mind that Barbara M. Walker wrote *The Little House Cookbook* (Harper) with some authority. Her two and a half pages of thanks and the considerable research they represent are as fascinating as the book itself. Ms. Walker certainly did her "homework"!

Please note, however, that properly satisfying your youngsters' curiosity about a specific subject depends less on the accuracy or currency of any *one* book than the access you provide to *many* books on that subject. Only by comparing information from a variety of sources will children learn for themselves that the printed word is not eternal. "Facts" can be ephemeral, as easily misstated as outdated.

4. Appropriateness

Is the author's style and language appropriate for the intended audience? Did the author start at the beginning and proceed to define, explain, and describe simply, clearly, and in a logical manner? Is there an index, a glossary, a bibliography where necessary? Do captions enhance photographs and diagrams? Are the illustrations well chosen and relevant?

When selecting for little ones, keep in mind that the simplest words in the shortest sentences do not necessarily equal the best books for the youngest reader. Vocabularies cannot grow on words of one syllable à la Dick and Jane. Teacher Susan Ohanian decries sanitized basal readers, with this marvelous prose: "Like Bartleby the Scrivener, modern reading textbooks are 'pallidly neat, pitiably respectable, incurably forlorn.' There is room in our children's literature for silliness, for unpleasantness, and for difficult words that children do not know. Above all, there is a place for detail and nuance and subtlety...."[14]

Enrich childrens' language and stretch their horizons with books like Ron Hirschi's *Who Lives in ... Alligator Swamp?* (Dodd), an outstanding read-aloud, look-together book for parents and preschoolers. Children will be held fast by the photographs as they wrap their tongues around "gallinule," "bobolink," "thrasher," and the names of other creatures in the habitat.

Seymour Simon's *The Smallest Dinosaurs* (Crown), another book addressed to primary-graders, is equally appropriate for older students. As with Mr. Hirschi, Mr. Simon neither talks down to nor at young readers. Acknowledging their intended audience only as to the amount of information they share, both write simply, clearly, and with respect for intelligent readers of any age.

Children must hear new words. They may not use them correctly at first, but that, too, is unimportant. (I could hardly keep a straight face when one of my neighbor's children said he was so cold he felt "isolated." Eventually he got it right.)

At a conference of the National Council of Teachers of English, I heard author/illustrator Jan Adkins remark, "Children should not get all of a book the first, the third, or even the fifth time they read it. It should become an old friend." A book that becomes "an old friend" will continue to intrigue and influence a child in a comfortable, nonthreatening way.

Word Length Is Not Proportional to Child Length

It's easy to assume that bigger kids need bigger words and that they'll remember what they've already been taught without review. When selecting books, particularly for intermediate grade and junior high readers, make certain that the author 1) has not written multisyllabic jargon or used a framework of compound-complex sentences and 2) has written as though the reader had no prior knowledge of the subject and is entering its territory for the first time.

On the other hand, I once taught an unusually gifted first-grader who was fascinated by sharks and could read and absorb information from books written for sixth-graders. There's nothing automatic about matching kids and books. You gotta know the territory!

It's when I start learning about a subject from scratch—as I did when I recently reviewed books about lasers—that I best appreciate what it feels like to be in my students' shoes. I had to read the simplest children's books many times to begin to understand the principles behind a laser's light, and even now I don't fully appreciate how it creates three-dimensional images. As parents and teachers, we forget that learning often takes a very long time, and that some things may never be learned.

Good Children's Books Teach Everyone

When writing ads, experienced copywriters approach new subjects or review old ones through children's nonfiction books. So do I. Writers for children assume the reader has no prior knowledge of the topic. They start at the beginning and proceed in a logical, gently paced sequence. Many writers of adult nonfiction assume the reader knows something about the subject and can learn it quickly, merely by virtue of adulthood. They start in the middle, move fast, and often leave their readers stranded.

Considerations of the reader's age should influence but not constrain the author. The key to good writing is clarity; a key to good teaching is starting at the beginning. Good nonfiction combines both.

5. Rhetoric

Does the author make a careful distinction between fact, theory, and opinion? Does the author talk down to and mislead readers with cute devices?

At sea level, water boils at 212 degrees Fahrenheit. That is a *fact.* Dinosaurs became extinct when the dust from meteorites struck the earth with great force and blocked sunlight long enough to prevent survival. That's a *theory.* Everybody needs milk. That's an *opinion.*

Children accept what they read as fact, unless counseled otherwise. In newspapers, the columnists' opinions are frequently flagged as "commentary." In children's books, authors generally have no such device and must use other means to differentiate fact from opinion. A writer of good nonfiction must carefully delineate between factual and editorial statements.

By the very nature of their craft, however, journalists and other writers of nonfiction must decide what to put in and what to leave out. That means their biases have influenced even the "facts" they choose to present. Once again, whether or not the bias is subtle or straightforward, it is more important that you provide children with many views of a particular subject rather than one, no matter how unbiased you believe it to be.

Watch Out for Rhetorical Rigamarole

Two rhetorical devices that should be avoided in children's books are teleology and anthropomorphism.

Teleology transforms an event that is natural into one that is planned. For example, "The sheep grows his long woolly hair so that you can have a nice warm coat to keep out the cold." Sheep do not decide to grow hair, let alone determine its use.

Anthropomorphism occurs when human characteristics are attributed to animals. "The lonesome baby foxes were happy to see their mother return to the den, but sad and disappointed that for the third day, she'd not brought back anything to eat." Loneliness, joy, despair, and tracking time are people's properties, not fox features.

6. Stereotypes

Are stereotypes avoided?

In Aliki's unstereotypical *Digging Up Dinosaurs,* the scientists, all of whom do *not* wear glasses, are young, old, male, female, and from many ethnic backgrounds. That's good! So are depictions of disabled people in mainstream jobs (Gail Gibbons's *Deadline!*); photographs of fathers and their children (Joanna Cole's *How You Were Born*);

skeletons in women's bodies (Drs. Ruth and Bartel Bruun's *The Human Body*).

Books about space exploration should acknowledge research other than NASA's (Moira Butterfield's *Space Stations and Satellites*); famous people can have unpleasant qualities (R. R. Knudson's *Babe Didrikson* and Natalie S. Bober's *Breaking Tradition*); there are poor people in "wealthy" nations, rich people in "poor" ones, and all countries have people living within a wide range of social, cultural, economic, and educational levels (Bookwright Press's "We Live in . . ." series).

Going to the doctor/hospital can be unpleasant (James Howe's *The Hospital Book*); boys cook (Jill Krementz's *The Joy of Cooking*); women drive semitrailer trucks (George Ancona's *Bananas*); and his *Dancing Is* is for everyone under the sun.

7. Tone

Does the author create an excitement for the subject, an enthusiasm for learning? Is the reader satisfied, yet inspired to read on?

I grasp little of what James Jespersen and Jane Fitz-Randolph write. Yet I relish their books and make certain that any junior high or high school teacher I meet hears about them. *From Quarks to Quasars,* for example, traces the development of physics, a subject for which I have little facility. I read the first sentence and couldn't put the book down. Through their analogies, illustrations, and anecdotes, I could follow, albeit primitively, what I was reading while I read it. I even read excerpts aloud to my husband. My handy physicist (next-door neighbor Jon Jerome) verified its factual worth and found it as exciting a "read" as I had.

I have retained few of the facts they shared, but I still feel the authors' excitement and enthusiasm. And I appreciate the romance, beauty, and allure of physics as I never had before. If this book about something I barely fathom grabs me, imagine what it will do to a budding physicist! Undoubtedly, it will stimulate as much curiosity as it satisfies.

In the same way, Patricia Lauber's *Volcano* propels kids into more books about volcanoes and natural catastrophes and make-your-own-volcano experiments; John Bonnett Wexo's *Eagles* sends them to raptors to food pyramids to endangered species to conservation projects; Vicki Cobb's and Kathy Darling's *Bet You Can* and *Bet You Can't* turn everyone into "experimenters" on the hunt for more "tricks that aren't"—about optical and sensory illusions, mathematics . . . and on and on.

8. Cautions

Are dangers noted and precautions advised where necessary?

If you do not have a science teacher on call to check and comment on the danger level of all but the most obviously safe experiments, then you must try them before youngsters do. If you discover errors or omissions in critical steps, measurements or ingredients, correct them—in writing—in the book.

Make certain children understand they are not to mimic the behavior of animal handlers pictured with venomous or dangerous creatures; that daredevil stunts take great skill and practice; that world records are generally made by experts who know what they are doing and who should not be willy-nilly emulated. Books on sports should advise youngsters of inherent dangers and proper gear.

On the other hand, warnings are sometimes overdone. For example, cookbooks written for middle-grade and older children do not need constant reminders to have an adult turn on the oven or stove, or to be wary of sharp knives. Chances are, children who can read recipes have been turning on stoves and ovens and using kitchen knives long enough to do all three properly. Better they should be reminded to turn OFF the stove or oven, and place sharp instruments flat, handle toward the user.

9. Format

Does the format enhance the text and contribute to its clarity? Is an index, a glossary, and a table of contents provided where appropriate? Are pages numbered?

Whenever we're brainstorming criteria, it's a librarian who inevitably asks, "Does the book have an index?" Probably because youngsters come streaming into the library with specific questions and the fastest way to find out whether or not a book holds the answer is to look in the index.

Unfortunately, many good books do not have indexes. A few years ago, I became so annoyed when I tried to find something in one of the "Brown Paper School" series, I decided that if the publishers weren't going to index the books, I would. Then I thought, "Why me? Better my students." And what was a negative turned into a positive. I assigned paragraphs, pages, or chapters to individuals or groups of children, and let them create an index. It's a super way to have them find key words, to understand the value of topic sentences and subheads, and to appreciate the organization of a chapter. I typed the finished index, had my students sign it, and affixed it to the book. Every few years, of course, I'd "lose" the index and it would have to be redone!

Do all books need indexes? It depends. I've seen well-illustrated, 32-page books with 22 pages of text, four lines per page, and an index that added little. It seemed to have been included so that the publisher could list "index" in the description. What very little information the book contains is easier and faster found flipping through the pages.

I've learned from my editor (Deborah Brodie, editor of the unindexed Viking and Puffin "Women of Our Time" biographies) that adding an index to that series would eliminate one or two pages of text and/or illustrations in a 64-page book. Under those circumstances, I, too, would opt for no index. Given the same choice, however, for the "Brown Paper School" series, I'd decide just the opposite.

As for page numbers—ALWAYS!

10. Book Design

Is the design appropriate for readers of all ages? Do the illustrations and typeface(s) enhance or extend the text? Are size relationships accurately portrayed? Are illustrations appropriately labeled and integrated with the text? Are charts relevant, clearly drawn, and easy to understand?

Good Design Works Well for Everyone

Well-designed and -written books with inoffensively large print and nonchildish illustrations make excellent introductions to a subject for all readers—from primary grades through junior high and beyond.

Beginning readers/writers or older hesitant ones can glean enough information from photographs or illustrations to prepare and deliver oral or written reports. They can select two or three books in a series, for example, and easily make comparisons that form a basis for discussion. Older, better readers can use the books as jumping-off points for further research. "Beginning" books provide basic information, are models for organizing reports on the subject, and often provide ideas for related topics.

Black-and-White Can Be Colorful

Color is a characteristic that appears early on a list of criteria for good nonfiction. It is essential if youngsters are fully to appreciate light's rainbow spectrum, a New England fall, or an apple's dramatic transition from cool green to rich red.

But color is not always required. Photo-essayist George Ancona told me that when color is not an essential part of the message, black-and-white photography can be used to unify a book—it provides a common denominator for a variety of subjects and backgrounds. He says that the way photos are used is as important as their color. He introduces variety, rhythm, and mood to a book with photos of contrasting characteristics such as tone, size, shape, and scene. You'll get the picture in Mr. Ancona's *Being Adopted* and *My Friend Leslie* (both Lothrop), where his focus is the love and warmth within families and between friends; in Hella Hammid's sensitive portrayal of preschoolers and infants in *A Is for Aloha* (U/Hawaii) and *The New Baby at Your House* (Morrow); in the vivid wildlife views of Hope Ryden's *Bobcat* (Putnam), Ozzie Sweet's photographs in Jack Denton Scott's *Alligator* (Putnam), and Nina Leen's *Rare and Unusual Animals* (Holt).

Open Kids' Eyes to Good Books

Many design elements that make a book pleasant to hold and read are not readily apparent to the average reader: book size, paper color and quality, typeface, spacing between lines, margin widths, illustration color, illustration size and placement, decorative embellishment, and page numbers. They are subtle features far more obvious when handled poorly than artfully.

The ultimate design test a book must pass is this: Does reading the book become as much an aesthetic as an intellectual experience? If so, you are holding an eye-opener.

11

A Guide to 500+ Children's Nonfiction Books, with 150 Tips

I've coded the entries in this Guide for easy reference. Here's an example:

THE PLANETS IN OUR SOLAR SYSTEM
Franklyn M. Branley ──────────▶ *Book is published in both*
Crowell (both), 1981   *hardcover and paperback*
Full-color illustrations by Don Madden and b/w photographs
[p] 32 pages

      ▶ *Age range:* [p] *for preschooler and primary (grades K–3)*
                     [i] *for intermediate (grades 4–6)*
                     [j] *for junior high school (grades 7–9)*

The age range is only to help, not limit, the linking of books to children. Junior high photoessays can be as enriching to primary-graders just looking as their "first" books can be to junior-highers just beginning new subjects.

☞ An idea for parents and teachers. Ideas particularly suitable for classrooms are labeled T (for teacher) TIPS.

TIP: ☞   TEACHER'S TIP: T☞

BOOKS FROM BRITAIN

In this guide, you will find books originally published in England and reprinted verbatim in the United States. In most of them, your children will find occasional "misspellings" and unfamiliar words: *traveller* and *petrol,* for example, instead of *traveler* and *gasoline.* Please don't let the minor differences between English and American keep you from using these worthwhile nonfiction works. In addition to providing your children with first-rate information sources, you can use the books to teach your youngsters that our language is both versatile and constantly changing.

CATEGORICALLY SPEAKING

Would that there were room in the Guide for more categories! I've had to leave out groups of books that I know kids love. If a subject you seek is not included, perhaps it will appear in a revised edition of *Eyeopeners!*

ABC Books

Babies, cities, dinosaurs—just about everything you can touch, taste, see, smell, or hear has been alphabetized. All in books that range from the smallest, simplest, one-item-per-page toddlers' board book to Mike Wilks's 10 x 13" *Ultimate Alphabet* (Holt) of 7,777 items he patiently painted over a period of four years for persistent perusers' pleasure. Short and fat, like *Baby's ABC* (Random House), or tall and thin, like the *Museum of Modern Art, New York, ABC* (Abrams), artful alphabet books are for readers of all ages—no matter their "intended" audience.

ANIMAL ALPHABET
Bert Kitchen
Dial, 1984
Full-color illustrations by the author
[all ages] 32 pages

This cleverly designed and executed set of animal-entwined letters will entrance everyone. The elegant elephant embracing an *E* on the cover is a teaser for the captivating creatures you'll find on the inside.

ALPHABATICS
Suse MacDonald
Bradbury, 1986
Full-color illustrations by the author
[p] 64 pages

Brightly colored letters are twisted, turned, and wittily transformed into objects—an upended *A* becomes an ark, for example, and the hole in a *b,* a balloon.

BUSY ABC
Colin and Jacqui Hawkins
Viking, 1987
Full-color illustrations by the authors
[p] 32 pages

Pert preschoolers portrayed in the process of—blowing, cooking, hopping, looking, whispering, zippering, and so on.

☞ This and Janet Beller's photoessay *A-B-C-ing* (Crown) are marvelous mime motivators: have youngsters dramatize their own alphabetical actions and see who can guess what they're doing.

ON MARKET STREET
Arnold Lobel
Greenwillow, 1981
Color illustrations by Anita Lobel
[all ages] 40 pages

Imagine a magical marketplace of twenty-six shops, one for each letter of the alphabet, where the shopkeepers *are* their wares: a woman of wigs, for example, and a man made of musical instruments. Sound wonderful? It is indeed!

☞ Use the Lobels' creative excursion to inspire youngsters to make their own merry merchandisers out of pictures they've drawn or cut from magazines.

A IS FOR ALOHA
Stephanie Feeney
U/Hawaii Press, 1980
B/w photographs by Hella Hammid
[p] 64 pages

Twenty-six evocative one- and two-page photographs capture Hawaiian preschoolers and the people, places, and experiences that make up their everyday island life.

☞ Hand youngsters a camera and let them photograph an alphabetical array of scenes for their own "A Is for . . ." book. Or have them illustrate the book with pictures they draw or cut from magazines.

FIND THE ANIMAL ABC
Demi
Grosset, 1985
B/w and full-color illustrations by the author
[p] 48 pages

A Demian catch-me-if-you-can test of visual acuity. Youngsters match a creature the artist has drawn in a box with its twin cavorting among dozens of other animals elsewhere on the page.

MOUSE NUMBERS AND LETTERS
MOUSE WRITING
Jim Arnosky
Harcourt, 1982; 1983
Two-color illustrations by the author
[p, i] each 48 pages

A jaunty little mouse bends twigs to construct upper-case printed letters in the first book; in the second, an intrepid pair of mouse skaters glide in perfect Zaner-Bloser cursive, ingeniously demonstrating where each upper- and lower-case letter begins and ends.

☞ Your children might enjoy knowing that the 1980 Winter Olympics in Lake Placid inspired Mr. Arnosky's *Mouse Writing*. His daughter Amber was having difficulty making a capital *S* in cursive, and he thought it would help to liken the motion of her hand to an ice skater's sweeping strokes. It did!

JAMBO MEANS HELLO
Muriel Feelings
Dial, 1974
Two-color illustrations by Tom Feelings
[p, i] 56 pages

Kiswahili (the prefix *Ki* denotes the language as opposed to the people who speak it) is spoken across more of Africa than any other language. Twenty-four of its words are listed, defined, and explained: one for each letter of the alphabet. There are no sounds for *Q* and *X*. This is a lovely introduction to the customs of many East Africans, as well as their language.

A, MY NAME IS ALICE
Jane Bayer
Dial, 1984
Full-color illustrations by Steven Kellogg
[p, i] 32 pages

"B, my name is Beverly, and my husband's name is Bob, we come from Boston. . . ." This alphabetical word game requires no equipment and can be easily adapted for rainy day activities or to help time pass on buses, in line at the supermarket, or in the doctor's waiting room.

NORTHERN ALPHABET
Ted Harrison
Tundra, 1982
Full-color illustrations by the author
[p, i] 32 pages

Boldly colored, full-page illustrations and brief descriptive sentences depict North American people, places, and things above the 55th parallel (roughly the latitude of Ketchikan, Alaska).

☞ Mr. Harrison found no places north of the 55th parallel in North America beginning with X. Ask youngsters to explore the world, via atlases, to find where X does mark the spot—the first letter of the spot's name, that is. (There are at least 20 below the 55th parallel, including two Xenias, in the United States.)

CITY SEEN FROM A TO Z
Rachel Isadora
Greenwillow, 1983
B/w illustrations by the author
[i] 32 pages

BIG CITY ABC
Alan Moak
Tundra, 1984
Full-color illustrations by the author
[i] 32 pages

The sights that make New York and Toronto, respectively, special places in the eyes of an artist who lives there.

☞ Ms. Isadora's book reminded me of the city in which I grew up. It's quite different from the one in which I live now. Have some children interview parents about their hometowns. Send others to the library to look up and photocopy local scenes from old newspapers, so they can discover how their town has changed over the years.

With Mr. Moak's book as a model, children can collaborate on a "Welcome to Our City ABC." They can paint scenes of parks, buildings, and other landmarks around the city, bind the pictures together, and keep the finished collection in the school library or office, readily available for the new kids on campus.

ALLIGATOR ARRIVED WITH APPLES
Crescent Dragonwagon
Macmillan, 1987
Full-color illustrations by Jose Aruego and Ariane Dewey
[p, i] 40 pages

Talk about potlucks! An alphabetical array of animals contributes culinary concoctions to a gastronomic gala.

ASTER AARDVARK'S ALPHABET ADVENTURES
Steven Kellogg
Morrow, 1987
Color illustrations by the author
[i] 40 pages

Warm and witty illustrations encapsulate the longest, most delightful, initially alliterative, nonsensical, yet grammatically correct, compound-complex sentences I've seen assembled anywhere.

☞ Help kids ease into writing compound-complex sentences with Steven Kellogg's humorous concoctions as models. Let them replace words noun by noun, adjective by adjective, and so on, until they have completely new sentences. Vocabularies will increase at the same time if the writers thumb through thesauri and dive into dictionaries for new words to create even sillier scenes.

ANIMALPHABET ENCYCLOPEDIA
Keith McConnell
Stemmer, 1982
B/w illustrations by the author
[i] 48 pages

Line drawings and a brief description of each of a dozen alphabetically grouped animals are on alternate pages of this coloring book. Companion coloring books *ReptAlphabet Encyclopedia* and *SeAlphabet Encyclopedia* feature reptiles and sea life, respectively.

☞ Challenge children to go on a "Big Game Safari" and track down every creature in *AnimAlphabet* or other similar coloring books, during spare moments throughout the year.

   Pass out illustrations, one page per week. When "hunters" have correctly "captured" the animals by accurately identifying and coloring the pictures, let them add a feather to a cap of their own design you've pinned to a bulletin board.

POSTAL WORKERS: A TO Z
TEACHERS: A TO Z
Jean Johnson
Walker, 1987
B/w photographs by the author
[i] each 48 pages

Clear photographs give youngsters interesting on-the-job and behind-the-scenes peeks at both professions. Other titles in the series include *Firefighters: A to Z* and *Police Officers: A to Z.*

☞ With any of Ms. Johnson's books as a model, suggest some children write a "Students: A to Z" and others interview family members for a brother, a sister, a parent, or a grandparent A to Z.

ALPHABET ART
Leonard Everett Fisher
Four Winds, 1978
Two-color illustrations by the author
[i, j] 64 pages

Chinese, Cyrillic, and Eskimo are among the thirteen alphabets found in this handsome volume. A brief history of the written language precedes each.

☞ Youngsters can collect alphabets from around the world if they request sample newspapers from family or friends living abroad or write to foreign consulates. As the collection of multilingual papers swells, cut out and put their mastheads on the walls. This unique "wallpaper" can inspire interesting discussions on diversity and uniformity in written communication.

MUSEUM OF MODERN ART, NEW YORK, ABC
MUSEUM OF FINE ARTS, BOSTON, ABC
Florence Cassen Mayers
Abrams, 1986
Full-color photographs and reproductions
[all ages] each 32 pages

These tall, thin books (5 x 14″) literally elevate abc's to fine art. Each contains an alphabetically representative sampling of the masterpieces in the permanent collections of both institutions.

☞ As you enter a museum with children, stop first at the shop and buy postcards of the items on display. Deputize your children "Museum Inspectors," hand them the cards, and let them locate the originals.

Adoption

BEING ADOPTED
Maxine B. Rosenberg
Lothrop, 1984
B/w photographs by George Ancona
[p, i] 48 pages

This is a sensitive look at three American families with adopted children of different racial and cultural backgrounds. The photographs capture the youngsters' exuberance; the text, their special concerns. Advice for parents with adopted foreign-born or minority children concludes the book.

WE DON'T LOOK LIKE OUR MOM AND DAD
Harriet Langsam Sobol
Coward, 1984
B/w photographs by Patricia Agre
[i, j] 48 pages

Brothers Eric and Joshua are adopted sons who have different Korean birth mothers. The book reflects the warm and loving family life in which Mr. and Mrs. Levin help the boys grow up as Levins with a Korean heritage.

THE ADOPTED ONE
Sara Bonnett Stein
Walker, 1979
B/w photographs by Erika Stone
[p, i] 48 pages

Two texts appear side by side in this "Open Family Book." The first, in small type, provides background information for adults; the second, in large type, is ideal for parents to read aloud with their youngsters. Both concern the difficulties a preschooler might have adjusting to and growing up in an adoptive family.

☞ When talking about families, point out that they come in all shapes and sizes. Norma Simon's *All Kinds of Families* (Whitman) nicely illustrates this point.

HOW IT FEELS TO BE ADOPTED
Jill Krementz
Knopf, 1982
B/w photographs by the author
[i, j] 112 pages

Nineteen youngsters, ages nine to sixteen, share their innermost thoughts about adoption. The boys and girls, from different socioeconomic backgrounds, were adopted at various ages into one- and two-parent homes; some adoptees became an only child while others acquired siblings.

☞ When you design activities that focus on the family, remain sensitive to children whose home life does not revolve around two biological parents. If family trees are on the agenda, allow youngsters to draw their own or that of a friend or neighbor; when studying inherited traits, let some students trace their own while others poll those of other kids on campus.

Airplanes

Suggest children design and budget a "Terrific Trip." Pick up brochures at a travel agency, write for packets of information from domestic or international tourist bureaus, and get travel schedules at airline, train, and bus counters. When junior travel agents take charge, reading, math, and map reading won't be the same. For fantasies featuring flights, they'll find a view of the real thing in the following.

AIRPORT
Byron Barton
Crowell, 1982
Full-color illustrations by the author
[p] 32 pages

Primary-graders will sense the hustle and bustle from arrival to takeoff when they embark upon this armchair trip to the airport.

AIRPORTS
Michael Jay and Mark Hewish
Watts, 1982
Full-color illustrations
[p, i] 32 pages

This contrasts early airports with contemporary ones and provides such details as sample tickets, boarding passes, and flight plans to interest preflight travelers of all ages.

☞ Use the Jay/Hewish *Airports* as a primer for a visit to an air terminal or a classroom visit from a pilot, traffic controller, or flight attendant. If a commercial airport isn't nearby, a request for help from a local flying club may net you a guest speaker to describe his/her career around airplanes.

THE BIG BOOK OF REAL AIRPLANES
Gina Ingoglia
Grosset, 1987
Full-color illustrations by George Guzzi
[p, i] 48 pages

This information-packed, fully illustrated 9 x 12" book explains what keeps planes up and how to maneuver them in the air, and gives a view from the cockpit. Readers will also learn about a wide variety of commercial and military planes—including helicopters—and their uses.

☞ You can't let kids contemplate planes without proposing flight lessons under Seymour Simon's expert instruction! Set out his super *Paper Airplane Book* (Viking and Puffin) and piles of used-on-one-side paper you've saved for recycling, step aside, and watch your "pilots" take off.

AIRLINERS
N. S. Barrett
Watts, 1984
Full-color illustrations by Tony Bryan
[i] 32 pages

The focus is on airliners of every ilk, from the small 5-passenger business planes to the over-500-passenger Boeing 747 and the faster-than-the-speed-of-a-bullet supersonic Concorde.

ULTRALIGHTS: THE FLYING FEATHERWEIGHTS
Charles Coombs
Morrow, 1984
B/w photographs
[i, j] 160 pages

With gusto and considerable emphasis upon safety, the author reviews the development of manned flight, details the construction of the collapsible miniplanes, and covers the basics of aeronautics, meteorology, and navigation. He puts readers in the pilot's seat with a vivid description of flight training and a first solo.

☞ Link kids to Huck Scarry's *Balloon Trip* (Prentice) for a flight of a different sort. The sketchbook journal describes two trips the author/artist made—one in a hydrogen balloon and the other in a hot-air balloon. Between trips, he recounts how the Montgolfier brothers began balloon travel in 1783. (Two hundred and one years later, my husband and son treated me to my own hot-air balloon trip on the occasion of my fiftieth birthday. It was wonderful!)

RECORD-BREAKING AIRPLANES
Don Berliner
Lerner, 1985
B/w and full-color photographs
[i, j] 48 pages

This engrossing history of fast planes begins with Santos Dumont's 1906 flight at 25.6 mph (in a biplane he piloted standing up) and includes the 2,193.6-mph Lockheed SR71-A. I found particularly interesting the story of Hitler's successful deception about the quality of his air force and that we may never know just how fast a jet can fly, since it is likely to be a military secret.

THE GLORIOUS FLIGHT:
ACROSS THE CHANNEL WITH LOUIS BLÉRIOT
Alice and Martin Provenson
Viking, 1983; Puffin, 1987
Full-color illustrations by the authors
[p, i] 40 pages

Louis Blériot broke the air-speed record in 1906 by piloting his monoplane an amazing 47.8 mph. That same year, he became the first man to cross the English Channel. This simple picture book re-creates the mood of turn-of-the-century France and Louis Blériot's determination to build and fly his own planes.

Alcohol

Alcohol is a problem for kids. Some have parents or older siblings who drink excessively. Reportedly 20 percent of sixth- to twelfth-graders consider themselves heavy drinkers; one out of four teenagers will become a problem drinker in high school. All children are exposed to seductive advertising and, at times, peer pressure to experiment.

Alcohol and its abuse, however, is not a subject to enter without adequate preparation and training. Young children tend to repress the fear, shame, and concern generated by an alcoholic in the family, and young drinkers are not easily counseled. Yet all adults in contact with children should be acquainted with literature about alcohol and alcoholism, if only to recognize clues and ask for help. Children of alcoholics might arrive at school disheveled and tense on Monday, relax by midweek, and become agitated again as they anticipate the weekend and its alcohol-related horrifics; drinking youngsters exhibit other symptoms, which should alert parents and teachers.

TEENS TALK ABOUT ALCOHOL AND ALCOHOLISM
Paul Dolmetsch and Gail Mauricette
Dolphin, 1987
[j] 144 pages

Though all of the teens "talking" are not alcoholics or from alcoholic families, all have witnessed or experienced the devastating effects of alcohol abuse. The editors begin with a discussion of alcohol's effect on the body and move to the social and emotional pressures, living with (an) alcoholic parent(s), and recovering from alcoholism. In conclusion, the teenagers review and recommend twelve books of fiction dealing with alcoholism.

☞ Provide multiple copies of *Teens Talk*... and let students enact the stories as readers theater or, working in small groups, role-play to practice and consider their reactions.

ALCOHOL: WHAT IT IS, WHAT IT DOES
Judith S. Seixas
Greenwillow (both), 1977
B/w illustrations by Tom Huffman
[i] 56 pages

In simple, straightforward terms, Ms. Seixas explains the effects of alcohol and refutes related misconceptions (an alcoholic can stop drinking by using willpower and most alcoholics are bums, for example). An excellent topic opener or quick reference for posters children can design about alcohol and its abuse.

COPING WITH AN ALCOHOLIC PARENT
Kay Marie Porterfield
Rosen, 1985

WHEN YOUR PARENT DRINKS TOO MUCH
Eric Ryerson
Facts on File, 1985
[j] 128 pages; 144 pages

These two books are the best I've read for teenage children of alcoholics.

Young adults will find it especially easy to relate to Mr. Ryerson, the son of an alcoholic. He urges them to appreciate three *C*s—that they didn't *cause* their parents' drinking, they can't *control* it, and they can't *cure* the disease. Both he and Ms. Porterfield stress the importance of letting go of the shame and embarrassment, discuss the effects of a parent on the mend, and conclude with suggestions for seeking help.

LETTERS TO JUDY
Judy Blume
Putnam, 1986
[i, j] 288 pages

Here, Judy Blume shares some of the 2,000 letters she receives each month from children. They write about parents, siblings, and friends; puberty, dating, and divorce; alcohol, drugs, and more. The popular children's author adds her comments and occasional advice. She concludes with a list of resources for additional help.

Every parent and teacher should read her book, if only to be reminded how difficult and often painful it is to be young. A copy belongs in every school library, ready for children when the need arises. (All royalties go directly to the Kids Fund, a nonprofit charitable and educational foundation.)

Alligators and Crocodiles

ALLIGATORS AND CROCODILES
John Bonnett Wexo
Wildlife, 1984 (paperback only)
Full-color illustrations and photographs
[p, i] 20 pages

Eyes will light up and imaginations jump into overdrive as kids find themselves face-to-face with an awesome American alligator. Moving on, they'll learn about crocodilian ancestry and other fascinating reptilian characteristics.

☞ The Wexo centerfold is perfect for creative writing: How did the photographer catch that image? What was the alligator doing before and after it was "shot"?

ALLIGATOR
Jack Denton Scott
Putnam, 1984
B/w photographs by Ozzie Sweet
[i] 64 pages

The collaborators describe this amphibious predator's beauty, from the tip of its tail (regrown if lost) to its forty-tooth snout. They cover its gentle mating ritual, nest-building activities, and remarkable survival through the millennia.

☞ No alligator agenda is complete without Thatcher Hurd's *Mama Don't Allow* (Harper). Stamp your feet, sing along, and delight with your youngsters as the smooth swamp dwellers are outsmarted.

THE CROCODILES STILL WAIT
Carol Carrick
Houghton, 1980
Two-color illustrations by Donald Carrick
[p] 32 pages

If children find today's crocodilians formidable, what would they think of their fifty-foot ancestors whose heads were six feet long? The giant comes to life in the dramatic scenes of a female's protection of eggs and young during one Mesozoic summer.

Art and Artists

Many adults consider themselves too uneducated about art to introduce the subject to children. Yet what could be simpler? Just say "I like that!" when something appeals to you, or "I don't like that" when it doesn't. Encourage children to do the same. Discuss what you do or don't like. Borrow a book about the artist and together learn more about his or her work. Explain that art is in the eye of the beholder, that tastes change over time. The more we look at art and read about it, the more we come to appreciate it.

MARC CHAGALL
PABLO PICASSO
Ernest Raboff
Lippincott (both), 1987
Full-color illustrations by the author and reproductions
[p, i, j] each 32 pages

Each volume contains 15 reproductions; a brief, simply written biographical sketch; and analyses of the artist's paintings in a colorful hand-lettered text. They're excellent starting places for youngsters on their way to appreciating art. Other titles in the series include *Pierre-Auguste Renoir, Vincent van Gogh,* and *Leonardo da Vinci.*

LINNEA IN MONET'S GARDEN
Christina Björk
R&S, 1987
Full-color illustrations by Lena Anderson and b/w and full-color photographs
[i, j] 56 pages

This blend of fact and fiction is a superb introduction to the Impressionist, his family, his home in Giverny, his art—and a little bit of Paris as well. Colorful drawings portray the fictional aspect. Black-and-white photographs of Monet and his family, as well as color photographs of his paintings and garden, show the factual ones. Author and illustrator re-create the life of the painter and a visit to Giverny as vividly as they create the enthusiasm of Linnea, his young admirer.

BREAKING TRADITION: THE STORY OF LOUISE NEVELSON
Natalie S. Bober
Atheneum, 1984
B/w photographs
[j] 192 pages

The author so completely drew me into the life of sculptor Louise Nevelson, I was certain I'd finished the book in minutes, though I'd been reading for more than an hour. Ms. Nevelson's unrelenting drive to create will absorb you and the young adults with whom you share this.

GRANDMA MOSES: PAINTER OF RURAL AMERICA
Zibby Oneal
Viking, 1986; Puffin, 1987
B/w illustrations by Donna Ruff and reproductions
[i, j] 64 pages

The author never met Grandma Moses but, within 64 short pages, she has brought her to life with the knowing warmth and affection of an old friend.

☞ Have your youngsters borrow a book of Grandma Moses reproductions from the library and use them as inspiration for pictorial autobiographies.

A HISTORY OF ART
Marshall B. Davidson
Random House, 1984
Full-color illustrations and reproductions
[j] 112 pages

This slim, 8½ x 11″, 112-page, under-$10 volume is an excellent addition to any home reference library. It surveys art from the ancient world to Jean Dubuffet and Jim Dine. The art is grouped according to period and all reproductions have brief anecdotal annotations.

GREAT PAINTERS
Piero Ventura
Putnam, 1984
Full-color illustrations by the author and full-color reproductions
[j] 160 pages

If you've seen the real *Mona Lisa,* your initial reaction was probably "It's so small!" Reproductions, from postage stamp to billboard, don't prepare you for the 20 x 30″ original. There will be no misconceptions, however, about the relative size of any painting in this book. The author has ingeniously placed each photographic reproduction within an illustrated setting, juxtaposing (to scale) the painting, its admirers, the artist, or his model(s). The narrative is for older readers, but the detailed pictures are for viewers of all ages.

THE TURN ABOUT, THINK ABOUT, LOOK ABOUT BOOK
THE LOOK AGAIN . . . AND AGAIN, AND AGAIN, AND AGAIN
BOOK
Beau Gardner
Lothrop, 1980; 1983
Full-color illustrations by the author
[p, i] each 32 pages

No matter how you look at it, we all see things differently. Rotate one of the books above, for example, and you'll see in turn, a teacup handle, a cat's tail, the letter *J*, and an elephant's tusk—perhaps!

☞ Distribute 6-inch squares of colored construction or origami paper and have youngsters create designs à la Gardner's turn-around books. Pin up their designs through the center, so everyone can enjoy twisting and turning the pictures, to see what they can see.

DRAWING FROM NATURE
DRAWING LIFE IN MOTION
Jim Arnosky
Lothrop (both) 1982; 1984
B/w illustrations by the author
[i, j] 64 pages

In each of these perceptive guides, the author/artist opens our eyes to the vibrant life about us. In the first, he explains and illustrates that nature is everywhere, at home and trekking through the woods. It is in the steam from a teakettle, the dewdrops on a spiderweb, a look between father and infant son. In the second, he focuses upon the geotropic twistings and turnings of seedlings; the subtle swaying of stems and leaves shadowing the sun; the rhythm of a falling leaf, a slithering snake, a swooping owl.

Australia

Ask youngsters to brainstorm things Australian and (after *Crocodile Dundee*) koalas and kangaroos will probably top the list. For absorbing close-ups of each, turn to . . .

KOALA
KANGAROO
Caroline Arnold
Morrow, 1987
Full-color photographs by Richard Hewett
[i] each 48 pages

Smoothly flowing texts and sharply focused photographs spotlight the popular marsupials' physical characteristics and conservation efforts on their behalf.

KOALAS
John Bonnett Wexo
Wildlife (paperback only), 1983
Full-color illustrations and photographs
[p, i] 20 pages

Color photographs, detailed illustrations, information-packed captions, and a conversational narrative explain how the koala is adapted to life in a treetop, for example, and why the kangaroo uses *less* energy the faster it hops. The author compares the development of marsupial and placental babies, introduces the platypus and the spiny anteater, and presents a fascinating juxtaposition of marsupials and their mammalian look-alikes.

☞ Koalas, though sometimes called koala bears, aren't. Have your children compare both mammals' physical characteristics and list why koalas are *not* bears.

AMAZING ANIMALS OF AUSTRALIA
S. L. Barry et al.
National Geographic, 1984
Full-color photographs
[i] 104 pages

At first sight of their names, I couldn't help wondering if bettongs, brolgas, and bilbies band together in bevies, broods, or bunches; quokkas and currawongs congregate in caches; perenties and pademelons parade in passels; or durrants deploy in droves! In spite of fine photographs and intriguing information, my immediate reaction to this absorbing book was more lexicological than zoological, you see.

☞ What fun children will have as they look through *Amazing Animals*... and discover the dozens of delightfully dubbed denizens (sorry) from Australia's sea to its outback. Use the creatures as inspiration for poetry, tongue twisters, word finds, crosswords, riddles, fanciful tales, and other wonderful wordplay.

WALLABY CREEK
TASMANIA
Joyce Powzyk
Lothrop, 1985; 1987
Full-color illustrations by the author
[i] each 32 pages

The beautiful watercolors add an artist's perspective to children's views of the flora and fauna of Australia within each ecological niche, from snowy highlands to the seashore.

☞ Pair Ms. Powzyk's wildlife portraits with photographs of the same creatures. Discuss the differences and similarities between images by artists who use paint and brush and those who use camera and film.

PASSPORT TO AUSTRALIA
Susan Pepper
Watts, 1987
Full-color photographs and illustrations
[i] 48 pages

Two-page articles, illustrated with photographs, maps, and charts, provide a clearly delineated, easily grasped overview of the country's geography, its people, and their form of government. They are a good starting point for young people, particularly hesitant junior high students, about to explore the world's smallest continent.

A FAMILY IN AUSTRALIA
AN ABORIGINAL FAMILY
Rollo Browne
Lerner, 1987; 1985
Full-color photographs
[i] each 32 pages

In the first title listed, readers "visit" the Northern Territory, home of bauxite miner Tom Baker and his family. In the second, they'll meet eleven-year-old Lynette, her brother, sisters, and parents who live in a Northern Territory town one hundred miles from the nearest public transportation.

☞ Browne's close-ups of "down under" family life offer many opportunities for discussion. Keep in mind, however, that the lifestyles depicted are the exception rather than the rule. Most Australians are city dwellers (60 percent of the population is concentrated in five coastal cities) and live lives not too different from their urbanized American counterparts.

WE LIVE IN AUSTRALIA
Rennie Ellis
Bookwright, 1983
Full-color photographs
[i] 64 pages

Twenty-eight two-page interviews, presented as personal statements and accompanied by photographs, provide a glimpse of the peoples who contribute to Australian culture.

☞ You or your children can add drama to vicarious Australian adventures by learning and telling folktales—in sand. You'll find two Aboriginal sand stories in Anne Pellowski's *The Story Vine* (Macmillan). The author includes directions for a special sandbox you can use on an overhead projector.

While some youngsters are practicing sand stories, others can perfect string figures, another Aboriginal storytellers' art. You'll find directions for figures that originated in Australia and nearby in Camilla Gryski's *Cat's Cradle, Owl's Eye* and *Many Stars and More String Games* (Morrow).

Authors and Illustrators

Whenever I meet with a class of youngsters for the first time, I have by my side a portable corkboard covered with photographs. Among them are baby and sixth-grade pictures of myself, shots of my husband and son as babies, and a photograph of my dad, the youngest of eight children, as a preschooler, in a formal studio portrait taken at the turn of the century.

The pictures illustrate that I, too, was once as young as my students, and that I have a life away from school—as a mom and a daughter. Children tend to forget that we have roles other than those in which they see us.

In a similar fashion, auto- or other people's biographies of children's book authors and artists help youngsters realize that some of their favorite books' creators are real people. They provide insight into the origins of characters, incidents, and scenes in those stories.

SELF-PORTRAIT: TRINA SCHART HYMAN
Trina Schart Hyman
Harper, 1981
Full-color illustrations by the author
[i, j] 32 pages

Ms. Hyman, the first art director of *Cricket* magazine and a Caldecott Award winner, tells how she was once Little Red Riding Hood, kept company with trolls in Norway, and now creates her books in a big farmhouse in Vermont.

    ☞ Where do artists find inspiration for many of their illustrations? Share Ms. Hyman's *Little Red Riding Hood* (Holiday), then the chapter of the same name from her self-portrait, and you and your children will discover the model for Red Riding Hood's mother. Grandmother and the woodsman are the artist's neighbors.

A GRAIN OF WHEAT
Clyde Robert Bulla
Godine (both), 1985
B/w photographs
[i] 49 pages

The author shares memories of his dog Carlo, learning to swim, and his determination since childhood to become a writer. The last two chapters are my favorites and I read them aloud at most workshops to remind teachers and parents to respect their children's dreams.

☞ Photographs of Mr. Bulla as a child illustrate his book. Have your students bring in pictures of themselves as babies. When you've collected them all, put them on a "Very Important People" bulletin board—unlabeled. See how well your children recognize who's who. At the first parent conference, ask parents to send you, in a sealed envelope, their pictures as elementary-graders. Display the photos and have your students guess who they are! Do the same with your faculty members.

WHEN I WAS NINE
HIGHER ON THE DOOR
James Stevenson
Greenwillow, 1985; 1987
Full-color illustrations by the author
[i] each 32 pages

In these sets of reminiscences, Mr. Stevenson writes about publishing a neighborhood newspaper, a family trip through the States, brotherly squabbles, and other ordinary childhood happenings in the 1930s. He illustrates both books with drawings appropriately fuzzy, like most memories of times past.

☞ When children have written about their favorite family trip, have them interview the other family members who went on the same trip. Do their memories resemble or differ from one another? Children can interview their parents to discover what their favorite family trip was—when they were children.

MY BAR MITZVAH
Richard Rosenblum
Morrow, 1985
B/w illustrations by the author
[i, j] 32 pages

The details are Jewish, but the surrounding events, catholic: the months of preparation for a momentous occasion; buddies' friendly heckling during a solemn event; and, of course, the gifts.

☞ Let youngsters describe their confirmation, Bar/Bat Mitzvah, or other similarly significant events, commenting on their most memorable aspects. Jon Mayled's *Initiation Rites* (Silver) contains colorful photographs and introductory information about coming-of-age ceremonies in seven religions, including Buddhism, Islam, and Hinduism.

HOMESICK: MY OWN STORY
Jean Fritz
Putnam, 1982
B/w illustrations by Margot Tomes and b/w photographs
[i, j] 200 pages

As vividly as she re-creates American history, Ms. Fritz recalls her two-year transition from leaving home in China (where she had been born to American missionaries) to coming "home" to America—from October 1925, when she was eleven, to September 1927. In *Homecoming* (Putnam) the author recounts her return visit to China some fifty-five years later.

☞ Ms. Fritz wrote about the handwriting exercises she had to do when she entered school in America. Have your children ask their parents how they learned handwriting in school. Have them send samples of their writing to school. Share Ms. Fritz's *Will You Sign Here, John Hancock?* and start a class collection of "John Hancocks" from family, friends, and acquaintances. When your bulletin board is filled with signatures, see what similarities children can note and if those similarities correspond to the ages of the signers.

ME ME ME ME ME: NOT A NOVEL
M. E. Kerr
Harper, 1983
[j] 224 pages

Her autobiography is as perceptive, forthright, and witty as anything Ms. Kerr has made up. Fans will recognize the source of some of the author's "fictional" plots and characters.

☞ When you focus on biographies, start with yours: use family photos to introduce yourself to your students. (My sixth-grade picture always elicits an incredulous "That's YOU?!") Chalk up answers to the questions your snapshots inspire, and your boys and girls will have notes from which they can then write a brief biographical sketch about you.

Make that sketch the first in a series of question-framing/note-taking/writing-rewriting activities that involve interviews with schoolmates and relatives. Follow those with "interviews" of notable people via their bio- or autobiographies.

ONCE UPON A TIME
Putnam (both), 1986
Full-color and b/w illustrations
[i, j] 64 pages

Such noted children's book authors and illustrators as Arnold Lobel, Natalie Babbit, Ashley Bryan, and Judy Blume contributed to this collection of anecdotes, stories, and reminiscences of books and reading. Proceeds from the book's sale go to Reading Is Fundamental.

☞ Have your children share their earliest memory of being read to or reading a book. Don't forget to share your own.

KIPLING: STORYTELLER OF EAST AND WEST
Gloria Kamen
Atheneum, 1985
Brown-and-white illustrations by the author
[i] 80 pages

Kipling's story has all the elements of a fairy tale, including a wicked witch (a grim "Aunty" Rosa) and a kindly mentor (the headmaster of a private school). Youngsters will enjoy "meeting" the man and discovering the genesis of Mowgli, Rikki-Tikki-Tavi, and other favorite Kipling characters.

A BABY FOR MAX
Kathryn Lasky and Maxwell B. Knight
Scribner's, 1984; Aladdin, 1987
B/w photographs by Christopher G. Knight
[p] 32 pages

Children with a new sibling on the way will quickly identify with Max's version of what it means to become an older brother. I'm recommending it here because it's also an introduction to photographer/ husband and author/wife photoessay collaborators Kathryn Lasky and Christopher G. Knight. Max is their son. The three are shown preparing for the arrival of the fourth Knight.

LAURA INGALLS WILDER: GROWING UP IN THE LITTLE HOUSE
Patricia Reilly Giff
Viking, 1987; Puffin, 1988
B/w illustrations by Eileen McKeating
[i] 64 pages

Ms. Giff follows Laura Ingalls Wilder from the start of her first book, *The Little House in the Big Woods* (Harper, 1932), at age sixty-three, to her death, just a few days before her ninetieth birthday. In a skillful interweaving of Wilder's past and present, Ms. Giff reveals the who, what, where, when, and why of the "Little House" series as some of them were created.

Babies

BEFORE YOU WERE BORN
Margaret Sheffield
Knopf, 1984
Full-color illustrations by Sheila Bewley
[p] 40 pages

Simple prose helps very young children appreciate what it is like for a baby growing inside its mother the few months before birth. Softly colored, nonclinical illustrations let readers peek at the infant warmly ensconced in the womb.

BEING BORN
Sheila Kitzinger
Grosset, 1986
Full-color photographs by Lennart Nilsson
[p, i, j] 60 pages

Striking photographs, set like jewels against a rich, black background, dramatically illustrate the beauty and wonder of human development from conception to birth. The author speaks directly to children as she describes what they heard, saw, and felt during their prenatal life and at birth. Her words are warm, gentle, poetic, and enlightening.

HOW YOU WERE BORN
Joanna Cole
Morrow (both), 1984
B/w photographs
[p] 48 pages

This simple, informative explanation of birth—from single cell to new-born—is reassuring and straightforward. It begins with sage advice to parents on dealing with children's questions about birth and a list of books for further reading. The photographs include moms *and* dads preparing for and holding their babies.

☞ Before the new sibling arrives, prepare children for the positive and negative feelings they may have when there is a *New Baby at Your House* (Morrow). As in her book above, Ms. Cole opens with advice to parents.

101 THINGS TO DO WITH A BABY
Jan Ormerod
Lothrop, 1984; Puffin, 1986
Full-color illustrations by the author
[p, i] 32 pages

The author/artist captures the warmth of family life as well as the joys and frustrations of a primary-grader as she gets to know her little brother. This is a delightful look at a family enjoying, and being enjoyed by, its newest addition.

☞ An excellent device for getting boys' and girls' creative "juices" flowing is to have them brainstorm 101 uses for a brick or a pencil or a marshmallow. Try babies and see how often your children and Ms. Ormerod agreed.

Ballet

For many youngsters, the Christmas season's live or televised productions of *The Nutcracker Suite* are a first exposure to ballet. Use the annual musical treat as inspiration for a closer look at the moving art form. Set the stage by playing a recording of the music and have handy . . .

THE NUTCRACKER
Ellen Switzer
Atheneum, 1985
Full-color photographs
[j] 112 pages

The author provides both a description of how E. T. A. Hoffmann's story was transformed into a ballet and full-color photographs as it was danced by the New York City Ballet. The photographs, annotated with the ballet's narrative, constitute the major portion of the book. On the last few pages, the principal dancers explain how they interpret their respective roles.

IF YOU WERE A BALLET DANCER
Ruth Belov Gross
Scholastic (paperback only), 1979
B/w photographs
[p] 64 pages

Ms. Gross's simple question-and-answer format, well chosen black-and-white photographs, and glossary of terms—with pronunciation guide—provide useful information for young would-be dancers or viewers.

☞ If any children in your school study ballet, ask one or two to speak to your class and describe their lessons. Invite a ballet teacher and a fellow dancer to visit. Aim for a man and a woman to discuss and demonstrate the similarities and differences in their respective roles and steps. Ask if you can audit a ballet class with a small group of children.

I LOVE TO DANCE!
Gerry Zeck
Carolrhoda, 1982
B/w photographs by the author
[i] 64 pages

Young boy dancers will easily identify with exuberant ten-year-old Tony Jones, whose goal is to dance with the American Ballet Theatre in New York City. His classes and experiences, perhaps even his dreams, will be quite familiar.

BALLET COMPANY: THE ROYAL BALLET
Kate Castle
Watts, 1984
Full-color photographs and illustrations
[i] 48 pages

Take a tour of the Royal Opera House in London's Covent Garden and meet the people, from stage doorkeeper to prima ballerina, who collaborate on each performance.

BALLET
Annabel Thomas
Usborne, 1986
Full-color illustrations
[i] 48 pages

This colorfully illustrated, information-packed introduction to ballet includes a brief history, an explanation of the Benesh notation system, hints for watching a performance, and miniprofiles of eighteen internationally known dancers.

BALLET STEPS: PRACTICE AND PERFORMANCE
Antony Dufort
C. N. Potter, 1985
B/w illustrations by the author
[i] 160 pages

The nondancer author/artist created this book to connect what he noticed in ballet classes with what he saw in performances. He beautifully captures the expressive language of dance in harmony with music, which readers cannot hear but will surely sense.

☞ Make Mr. Dufort's "illustrated vocabulary of classical ballet" available for Sustained Silent Reading time. It is ideal for dancers and nondancers alike.

Bats

Make bats "Pet-of-the-Month" (figuratively speaking, of course) and counter the image of a dirty, demonic, winged nuisance with the truth about the world's only flying mammals. None of the more than eight hundred species harass humans; some help keep insect populations pared, others pollinate flowers, and all preen themselves fastidiously.

BATS
Sylvia A. Johnson
Lerner, 1985
Full-color photographs by Modoki Masuda
and drawings by Masayuki Yabuuchi
[i, j] 48 pages

Start here when introducing children to the much-maligned mammals. The photographs and clear descriptions of various bat attributes and their habitats and diets will absorb even reluctant readers.

☞ Bats belong to the scientific order *Chiroptera,* which means "hand-wing." As you read aloud Ms. Johnson's description of a bat wing and how the animal flies, have youngsters close their eyes and visualize their hands becoming wings. Let them enjoy the imagined sensation of flying like a bat.

BILLIONS OF BATS
Miriam Schlein
Lippincott, 1982
B/w illustrations by Walter Kessell
[p, i] 48 pages

This look at more than twenty species explains how certain of them maneuver via sonarlike echolocation and migrate or hibernate when the weather turns cold.

☞ Let youngsters get their hands on a bat. Show them Kenneth Lilly's life-size illustration of a greater Indian fruit bat in Joanna Cole's *Large As Life: Nighttime Animals* (Knopf).

THE BAT
Nina Leen
Holt, 1976
B/w photographs by the author
[i, j] 80 pages

Ms. Leen spent over three years capturing twenty-two species of bats on film. In an appendix, as absorbing as the book itself, she tells exactly how she was able to "shoot" a flying fox swimming, vampire bats hopping about, and the fishing bulldog bat catching a fish.

VAMPIRE BATS
Laurence Pringle
Morrow, 1982
B/w photographs
[i] 64 pages

These bats were first recorded in 1498, after Columbus landed in Trinidad. Europeans who believed in vampire myths named them after the mythical creatures. Here, the author describes what scientists have learned about one species of the leaf-nose bats that dine on blood.

Bears

Bears captivate children as soon as they meet "Momma, Poppa and Baby": Almost everyone knows Pooh and Paddington, today's tots can turn to *Albert the Running Bear's Exercise Book* (Clarion) to keep fit, and there are few without a teddy bear or two. But it's the real ones, the largest meat-eating land animals on earth, who are truly fascinating. They come in black, blue, brown, and white, can weigh less than 100 or more than 2,200 pounds and stand from 4 to 11 feet tall. The black ones can be white or blue, the brown ones silver-tipped or almost black, and the white ones are really yellowish.

BEARS
John Bonnett Wexo
Wildlife, 1982
Full-color photographs and illustrations
[p, i] 20 pages

This is the place to start when you share the bear facts of life. Absorbing artwork provides visual details that make youngsters want to read every accompanying word. The simple text introduces readers to what we know and have yet to learn about brown and black bears in general, the polar and three smallest bears (spectacled, sun, and sloth) in particular.

GRIZZLY BEARS
John L. Weaver
Dodd, 1982
B/w photographs
[p] 64 pages

Primary-graders can easily bear grizzly specifics from Mr. Weaver's look at a mother and her three cubs' first fifteen months.

THE WAY OF THE GRIZZLY
Dorothy Hinshaw Patent
Clarion, 1987
B/w photographs by William Muñoz
[i, j] 64 pages

The zoologist author has written an absorbing and insightful account of this awesome animal's physical, social, and territorial characteristics and the impact of humans upon its existence.

☞ If children become particularly intrigued by grizzlies, read aloud excerpts from Thomas McNamee's excellent book for adults, *The Grizzly Bear* (Knopf).

ANDY BEAR
Ginny Johnston and Judy Cutchins
Morrow, 1985
B/w and full-color photographs by Constance Noble
[i] 64 pages

Constance Noble is one of the few zookeepers to raise successfully polar bear cubs born in captivity. Follow Ms. Noble's round-the-clock, surrogate-mother activities as she nurtures an under-one-and-a-half-pound cub from birth to his first birthday—at 150 pounds.

SEVEN TRUE BEAR STORIES
Laura Geringer
Hastings, 1979
B/w illustrations by Carol Maisto
[i] 88 pages

What happens when human meets bear? Seven such confrontations are recounted as stories short enough to tempt the most reluctant readers and exciting enough to keep them turning the pages. Each is also an excellent read-aloud.

☞ Pair the true stories above with Alvin Schwartz's *Fat Man in a Fur Coat* (Farrar), a collection of tales true and tall, legends, humorous stories, and facts about bears. Be sure children note the notes Mr. Schwartz has included along with his list of sources and bibliography. They enhance the collection and help youngsters appreciate what's involved in gathering material for such a work.

THE FIRST TEDDY BEAR
Helen Kay
Stemmer, 1985
Brown-and-white and full-color illustrations by Susan Detwiler
[p, i] 40 pages

Had Mississippi and Louisiana been able to settle their border dispute without President Teddy Roosevelt's help, there might never have been a teddy bear—perish the thought! Teddy-bear companions of all ages will enjoy this charming account of the stuffed animal's fortuitous (for us) origins.

☞ All teddy bears (and friends) should be familiar with William Pène du Bois's fictional "biography" *Gentleman Bear* (Farrar), whose daring trans-Channel flight helped win World War II. Gentleman Bear had an outfit for every occasion. Suggest youngsters dress their teddy bears for a special picnic—and have one.

Bicycles, BMX, and Motorcycles

TWO HUNDRED YEARS OF BICYCLES
Jim Murphy
Lippincott, 1983
B/w photographs
[i, j] 64 pages

Mr. Murphy's history helps children better appreciate the comfort of their modern bikes—earlier two-wheelers had no pedals, brakes, or any form of shock absorption. He concludes with a detailed look at modern bicycle design.

BIKE FACTORY
Harold Roth
Pantheon, 1985
B/w photographs by the author
[i] 48 pages

To make the average bicycle, hydraulic cutters, benders, coilers, and expanders "nibble," twist, round, and punch steel tubing and ribbon into hundreds of parts—more than 400 with nuts and bolts. Youngsters can follow the process in this trip through the Columbia Manufacturing Company's Massachusetts plant.

☞ Alan Say's *Bicycle Man* (Houghton) and Mary Scioscia's *Bicycle Rider* (Harper) are based upon real incidents. After I'd read both stories aloud, my youngsters and I wondered what was true and what was made up. Your children might enjoy learning—as we did—where the facts end and the fiction begins in these two instances.

I phoned Mr. Say and learned that the bicycle man looked and performed as described, but his red-headed buddy never existed. Ms. Scioscia told me that champion racer Marshall Taylor grew up in the warm and loving family she'd described. She made up his siblings' names, however, since she was unable to find them listed anywhere.

BICYCLE MOTOCROSS IS FOR ME
Tom Moran
Lerner, 1982
B/w photographs by the author
[i, j] 48 pages

A preteenager introduces readers to the sport of BMX. He describes its special terms, equipment, and strategies. This is a first-rate look at an activity many elementary-grade girls and boys enjoy.

☞ Motocross bikers cannot race without helmets. For safety's sake, encourage youngsters to wear them whenever they ride. Teachers can contact the person in the police department responsible for information about bicycles (in my town it's a "bike technician") and arrange a class visit to bring youngsters up to date on rules and regulations of the road and good safety procedures.

BMX
Charles Coombs
Morrow, 1983
B/w photographs
[i, j] 144 pages

Readers will find detailed advice on the choice and care of motocross bikes, protecting oneself from injury, and improving riding technique. This book is particularly valuable for its emphasis on good sportsmanship and trying one's best. In the last chapter, a racer concludes, "First or second place, you have qualified for . . . another chance to race. And that's what really counts, the racing."

BIKES
Stephen Hoare
Warwick, 1985
Full-color and b/w illustrations and photographs
[j] 96 pages

This pocket-size (4¾ x 7½") volume is neatly crammed with facts on the history of motorcycles, how the engine and other systems work, classic and contemporary machines, stunt riding, and more. Format and contents will delight readers—reluctant and otherwise.

MOTORCYCLE: THE MAKING OF A HARLEY-DAVIDSON
William Jaspersohn
Little, 1984
B/w photographs by the author
[j] 127 pages

Youngsters can follow the production of a Harley-Davidson motorcycle, from design to delivery, in this detailed tour of the manufacturing plant in Milwaukee, Wisconsin.

☞ Link elementary-graders to Beverly Cleary's humorous *Lucky Chuck* (Morrow). As they follow the teenager on his new secondhand motorcycle, they'll learn about the protective riding gear, how the bike is driven, pertinent Motor Vehicle code rules and regulations, and the importance of road safety.

Biographies

Biographies are natural links to other subjects, and I've chosen to weave many of them throughout the Guide, rather than group them all into this section of *Eyeopeners!* For example, I've linked readers to chemist Antoine Lavoisier, "the father of chemistry," in the Science Experiments section, astronaut Guion Bluford in the Space and Astronomy section, and Queen Eleanor of Aquitaine in Medieval Days. The Quick-Link Index will lead you to other biographies in a variety of the Guide's sections.

AND THEN WHAT HAPPENED, PAUL REVERE?
Jean Fritz
Coward, 1973; 1982
One- and four-color illustrations by Margot Tomes
[i] 48 pages

Mention biographies for children to anyone familiar with the subject, and immediately the name Jean Fritz pops up. Her focus is mostly American history and when she describes the people who shaped our country's growth, Ms. Fritz creates a sense of time and place. She makes up none of the particulars, reveals her subjects' strengths and frailties, and quotes conversation only when research documents it. Her words enlighten, enrich, and engage young readers. Those characteristics should be reflected in all of the biographies you select for your children.

Among her more than a dozen biographies are *Can't You Make Them Behave, King George?*, *What's the Big Idea, Ben Franklin?*, *Make Way for Sam Houston* (all Coward; both), and *The Double Life of Pocahontas* (Coward and Puffin). Let youngsters' fingers do the walking through the card catalogue for her others—all worth reading.

LANGSTON: A PLAY
Ossie Davis
Delacorte, 1982
[j] 144 pages

Assign the parts to specific people and produce them as plays or readings, have youngsters read them aloud as you alternate roles during class, or assign this as a book to be read. Any way, youngsters will enjoy this introduction to noted black writer Langston Hughes. The play is set in a church basement, where he happens upon a rehearsal of one of his plays. Using the actors to re-create scenes from his memory, Hughes tells how he became a poet.

WOMEN WHO CHANGED THINGS
Linda Peavy and Ursula Smith
Scribner's, 1983
B/w photographs
[j] 208 pages

Did you know that federal legislation regulating food additives is largely the result of a campaign waged by one, almost anonymous woman? Motivated by the assumption that there must be many unknown women whose lives have had a significant effect on generations of people, the authors have written about nine who were active between 1880 and 1930. Among them are Leta Stetter Hollingworth, whose research shattered the male-framed theory of woman's innate inferiority, and Sara Josephine Baker, who revolutionized public health care.

DOLLY PARTON: COUNTRY GOIN' TO TOWN
Susan Saunders
Viking, 1985; Puffin, 1986
B/w illustrations by Rodney Pate

CAROL BURNETT: THE SOUND OF LAUGHTER
James Howe
Viking, 1987; Puffin, 1988
B/w illustrations by Robert Masheris
[i, j] each 64 pages

More than the media "hype" of famous names, dates, and places too often seen in books about popular entertainers, these biographies reveal the person behind the personality. Both are in the fine "Women of Our Time" series that includes Milton Meltzer's *Winnie Mandela: The Soul of South Africa*, James Haskins's *Diana Ross: Star Supreme*, Kathleen V. Kudlinski's *Rachel Carson*, and Patricia Reilly Giff's *Mother Teresa: Sister to the Poor.*

☞ During my first class with them, I jot the answers to questions youngsters ask me about myself on the board. When they've finished, I ask them to use the "notes" I chalked up during their interview as the basis for my biography—the first of a series I have them write. Others include biographies of each other, their best friends, a parent or sibling, their pets.

THE SHORT LIFE OF SOPHIE SCHOLL
Hermann Vinke
Harper, 1984
B/w photographs and illustrations
[j] 192 pages

On February 22, 1943, twenty-one-year-old Sophie Scholl, her twenty-four-year-old brother, Hans, and their friend Christoph Probst, twenty-three, all members of a student nonviolent resistance organization called the White Rose, were guillotined by the Nazis for "smearing house walls with subversive incitements and disseminating fliers fomenting high treason." Creating a "collage" of interviews with Sophie's surviving relatives and friends, excerpts from her diary, and contemporary documents, Mr. Vinke pieces together the compelling story of a sensitive young woman's moral development: a woman whose conscience would not let her ignore the injustices of tyranny, whatever the cost.

ISAAC NEWTON: RELUCTANT GENIUS
D. C. Ipsen
Enslow, 1985
B/w photographs and illustrations
[j] 96 pages

The author discusses Newton's theory of optics, laws of motion, and the invention of calculus within the context of the jealous scholarship of the seventeenth and eighteenth centuries. Newton's unwillingness to share his ideas with rival scholars explains the "reluctant" in the title.

EARTH, SEA, AND SKY: THE WORK OF EDMOND HALLEY
Linda Walvoord Girard
Whitman, 1985
B/w illustrations by James Watling and reproductions
[i, j] 64 pages

This vivid and compelling biography reveals Edmond Halley as a brilliant, innovative, insatiably curious scientist. He charted previously unrecorded stars of the Southern Hemisphere and wrote papers on numerous other subjects in addition to comets.

Boats

LIFE ON A BARGE
Huck Scarry
Prentice (both), 1982
B/w illustrations by the author
[i, j] 72 pages

Mr. Scarry's sketchbook-journal of his trip along the Rhine River aboard a Dutch barge is enriched with fascinating details. He also includes scenes of early America's Erie Canal. The author/artist's *Life on a Fishing Boat* (Prentice) is equally absorbing.

☞ Youngsters can keep a sketchbook-journal of family trips. When they get back, they can research more about what they've seen and add historic detail or other information, in the style of Mr. Scarry.

THE ERIE CANAL
Peter Spier
Doubleday, 1970
Full-color illustrations by the author
[p, i, j] 36 pages

A history of the canal and answers to questions children most often ask about it accompany the lyrics and melody of the song of the same name.

☞ Barges are workboats of the inland waterways. Share Jan Adkins's *Workboats* (Scribner's) to give youngsters a look at their open sea counterparts: tugs, trawlers, lobster boats, Coast Guard cutters, and others. The story of a search for a lost fisherman is made up; most of the people, the places, the boats, the fishing and search details, and the procedures are real. The illustrations are outstanding.

GREAT RED RIVER RAFT
Peter Zachary Cohen
Whitman, 1984
Brown-and-white illustrations by James Watling
[i, j] 40 pages

In 1838, after five years' perseverance, Henry Miller Shreve and his two-bottomed, iron-coated, steam-driven snagboat broke through a 200-mile logjam on the Red River. This fascinating book recalls that event and the man for whom Shreveport, Louisiana, is named.

CANOEING IS FOR ME
Tom Moran
Lerner, 1984
B/w photographs by the author
[i] 48 pages

Brothers Adam and John Paul, who are pictured as they demonstrate the sport, describe equipment, define special terms of canoeing, and detail the strokes that keep the craft on course.

☞ Vera B. Williams's *Three Days on a River in a Red Canoe* (Green-willow) so entranced my students and me I had to find out if it happened. The author told me she had spent many weekends canoeing and had, in fact, taken a three-week river trip from White Horse to Dawson in the Yukon Territory. (I forgot to ask if her canoe was red!)

After they've enjoyed this delightful tale of two youngsters' adventures with their mom, an aunt, and a new canoe, children can try the fruit stew and dumpling mix the foursome made during their journey. The simple recipes are included along with the other factual information about camping and canoeing.

Bodies

YOUR WONDERFUL BODY
Donald J. Crump, ed.
National Geographic, 1982
Full-color photographs and illustrations
[i] 104 pages

Youngsters are led on a tour of their bodies by the "Bod Squad," car-toon characters who can shrink to microscopic size. Photographs taken with a scanning electron microscope provide dramatic sites to visit. The emphasis is on how to keep fit with exercise and proper nutrition.

☞ Children can create a travel brochure and itinerary for a trip through the body, similar to the Bod Squad's in the book above. "A Day's Drive Through the Digestive System," for example, might begin with descriptions of the sights and sounds encountered as travelers proceed over the teeth, across the tongue, past the epi-glottis-sealed entrance to the windpipe, and down the esophagus.

THE HUMAN BODY
Ruth D. Bruun and Bertel Bruun
Random House, 1982

LIFE ON EARTH: BIOLOGY TODAY
Donald M. Silver
Random House, 1983
Full-color illustrations by Patricia J. Wynne
[i, j] each 96 pages

Colorful, detailed illustrations make these "musts" for readers of all ages. The Drs. Bruun discuss the body's regions and systems; Dr. Silver highlights similarities and differences between and among plants and animals. Both volumes are under $10 and worth adding to your basic home reference library.

☞ Highlight hands: begin with Gilda and Melvin Berger's *The Whole World of Hands* (Houghton) for simple experiments and activ-ities on the form and function of hands, left/right-handedness, and finger math. Then let youngsters paint hands *(Hanimals)*, tie knots *(Klutz Book of Knots)* and string figures *(Cat's Cradle, Owl's Eyes)*, sign from one to one hundred or any ten words on their spelling lists *(My First Book of Sign, I Can Sign My ABCs)*, sing finger-twisting ditties *(Hand Rhymes* and *Finger Rhymes)*, and fold paper *(Easy Origami)*.

THE HUMAN BODY
Giovanni Caselli
Grosset, 1987
Full-color illustrations by the author and others
[p, i] 64 pages

Though addressed to elementary-graders, junior high students will find this tour of the body intriguing. It begins at skin level, moves from head to toe, and includes views of a man at six stages of life between age one and seventy, as well as portraits that illustrate how genetic characteristics pass from generation to generation. Each two-page "chapter" highlights specific facets of the topic with attractive, easy-to-grasp, well-labeled, and annotated diagrams.

THE HUMAN BODY
Jonathan Miller
Viking, 1983
Full-color pop-up illustrations designed by David Pelham
[i, j, adult] 12 pages

I'll bet you can't keep your mouth closed when you turn to the first page of this book! The opening jaw-in-motion pop-up is irresistible. In addition to that moving illustration, readers manipulating the book and its tabs will see the heart flub-dub, an eardrum vibrate, and the lungs expand and contract.

BLOOD AND GUTS: A WORKING GUIDE
TO YOUR OWN INSIDES
Linda Allison
Little (both), 1976
B/w illustrations by the author
[i, j] 128 pages

In an upbeat, imaginative style that attracts and challenges young readers, the author suggests experiments, tests, and ideas for projects and manipulative devices that will encourage kids to discover more about themselves and their bodies.

CUTS, BREAKS, BRUISES, AND BURNS
Joanna Cole
Crowell, 1985
Two-color illustrations by True Kelley
[p, i] 48 pages

Ms. Cole introduces young readers to the ways in which the body heals itself. She identifies simple injuries and explains what is damaged and how it mends. And she provides first-aid hints for minor injuries.

INSPECTOR BODYGUARD PATROLS THE LAND OF U
Vicki Cobb
Messner (both), 1986
Full-color illustrations by John Sandford
[i, j] 128 pages

Fact and fantasy enlighten older readers about the body's healing processes. In the first half of each chapter, Inspector Bodyguard deploys troops to cope with threats to the well-being of his home-body. In the second half, the author explains how the body actually defends itself in each situation. "Red River Flood at Skin Frontier," for example, is paired with "How Your Blood Clots to Stop Bleeding." Youngsters viewing photomicrographs in *The Body Victorious* (below) will appreciate that Ms. Cobb's fictional versions are not so farfetched.

THE BODY VICTORIOUS
Kjell Lindqvist and Stig Nordfeldt
Delacorte, 1987
Full-color photographs by Lennart Nilsson
[j, adult] 196 pages

Rife with rich analogies and mesmerizing photographs taken with an electron microscope, this volume will impress browsers and read-aloud listeners of all ages with the beauty of the body's inner workings. The authors compare the fibrin in blood to reinforcing bars in concrete, for example, and that's exactly what it resembles 75,000 times life-size!

EMERGENCY ROOM
Bob and Diane Wolfe
Carolrhoda, 1983
B/w photographs
[i] 40 pages

Youngsters' eyes are opened to the goings-on when emergency room doctors and nurses attend to injuries needing immediate care.

☞ Much of children's apprehension about a hospital stay (their own, a friend's, or a family member's) comes from fear of the unknown. Use James Howe's *The Hospital Book* (Crown) to allay some of that anxiety. His words and black-and-white photos provide youngsters a preview of the experience by describing check-in routines, hospital personnel, and equipment. The author also discusses the anger and discomfort that are often a natural part of hospital stays.

CAN YOU GET WARTS FROM TOUCHING TOADS? ASK DR. PETE.
Peter Rowan
Messner, 1986
B/w illustrations by Quentin Blake
[i] 95 pages

WHY DOES MY NOSE RUN? AND OTHER QUESTIONS
KIDS ASK ABOUT THEIR BODIES
Joanne Settel and Nancy Baggett
Atheneum, 1985
[i] 80 pages

Have you ever told your children not to walk around with wet hair because they might catch cold? Dr. Peter Rowan collected and commented on ninety-four of the admonitions we heard as children (and often find ourselves repeating) in an entertainingly informative book. Dr. Settel and Ms. Baggett answer questions that reflect the natural curiosity kids have about themselves and their bodies.

There were no books available to help my parents explain what was happening to me as I went through puberty. Nor were there such books to guide Don and me and our son as he matured. Today's parents have a wealth of material to ease that often-awkward task of explaining human sexuality to children.

STRAIGHT TALK: SEXUALITY EDUCATION
FOR PARENTS AND KIDS 4–7
Marilyn Ratner and Susan Chamlin
Viking Penguin (both) 1987
B/w illustrations
[p with adults] 48 pages

This "family handbook," originally published by Planned Parenthood® of Westchester, Inc., is designed to educate adults about sexual matters, so they can educate their children. The authors suggest simple, commonsense answers to youngsters' questions and provide a list of "Dos and Don'ts," a bibliography for additional reading, and an 8-page pullout of children's activities.

WHAT'S HAPPENING TO MY BODY? BOOK FOR BOYS:
A GROWING UP GUIDE FOR PARENTS AND SONS
Lynda Madaras and Dane Saavedra
Newmarket (both), 1984

WHAT'S HAPENING TO MY BODY? BOOK FOR GIRLS:
A GROWING GUIDE FOR PARENTS AND DAUGHTERS
Lynda Madaras and Area Madaras
Newmarket (both), 1983
B/w illustrations
[i, j] 240 pages; 208 pages

Lynda Madaras teaches classes in puberty and sex education to teens and preteens, and these compelling guides reflect her insight and expertise. Whether they read the books alone or with an adult, young adults will learn about puberty in language they'll understand, with humor they'll appreciate, and a thoroughness they will find enlightening and comforting.

Buildings

Children (and adults) take for granted the buildings in which they eat, sleep, and play. But buildings reflect an evolutionary process as fascinating as any other aspect of human culture. Awaken youngsters to the excitement implicit in any structure—a marvelous amalgam of architecture, engineering, and labor, whether primitive or sophisticated, natural or manufactured, for one or many inhabitants.

BUILDING A HOUSE
Byron Barton
Greenwillow, 1981; Puffin, 1984
Full-color illustrations by the author
[p] 32 pages

Where does a house begin? What happens next? How does it "grow"? Boldly colored drawings simply and clearly illustrate the overall sequence for the very young.

☞ Use any opportunity to have your children meet and talk with skilled crafts people about their trades. When a carpenter or repair person is working around the house, ask him or her to spend a few minutes explaining his craft to your children. Arrange for a plumber or other skilled laborer to visit your classroom to describe the work and tools of the house-building trade. Visit a hardware store and discover the myriad sizes of nails, screws, bolts, and nuts and their respective functions.

HOW A HOUSE HAPPENS
Jan Adkins
Walker, 1972
B/w illustrations by the author
[i, j] 32 pages

With humor, insight, and superb book design (each page resembles an architectural drawing), the author/artist, an ex-architectural illustrator, makes the complex appear simple as he leads readers step by step through the many stages of house construction.

☞ With the above step-by-step books—and Ken Robbins's photo-essay *Building a House* (Four Winds)—for guides, have children write similar "construction projects": making a peanut butter and jelly sandwich; making a bed; wrapping a present; brushing teeth; getting dressed.

THE TOWN THAT MOVED
Mary Jane Finsand
Carolrhoda, 1983
Two-color illustrations by Reg Sandland
[p, i] 48 pages

Would you move to a new house if your old one sat atop a valuable mine? The people of Hibbing, Minnesota; discovered a rich vein of iron ore beneath their homes and, rather than destroy them, they used tree trunks to roll every building in town to new locations.

☞ Suggest youngsters study real estate sections of the local newspaper, list those things that make their houses special, then transform their lists into advertisements they can post under pictures of their houses. Pin these "ads" on a "Better Homes and Yards" bulletin board. Or collate them all into a hometown real estate guide.

A HOUSE IS A HOUSE FOR ME
Mary Ann Hoberman
Viking, 1978; Puffin, 1982
Full-color illustrations by Betty Fraser
[p, i] 48 pages

A sublime rhyme about all sorts of houses, including a shell for a clam, a dog for a flea, a barn for a lamb, and a pod for a pea.

☞ Let youngsters pretend they are tenants or landlords of any house in *A House Is a House for Me:* a pocket, a pen, a trashcan, or a den, for example. Ask them to describe without identifying their "house" and challenge classmates to guess who the landlord or tenant might be.

GRANDMOTHER'S ADOBE DOLLHOUSE
MaryLou Smith
New Mexico Magazine (both), 1984
Full-color illustrations by Ann Blackstone
[i] 32 pages

A guided tour of a dollhouse, as warm and inviting as the adobe house it models, highlights its distinctive features, multicultural origins, and the food and art of New Mexicans.

☞ With parents' permission, youngsters can bring their dollhouses or model cars to school for everyone to enjoy. While in the classroom, the miniature abodes can become the focus for writing assignments: descriptive narratives on their design or stories about their imaginary inhabitants.

THE TIPI
THE PUEBLO
Charlotte Yue
Knopf, 1984; 1986
B/w illustrations by David Yue
[j] 96 pages; 117 pages

These are insightful views of two very different "houses" and the daily lives of their ingenious designer/builders, respectively American Plains Indians and Southwest Native Americans. Both transformed materials at hand into unique dwellings perfectly suited to the land, its climate, and their needs.

THE CHILDREN'S BOOK OF HOUSES AND HOMES
Carol Bowyer
Usborne, 1978
Full-color illustrations
[p, i] 32 pages

A book filled with full-color, detailed drawings of peoples around the world and the places they call home. Each reading of this useful reference reveals (it seems) something new.

☞ Let youngsters draw pictures of their real and dream rooms, at home and at school. Inspire little ones with Beatrice Schenk de Regnier's imaginative book *A Little House of Your Own* (Harcourt).

SKARA BRAE
Olivier Dunrea
Holiday House, 1985
B/w illustrations by the author
[i] 40 pages

Neolithic settlers on the Orkney Islands (north of Scotland) built their neat, efficient houses out of the stone strewn along the beach. The author/artist re-creates the village, its people, and their artifacts.

UP GOES THE SKYSCRAPER
Gail Gibbons
Four Winds, 1986
Full-color illustrations by the author
[p, i] 32 pages

Bet your children (and you) can't pass a construction site without stopping to watch a new building go up. You'll find yourselves equally transfixed as workers constructively occupy themselves while this high rise takes shape. The view is one of Ms. Gibbons's best. (And I'd say that even if it weren't dedicated to me, my husband, and my son!)

☞ What's the tallest building in your town? When was it built? If possible, visit it with your children and note the number of floors, elevators, windows, ground floor entrances and exits, businesses it houses, the material on its face and in the lobby, and any other particularly interesting aspects of its architecture.

THE SKYSCRAPER BOOK
James Cross Giblin
Crowell, 1981
[i, j] 96 pages

Skyscrapers come to life as success symbols of the people who financed them, state-of-the-art representatives of the architects who designed them, and friends or foes of the people who live and work around or in them. The writing sparkles with historical anecdotes.

☞ Youngsters may not be able to build a skyscraper, but they can certainly set up ceilingscrapers. With playing cards or blocks, let them attempt a structure stable enough to reach from floor to ceiling.

A DAY IN THE LIFE OF A HIGH-IRON WORKER
John Harding Martin
Troll (both), 1985
Full-color photographs by Gayle Jann
[p, i] 32 pages

Want to know what it's like to work on a skyscraper? Accompany Robert Cameron as he manipulates monstrous metal beams on a high-rise building-in-progress—and learn.

☞ Contrast building a skyscraper with *Unbuilding* (Houghton) one. David Macauley's drawings for his fictional dismantling of the Empire State Building make clear that it takes as much knowledge and skill to demolish as to erect one. (On page 51 you'll discover a partial portrait of the world famous movie star without whom no Empire State Building book is complete.)

HOW THEY BUILT LONG AGO
Christopher Fagg and Adrian Sington
Warwick, 1981
Color and b/w illustrations
[j] 80 pages

This well-designed book includes a time line of relevant historical events that makes it easy to compare buildings within a period and over time. Readers will be intrigued by the sharp contrast between contemporary superstructures and those built before the fourteenth century. A glossary and a complete index increase the book's utility.

THE ELEVATOR
Barbara Ford
Walker, 1982
B/w illustrations
[i] 64 pages

Faced with the problem of moving furniture from one floor to another in a two-story factory, Elisha Graves Otis demonstrated the first safety hoist in 1852. This book chronicles the evolution of the elevator and introduces its inventor, whose works (unlike Thomas Edison's) represented 98 percent inspiration and 2 percent perspiration.

BUILDING: THE FIGHT AGAINST GRAVITY
Mario Salvadori
Aladdin, 1985
B/w illustrations by Saralinda Hooker and Christopher Ragus
[i, j] 152 pages

Learn why buildings stand up, through lucid explanations of architectural principles. Simple projects include making columns, beams, arches, bridges, and buildings out of paper and tongue depressors.

☞ Get out telephone books and city maps. Have youngsters pretend their house needs repair: perhaps it has to be reroofed, a window needs replacing, or a water pipe has burst. Have them find the closest appropriate roofer, glazier, or plumber in the yellow pages and write out directions from her shop to the house.

MESSING AROUND WITH DRINKING STRAW CONSTRUCTION
Bernie Zubrowski
Little, 1981
B/w illustrations by Stephanie Fleischer
[i] 64 pages

Easy-to-follow instructions show how to make model houses, bridges, and towers out of straws and paper clips or dowels and rubber bands. These worthwhile and enjoyable activities were tested by the youngsters who visit the Children's Museum in Boston.

Cars

The family car is the focus in this section. Talk cars with kids, however, and inevitably the discussion turns from the standard model to everything else: custom, sports, vintage, or toy cars; road, track, or ice racing; karting, rallying, or the drivers themselves. Fortunately, there are literally scores of worthwhile books on those and other related subjects.

CARS AND HOW THEY GO
Joanna Cole
Crowell (both), 1983
Full-color illustrations by Gail Gibbons
[p, i] 32 pages

This simplified description of the internal combustion engine and its related systems will help elementary-graders understand why motorists can turn on the ignition, step on the gas, and drive away.

THE INTERNAL COMBUSTION ENGINE
Ross Olney
Lippincott, 1982
B/w illustrations by Steven Lindblom
[i, j] 48 pages

Follow the book above with this more detailed exposure of the power behind most vehicles. The author uses analogies that make basic principles easy to grasp.

☞ Children learn more about automobiles and the responsibilities that come with them when they help maintain the family car. With *Car Care for Kids and Former Kids* (Atheneum) as a guide, suggest girls and boys assist parents with such basic procedures as changing motor oil, cleaning air filters, and checking the tires.

FILL IT UP!
Gail Gibbons
Crowell (both), 1985
Full-color illustrations by the author
[p] 32 pages

Where does the gas come from? What makes the lift go up? How is a flat tire changed? Youngsters can peek below ground and behind the garage doors at a busy gas station.

☞ After children meet service station operators, introduce them to another group of workers who help keep their cars running smoothly—without bumps, that is: the planners, surveyors, heavy equipment oprators, and others Gail Gibbons portrays as they build a *New Road!* (Crowell).

☞ My dad taught my mom to drive on a Model T. He taught me on a three-quarter-ton Ford pickup. Were there any Fords in your youngsters' past? Ask children to find out. Have them also poll the drivers in their family to learn how each was taught to drive, on what kind of car, and whether or not that brand of auto is still manufactured.

If any of their relatives were driving between 1945 and 1966, children may hear some strange names: Nash, for instance, or Studebaker or Packard. Have John Struthers's *Dinosaur Cars* (Lerner) handy to introduce them to those late great cars.

THE PRESIDENT'S CAR
Nancy Winslow Parker
Crowell, 1981
B/w illustrations by the author
[i] 64 pages

George Washington rode in a yellow-and-white, round-bottomed, crane-neck coach whenever and wherever he wished. The current U.S. president rides in an armored, specially equipped, secret-service-guarded Lincoln he is never allowed to drive. Youngsters will gain a novel perspective on the presidency and how it has changed when they learn about these and the other vehicles that have carried presidents from here to there.

THINGS ON WHEELS
Kate Little
Usborne, 1987
Full-color illustrations by Peter Bull
[p, i] 24 pages

Readers and nonreaders alike will be attracted by the abundant illustrations and diagrams. They clearly identify basic car parts and engine operations, racing and off-road vehicles, motorbikes and trains.

☞ Two series contain titles on just about every permutation of four-wheeler conceivable. I've opted to cite one title from each (below) by way of recommending both series generally and automobile-related titles specifically.

RACING YESTERDAY'S CARS
Richard L. Knudson
Lerner, 1986
Full-color photographs
[i, j] 48 pages

One of more than fifty 48-page books in the Lerner "Superwheels & Thrill Sports" series on almost every vehicle people manipulate in the air, on land, or on water. In each, an interesting, conversational narrative contains a wealth of historical and contemporary information. Full-color and b/w photographs are on almost every page.

☞ Did you know that Henry Ford designed, built, and raced cars to attract investors in his dream automobile? Barbara Mitchell's *We'll Race You, Henry* (Carolrhoda) traces Ford's boyhood proclivity for mechanical things through the creation of the rugged, affordable, easily repaired, family-size gas buggy.

RACING CARS
N. S. Barrett
Watts, 1985
Full-color photographs and illustrations
[p, i, j] 32 pages

The Watts "Picture Library" series is designed for the poor or reluctant older reader. Thirty-two pages of full- or almost full-page brightly colored, well-annotated photographs and line drawings highlight important details; two- to four-page topic areas of relatively little text are set in inoffensively large type; a brief history of the subject, a facts and records section, and an index conclude each work.

Cats—Wild and Domestic

Wild Cats

How do scientists differentiate between wild big cats and little cats? Not on the basis of size, surprisingly enough, but on an ability to roar. Big cats can, little cats can't. The more flexible bones inside the voice boxes of lions, tigers, leopards, and jaguars create louder sounds than those in their "little" relatives, mountain lions, snow and clouded leopards, and cheetahs.

BIG CATS
LITTLE CATS
John Bonnett Wexo
Wildlife, 1981, 1984 (paperback only)
Full-color illustrations and photographs
[p, i] each 20 pages

In both paperbacks, photographs (some two pages across) and illustrations highlight the similarities and differences of several wild cat species and their interaction with people.

☞ Link youngsters to Robert McClung's *Rajpur: Last of the Bengal Tigers* (Morrow) for a vibrant story of a typical male Bengal tiger's birth and maturation and an introduction to current tiger research and conservation programs.

BOBCAT
Hope Ryden
Putnam, 1983
B/w photographs by the author
[i, j] 64 pages

The naturalist/author tracked through four states to "shoot" the wild cat hunting, rearing its young, and surviving. Her sensitively written narrative and striking photographs reveal the nature of a rarely seen native North American predator.

CLOSE TO THE WILD: SIBERIAN TIGERS IN A ZOO
Thomas Cajacob and Theresa Burton
Carolrhoda, 1986
Full-color photographs by Thomas Cajacob
[i, j] 48 pages

Visit behind the scenes at the Minnesota Zoo for close-ups of Siberian tigers as they roam their three-acre natural-habitat enclosure. This engrossing photoessay shows and tells how these biggest of all tigers are cared for as part of a program to preserve the endangered species.

☞ Feature felines. Encourage children to read, write, sing, speak, and paint pictures about cats—real and storybook, domestic and wild—for four weeks. If you start on April 12, you can end on May 12 and celebrate Cat Festival Day, as they do in Belgium. There, people parade costumed as cats from literature.

Here, youngsters can march through neighboring classrooms after they've donned cat masks of their favorite fact or fictional feline. (Ron and Marsha Feller's *Paper Masks and Puppets* [Art Factory] has step-by-step directions they can easily follow.) Let the students in each class play "20 Questions" and try to identify the cat breed or character represented by the masks.

Domestic Cats

CATS AND KITTENS
Rose Hill
Usborne, 1982
Full-color illustrations
[p, i] 24 pages

Along with suggestions for choosing a healthy kitten and keeping it fit, youngsters are wisely reminded of "pethood's" duties as well as its pleasures. Suggestions include taking kittens to the vet, and spaying or neutering them to avoid unwanted offspring.

UNDERSTANDING CATS
Bridget Gibbs
Usborne, 1978
Full-color illustrations
[i] 32 pages

Children learn what to expect when kitten becomes cat as they read about adult feline behavior, body language, courtship, and reproduction.

☞ Ms. Gibbs's book provides directions for a catnip mouse. Youngsters interested in making one can grow their own catnip. Refer them to Millicent E. Selsam's and Jerome Wexler's photoessay *Catnip* (Morrow), where they'll also learn about the plant's physical structure, its history, and why it affects cats and other animals.

CATS
Cynthia Overbeck
Lerner, 1983
Full-color photographs by Shin Yoshino
[i, j] 48 pages

Words and photos compare a house cat's physical characteristics and developmental stages to those of its wild relatives.

A CAT'S BODY
Joanna Cole
Morrow, 1982
B/w photographs by Jerome Wexler
[i, j] 48 pages

The focus is on attributes that make cats the perfect small rodent predator: a flexible spine, retractable claws, canine teeth, and keen eyesight.

☞ Let youngsters *Paws* (Archway) a few moments for Mike Thaler's cat-chy jokes, riddles, and "catoons." Among them they'll find such famous felines as Dwight D. Eisenmeower and Catrin Hepburn and learn about interesting lo-cat-ions like Perru and Connecticat.

A KITTEN IS BORN
Heiderose Fisher-Nagel
Putnam, 1983
Full-color photographs by Andreas Fisher-Nagel
[p, i] 40 pages

A simple, straightforward text accompanies captivating views of natural kittenbirth and the growth of three little ones into ready-for-adoption kittenhood.

Children—Near and Far

THE LAND I LOST
Huynh Quang Nhuong
Harper, 1982; Trophy, 1986
B/w illustrations by Mai Vo-Dinh
[i] 128 pages

Add this to your list of read-aloud books. Mr. Huynh's boyhood adventures on the central highlands of Vietnam—among them incidents with horse snakes, dangerous crocodiles, killer hogs, and a karate expert grandmother—are exciting tales your children will enjoy hearing more than once.

THE ROAD FROM HOME
David Kherdian
Greenwillow, 1979; Puffin, 1987
B/w photographs
[i, j] 256 pages

August 22, 1939. "... After all, who remembers today the extermination of the Armenians?"
   Adolf Hitler's statement, preceded by the Turkish order of 1916, "to destroy completely all the Armenians living in Turkey," begins the author's moving biography of his mother, Veron Dumehjian. It is a lyrical tribute to the ingenuity, perseverance, and endurance of the relatively few Armenians who were able to survive the horrors of their planned annihilation—and the memory of those who didn't.

☞ Upon the acceptance of an award for this book, Mr. Kherdian told of the dilemma he faced before writing his mother's story and of the peace she felt when he had finished. When you and your students have finished the book, share his speech. A copy is in the February 1980 issue of *The Horn Book* magazine.

SOME OF US SURVIVED
Kerop Bedoukian
Farrar, 1979
B/w photographs
[i, j] 186 pages

Though nine when he and his Armenian family were uprooted by the Turks more than 60 years ago, Mr. Bedoukian manages to recall his experiences as he lived them. They are " . . . true to the memories of a young boy, who, in the manner of a child, was curious about the nature of the world around him": at once a part of yet distant from the horrors surrounding him.

IMMIGRANT KIDS
Russell Freedman
Dutton, 1980
B/w photographs
[i] 64 pages

Your children will find it interesting to compare their lives, or those of their parents or grandparents, with the lives of the youngsters pictured in this photographic essay. These children grew up in America during the turn of the century. The period scenes in school, at home, and at play will provoke many lively discussions.

DMITRY, A YOUNG SOVIET IMMIGRANT
Joanne Bernstein
Clarion, 1981
B/w photographs
[i, j] 80 pages

The author follows the first few difficult years in America of Dmitry, a young Soviet Jew, who emigrated with his parents in 1976.

☞ Ask students who have moved to new schools to describe what it was like. Have them trace the move on a map. What was the worst part? The best? What did they learn from the experience? If they were to advise classmates about a move, what one bit of advice would they offer?

MY LITTLE ISLAND
Frané Lessac
Lippincott, 1985; Trophy, 1987
Color illustrations by the author
[p, i] 48 pages

Primitive paintings and simple text describe the friends, flora, and fauna the author sees on a visit home to Montserrat in the Lesser Antilles.

SO FAR FROM THE BAMBOO GROVE
Yoko Kawashima Watkins
Lothrop, 1986; Puffin, 1987
[i, j] 160 pages

This moving autobiographical account tells of the harrowing journey that the author, her mother, and sister made from Korea to their homeland Japan after World War II.

GAVRIEL AND JEMAL
Brent Ashabranner
Dodd, 1984
B/w photographs by Paul Conklin
[i, j] 96 pages

Alternate chapters tell of the family life, religious beliefs, schooling, and aspirations of two boys of Jerusalem: one a twelve-year-old Jew, the other a fourteen-year-old Palestinian. The similarities are striking.

THE CHILDREN WE REMEMBER
Chana Byers Abells
Greenwillow, 1983
B/w photographs
[i, j] 48 pages

The words are easy to understand; the pictures (from the Archives of Yad Vashem in Israel) of the Jewish children who lived and died during the Holocaust aren't.

HELLO, AMIGOS!
Tricia Brown
Holt, 1986
B/w photographs by Fran Ortiz
[p] 48 pages

A birthday day in the life of primary-grader Frankie Valdez, a young Mexican-American in San Francisco.

DAYDREAMERS
Eloise Greenfield
Dial (both), 1981
Brown, black, and white illustrations by Tom Feelings
[p, i] 26 pages

The artists' portraits of black children capture them "holding their bodies still/for a time/letting the world turn around them." The author's words, inspired by the illustrations, capture the essence of childhood introspection.

Children—with Disabilities

MY BROTHER STEVEN IS RETARDED
Harriet Langsam Sobol
Macmillan, 1977
B/w photographs by Patricia Agre
[i] 32 pages

The illustrations and spare, straightforward text describe eleven-year-old Beth's often conflicting feelings toward her older brother. Youngsters with brothers or sisters will recognize these feelings.

DON'T FEEL SORRY FOR PAUL
Bernard Wolf
Lippincott, 1974
B/w illustrations by the author
[i] 96 pages

Though born without complete arms and legs, elementary-grader Paul is becoming a self-sufficient person. The book begins as Paul dresses himself, a task complicated by the donning of prosthetic devices, then shows him at a horse-riding lesson, in school, at his birthday party, and on a trip to the Institute of Rehabilitation Medicine. After seeing a few days in Paul's life, children will understand why the last photograph is captioned "The Beginning" instead of "The End."

☞ Pair the photoessay about Paul with Curt and Gita Kaufman's *Rajesh* (Atheneum), who was born missing both legs and an arm and also wears prosthetic devices. The Kaufmans depict Rajesh's kindergarten experiences as he and his classmates learn to know one another.

MY FRIEND LESLIE: THE STORY OF A HANDICAPPED CHILD
Maxine B. Rosenberg
Lothrop, 1983
B/w photographs by George Ancona
[p, i] 48 pages

Karen, the author's daughter (and one of the youngsters featured in *Being Adopted*), talks about her friend and first-grade schoolmate, who was born with many physical impairments.

MOVE OVER, WHEELCHAIRS COMING THROUGH
Ron Roy
Clarion, 1985
B/w photographs by Rosemarie Hausherr
[i, j] 96 pages

Seven young people, ages eight to nineteen, overcome the constraints imposed by the disabled bodies that house their active minds.

THINKING BIG: THE STORY OF A YOUNG DWARF
Susan Kuklin
Lothrop, 1986
B/w photographs by the author
[i] 48 pages

Eight-year-old Jaime Osborn is an achondroplastic dwarf, which means that she has short arms and legs on a normal-size body. The author's sensitive portrait reveals what the youngster can and cannot do and how her dwarfism will affect her physically and socially as she matures. At the same time that readers note the more obvious differences between Jaime's world and theirs, they'll discover the many similarities and that, all things considered, Jaime is "like everybody else, just smaller."

FEELING FREE
Mary Beth Sullivan
Harper (both), 1979
B/w illustrations and photographs
[i, j] 192 pages

This joyous potpourri of interviews, commentary, stories, puzzles, cartoons, dramatizations, and the like began as a television series to help people get to understand, appreciate, and know children and adults with disabilities. It succeeds beautifully in its transition to a book.

OUR TEACHER'S IN A WHEELCHAIR
Mary Ellen Powers
Whitman, 1986
B/w photographs by the author
[p, i] 32 pages

Youngsters will meet Brian Hanson, whose partial paralysis doesn't interfere with his activities as a day-care teacher.

Children—on Their Own

THE OFFICIAL KIDS' SURVIVAL KIT
Elaine Chaback and Pat Fortunato
Little, 1981 (paperback only)
B/w illustrations by Bill Ogden
[i] 224 pages

Intermediate and junior high school homerooms should have at least one copy readily available for reference and casual browsing. This guide on "how to do things on your own" offers practical tips on becoming self-sufficient that all youngsters can use. Entries contain suggestions on how to deal with personal concerns—fears, brothers and sisters, and acne are examples; how to help with household chores; and how to handle emergencies—illustrated directions for the Heimlich Maneuver are included.

THE COMPLETE BABY-SITTER'S HANDBOOK
Carol Barkin and Elizabeth James
Wanderer, 1980 (paperback only)
[i, j] 160 pages

The authors suggest ways of breaking into the job market, speaking to prospective clients, dressing appropriately, and handling emergencies. They've also provided an excellent, reproducible 6-page client worksheet parents and sitters fill out together. After completion of that checklist, parents will feel certain that the person they've hired to care for their children is tackling the job in a professional manner.

☞ Let children role-play emergency situations to practice appropriate reactions. Have them create a *What to Do If . . .* book for emergencies.

KID CAMPING FROM AAAAIII! TO ZIP
Patrick McManus
Lothrop, 1979
B/w illustrations by Roy Doty
[i] 128 pages

Few experiences require that youngsters be responsible for their own behavior to the extent that camping does. Mr. McManus, who knows children, is an experienced camper concerned about the environment. He is a very witty man who's written a very funny book that also happens to be a superb guide to camping. Beginning, experienced, and even non-campers will love it.

IN CHARGE: A COMPLETE HANDBOOK
FOR KIDS WITH WORKING PARENTS
Kathy S. Kyte
Knopf, 1983
B/w illustrations by Susan Detrich
[i, j] 96 pages

Have a copy of this "handbook for kids with working parents" available for youngsters who go home to empty houses after school. Children, whether new at assuming responsibility or old hands at it, will find it a well-organized and practical guide to self-sufficiency. The author outlines sensible steps for getting organized, for coping with minor annoyances and major emergencies, for preparing meals, and for keeping clothes in order.

PLAY IT SAFE: THE KIDS' GUIDE
TO PERSONAL SAFETY AND CRIME PREVENTION
Kathy S. Kyte
Knopf, 1983
B/w illustrations by Richard Brown
[i] 128 pages

This guide begins with advice for changing one's body language to signal "in control" rather than "victim." The author continues with effective strategies for self-protection and for protecting belongings when at home alone or moving around the city; she offers sound advice for getting help if there is household violence and abuse. The conversational writing, enthusiasm, and supportive tone in both of Ms. Kyte's books inspire self-confidence.

THE KIDS' COMPLETE GUIDE TO MONEY
Kathy S. Kyte
Knopf, 1984
B/w illustrations by Richard Brown
[i] 96 pages

In a creative upbeat approach, Ms. Kyte helps youngsters adopt a practical approach to earning, saving, and spending money. She provides tips on becoming a knowledgeable consumer, bartering, swapping, and taking advantage of free and inexpensive entertainment.

☞ Have your whole class participate in the advertising awareness research suggested in *The Kids' Complete Guide to Money*.

THE GIFTED KIDS SURVIVAL GUIDE: AGES 11 TO 18*
THE GIFTED KIDS SURVIVAL GUIDE: AGES 10 AND UNDER**
THE GIFTED KIDS SURVIVAL GUIDE, II*
Judy Galbraith
Free Spirit, 1983; 1984; 1987
B/w illustrations
[j] *
[i] **

Children identified as "gifted and talented" who are uncomfortable with that label will find these well worth reading. Beginning with gripes common to gifted children ("the stuff we do in school is too easy and it's boring," for example), she proceeds to demolish such myths as G/T children will always succeed, or get good grades, and to explain what "gifted and talented" means and how it affects one's education.

Ms. Galbraith offers sound advice for coping with boring classes, unrealistic expectations, teasing, family, and stress, punctuating her text with comments of the children she interviewed for her books.

Cookbooks

There are few easier ways to help children learn to read carefully and follow directions than to ask them to prepare something from a recipe. My favorite Non-Book-Report assignment for youngsters who select a cookbook as recreational reading is the preparation of any recipe they choose. I've received some marvelous notes from family members commenting on delicious successes—or spectacular failings!

DINNER'S READY, MOM
Helen Gustafson
Celestial, 1986 (paperback only)
B/w illustrations
[i] 80 pages

There are more than fifty recipes in this tasteful, uncluttered, easy-to-read 11 x 8″ paperback. They provide youngsters the what and how-to of simple, mostly one-dish dinners that require little or no adult assistance.

☞ If you've access to a school oven and refrigerator, provide the ingredients for Ms. Gustafson's dry cookie mixture for young-sters to mix together and store in the fridge for future use. When it's time to reward someone for being thoughtful, working co-operatively, or demonstrating other desirable behavior, hand that child the mix, an egg, and milk (also on hand for just such an occasion) and set him or her to baking a batch of "Everyday Cookies" the whole class can enjoy.

JUST DESSERTS
Marilyn Linton
Kids Can, 1986 (paperback only)
[i] 64 pages

The fifty-seven one-to-a-page mouth-watering recipes in this spiral-bound paperback use everyday ingredients, contain directions for mi-crowave and conventional ovens, and are preceded by a glossary of cooking terms and utensils.

MY VERY FIRST COOKBOOK
Rena Coyle
Workman, 1985 (paperback only)
Full-color illustrations by Jay Joyner
[p, i] 128 pages

The colorful illustrations of a teddy bear chef will attract and help children follow each step of the fifty recipes for everyday meals, snacks, and foods for special occasions and holidays. Most are simple enough for completion with a minimal amount of adult assistance.

☞ When next camping or on an overnight hike with children, take along Jean Craighead George's *Wild, Wild Cookbook* (Crowell/ Harper Jr.). Her guide will help you forage wild fare to supplement your outdoor feasts. You might even be able to practice before you leave home—some of the plants (dandelions, for example, oxalis, or daylilies) could be in your own backyard.

COOKING THE KOREAN WAY
Okwha Chung and Judy Monroe
Lerner, 1988

COOKING THE ISRAELI WAY
Josephine Bacon
Lerner, 1986
Full-color photographs and b/w illustrations
[i, j] each 48 pages

If multicultural units are on the "table," let youngsters season their studies, flavor their facts, and, in general, further research with repasts linked to the countries under discussion. The titles cited are two of the more than twenty "Easy Menu Ethnic Cookbooks." All begin with an introduction to characteristic foods and customs, special ingredients, and cooking terms and provide simple menus for soups, meals, and desserts.

☞ Think *food* when you read aloud any of the "Anne of Green Gables," "Little House on the Prairie," or "Little Men/Little Women" books. Link your listeners to the appropriate volume—*The Anne of Green Gables Cookbook* (Oxford), *The Little House Cookbook*

(Harper), and *The Louisa May Alcott Cookbook* (Little) and suggest they pick and prepare any recipe.

If youngsters complete any of the books for recreational reading at school, teachers can accept a note from parent, grandparent, sister, or brother on the specially made treat as ample proof that another book has been read and "digested."

Cowboys and Cowgirls

Who were the cowboys of the Wild West? Definitely not the romantic heroes seen in movies. They were often black, Mexican, or Native American, seldom wore a gun (never carried two), and were killed more frequently in job-related tasks (trampled in a stampede, drowned crossing a river, or struck by lightning while herding) than by outlaws or Indians.

COWBOYS OF THE WILD WEST
Russell Freedman
Clarion, 1985
B/w photographs
[i, j] 128 pages

Return to the days of yesteryear when a cowboy was a transient, hard-working, low-paid, highly skilled individual. Fine research and archival photographs vivify the era of cattle drives.

COWBOY
Bernard Wolf
Morrow, 1985
B/w photographs by the author
[j] 80 pages

Many of today's cowboys face challenges other than those presented by livestock and nature. This powerful photoessay portrays a modern cowboy's efforts to conserve his way of life, despite coal companies that would rather mine the land around him than graze it.

COWBOYS
Teri Martini
Children's, 1981
B/w and full-color photographs
[p] 48 pages

Beginning readers will learn about cowboys' seasonal responsibilities, their recreation, and their uniform in this simple yet interesting and informative introduction.

☞ Use a coloring book to call attention to specifics youngsters might otherwise miss. Forty detail-laden pictures in David Rickman's *Cowboys of the Old West* (Dover) illustrate the cowboy's evolution from Spanish stockman with Columbus's 1494 expedition to fancy-dress cowboy in 1985 parades. Short descriptive paragraphs appear at the bottom of each illustration.

ROUND-UP
RODEO
Cheryl Walsh Bellville
Carolrhoda, 1982; 1985
Full-color and b/w photographs by the author
[i] each 32 pages

In *Round-Up,* follow cowboys as they catch their daily mounts, bring in cattle, dehorn, ear-notch, inoculate, and castrate bull calves, and relax after the hard springtime work. In *Rodeo,* the author, a once-professional rider, leads readers comfortably along the trail from rodeo's first loosely organized days to today's smoothly run events.

LET'S RODEO
Charles Coombs
Holt, 1986
B/w photographs
[i] 128 pages

The "feel" of a rodeo is inescapable in this behind-the-scenes and in-the-saddle account of skilled cowgirls, cowboys, and horses doing what they do best. Readers will burst through gates for a breathless eight seconds on a bucking bronco, and bounce atop a leaping, kicking, spinning bull until time's up!

LITTLE BRITCHES RODEO
COWGIRL
Murray Tinkelman
Greenwillow, 1984; 1985
B/w photographs by the author
[i] 56 pages; 32 pages

The first book contains full- and half-page pictures and an event-by-event description of the National Little Britches Association Finals for youngsters eight to eighteen years old. Readers of the second title follow an elementary-grader as she happily places second in barrel racing.

☞ Joseph Rosenbloom's *Wild West Riddles and Jokes* (Sterling) will enliven "cowboy" language arts activities. For example, children can create Cowboy Classics as corny as the titles in Mr. Rosenbloom's "Best Seller Lists." Two of his are "My Life as a Cowboy" by Rhoda Horse and "Protect Your Ranch" by Bob Dwyer!

Death

As with most important issues, children need to be told the truth about death when they have questions or concerns. The books that follow do so with sensitivity and compassion. Their authors wisely divide their attention between death and life—making the point that all living things die, that death is a part of life.

It is important that you also read these books. Though written for children, they will help you frame answers to questions they ask in ways the young can understand. They remind readers that we all grieve differently and encourage adults to be supportive, but not intrusive, as children work to accept death.

LIFETIMES
Bryan Mellonie
Bantam, 1983
Full-color illustrations by Robert Ingpen
[p, i] 40 pages

Author and artist use plants, insects, and even sand crabs to acquaint young readers with the concept of a life cycle. In a quiet, nonthreatening manner, they explain that nothing lives forever. They illustrate their simple text with serene images that will not upset young children.

DEATH IS NATURAL
Laurence Pringle
Four Winds, 1977
B/w photographs by the author
[i] 64 pages

With the demise of a cottontail, the author begins his gentle, straightforward discussion of death as part of the continuous recycling of the earth's elements. He divides readers' attention between death and life, making the point that all living things die—plants and animals, individuals and species—that death is a part of all life.

☞ As adults, many of us visit cemeteries when traveling, to read epitaphs and learn about the people of the area across an extended period of time. To give them perspective about people in their hometown, consider a similar visit to a local cemetery with children. They will be intrigued by the birth/death dates and ages of people with familiar names. The trip can serve as a jumping-off point for a discussion of local history, cultural diversity and change, and other topics that can be vivified by knowledge of individuals who have preceded them.

A LOOK AT DEATH
Rebecca Anders
Lerner, 1978
B/w photographs by Maria S. Forrai
[i] 36 pages

The author explores the various ways people die: some quickly, some over time; some by illness, others by accident. She also explains the process of grieving—how people handle grief in different ways and the eventual end of the period of sadness.

☞ Ms. Anders points out that many people believe life does not end with death. Supplement her comments with Jon Mayled's photoessay *Death Customs* (Silver). Written for upper-elementary-grade youngsters, it introduces the beliefs and rituals of seven religions.

THE KIDS' BOOK ABOUT DEATH AND DYING
Eric Rofes, ed.
Little, 1985
[i, j] 119 pages

This is a collaboration between the editor, a teacher, and fourteen of his eleven- to fourteen-year-old students. The boys and girls searched their own lives, talked with others, and consulted authorities to learn how to talk about death, how funerals are conducted, and how people react to the death of pets, adults, parents, children. They speculate about life after death.

☞ Remember that the terms we take for granted, such as *funeral, burial, cremation,* and *gravestone,* frequently have little or no meaning to children. When the need arises, discuss death openly, honestly, and in language that matches the child's understanding.

You'll find a note to parents on the inside cover of *I'll Miss You, Mr. Hooper* (Random House) that encourages appropriate dialogue. Based on a "Sesame Street" television script prepared after the death of actor Will Lee, the sensitively written book helps children understand that someone else will be there to care for them if a cherished one should die.

HOW IT FEELS WHEN A PARENT DIES
Jill Krementz
Knopf (both), 1981
B/w photographs by the author
[i, j] 128 pages

Ms. Krementz sought out and interviewed boys and girls who had lost a parent: eighteen seven- to sixteen-year-olds from various ethnic and socioeconomic backgrounds. Without exception, all of them were eager to share their thoughts and feelings of bereavement with the unfamiliar but obviously concerned author/photographer. Reading their statements will help older readers appreciate that children want to be told the details about the death of a parent. Not knowing is harder to live with.

☞ For fine examples of humor with death as a theme, share Robert W. Service's classic poem *The Cremation of Sam McGee* (Greenwillow), with vibrant illustrations by Ted Harrison, and the tale of "Old Dry Frye," as retold by Richard Chase in his *Grandfather Tales* (Houghton, 1948).

LEARNING TO SAY GOOD-BYE
Eda LeShan
Macmillan, 1976
B/w illustrations by Paul Giavanopoulos
[i, j] 96 pages

As Mrs. LeShan comfortingly explains, there is no right or wrong way to feel after the death of a parent. Everyone reacts differently. Her sage advice, framed within illustrative vignettes, helps children understand that anger, guilt, fear, or even relief can be natural reactions to the trauma of death. With understanding and compassion, she helps children adjust to the changes that may occur, including a parent's second marriage.

LOSS AND HOW TO COPE WITH IT
Joanne E. Bernstein
Clarion (both), 1977
[i, j] 160 pages

This will be a great help to anyone who has suffered a bereavement. The author relates death to losses of other kinds, from the infant's temporary loss as a parent leaves the room to the adult's permanent loss of a favorite necklace or a job. She explains that, from childhood, experiencing inevitable losses helps prepare us to handle death. She then alerts the reader to the succession of feelings that accompanies mourning and provides sound advice about coping. She also provides an extensive bibliography and a useful index.

☞ Judith Viorst's *The Tenth Good Thing About Barney* (Macmillan and Aladdin), Jean Little's *Mama's Going to Buy You a Mockingbird* (Viking and Puffin), and Katherine Paterson's *Bridge to Teribithia* (Crowell and Trophy) are three of the many sensitively written stories for children that concern death. They were written, respectively, for primary grade, older elementary, and middle or junior high school readers.

Dinosaurs

Dinosaurs head kids' lists of awesome creatures. And well they might! Brontosaurus was bigger than two schoolrooms; diplodocus, as long as five cars; ultrasaurus, taller than a telephone pole. They were the *real* giants. And therein lies their attraction.

DIGGING UP DINOSAURS
DINOSAURS ARE DIFFERENT
Aliki
Crowell (both), 1981; (both), 1985
Full-color illustrations by the author
[p, i] each 40 pages

With a light, often humorous touch, the author/artist helps youngest readers appreciate what's involved in digging up and reconstructing dinosaur skeletons. Her first book is a simple yet informative, behind-the-scenes look at the people and procedures of paleontology. In a similar manner, her second book shows how differences and similarities in bone structure help scientists classify dinosaurs.

☞ Design a fancy "Dinosaur Hunting License" for children who want to stalk the saurians. If you need help drawing dinosaurs to decorate it, follow Michael Emberley's directions in *Dinosaurs* or *More Dinosaurs* (both Little). When they have a license, kids can make themselves Emberley-inspired "Dinosaur Badges" to wear while digging up dinosaur data.

THE SMALLEST DINOSAURS
Seymour Simon
Crown, 1982
Full-color illustrations by Anthony Rao
[p] 48 pages

In a noteworthy blend of fine writing, illustration, and book design, young readers will discover what is known, unknown, and conjectured about the dinosaurs that weren't giants. Pair this with the author's book on those who were, *The Largest Dinosaurs* (Macmillan).

☞ Link kids to Colin Caket's *Model a Monster* (Sterling) for easy-to-follow directions on how to make dinosaurs out of pipe cleaners, aluminum foil, cardboard, papier-mâché, and other readily available materials.

SUPERSAURUS
Francine Jacobs
Putnam, 1982
B/w illustrations by D. D. Tyler
[p] 48 pages

In short, simple sentences for beginning readers, Ms. Jacobs describes Dinosaur Jim Jensen's discovery of a six-foot-wide hip bone and other fossils from the largest ever unearthed.

☞ Have youngsters trace a dinosaur picture on graph paper, enlarge it to life size, and paint a mural on a bedroom, basement, or school wall or ceiling—or the driveway or patio hardtop. Look up David Peters's *Giants of Land, Sea and Air* (Knopf) for dramatic illustrations of the relative sizes of dinosaurs, people, and other creatures.

HOW BIG IS A BRACHIOSAURUS?
Susan Carroll
Platt & Munk (both), 1986
Full-color illustrations by Frederic Marvin
[p, i] 32 pages

This information-packed, well-illustrated, 8-inch-square, under-$3 paperback is first-rate. The author covers the size, physical characteristics, diet, and habitat of dinosaurs and their contemporaries within a simple, stimulating question-and-answer format. And she makes it clear that there is still much to learn about the creatures.

☞ Make decorative pillows. On plain fabric or ready-made pillows, let youngsters 1) draw their favorite dinosaurs with indelible markers, 2) sketch in pencil and then embroider them, 3) cut them out of fabric for appliqué, or 4) combine all three techniques. The ones youngsters make in Janet Wright's class in Friday Harbor, Washington, become treasured keepsakes.

DINOSAURS
John Bonnett Wexo
Wildlife, 1985
Full-color illustrations and photographs
[i, j] 20 pages

In this skillful blend of what we do and don't know about dinosaurs, the author explores current theories on dinosaurs' appearance, disappearance, social structure, and descendants. Readers of all ages will be intrigued by illustrations that spread across two and three pages as well as a four-page centerfold of thirty-nine dinosaurs (with mom, dad, and child for scale). Mount them on a bulletin board and design scavenger-hunt activities around them.

☞ After they've discussed how colors differ among extant wildlife species, ask each youngster to color the same dinosaur picture you've outlined. (They'll find interesting comments on coloring in Mr. Wexo's *Dinosaurs.*) When they've finished, have them justify the colors. Did they portray a brightly colored male or a drab female, an old or a young dinosaur? Since no one knows what color they were, all versions will be "right."

RANGER RICK'S DINOSAUR BOOK
Howard F. Robinson, ed.
National Wildlife Federation, 1984
Full-color illustrations and photographs
[i, j] 96 pages

This is an oversize, lavishly illustrated look at what scientists know and postulate about dinosaurs from iguanodon to ultrasaurus. It's an excellent guide to saurians.

☞ Color your "prose-aic" views of prehistoric creatures with the choice poetry Lee Bennett Hopkins selected for *Dinosaurs* (Harcourt).

DINOSAURS AND THEIR YOUNG
Russell Freedman
Holiday House, 1983
B/w illustrations by Leslie Morrill
[p, i] 32 pages

Scientists once believed that dinosaurs, like snakes and turtles, buried their eggs and left them to hatch unattended. Mr. Freedman reviews the 1978 discoveries that suggest hadrosaurs may have cared for their young much as crocodiles do.

☞ No one knows whether it was the female, male, or both dinosaur parents who hatched eggs or watched babies. Suggest youngsters read about parental roles of other animals and present their own theories on how young hadrosaurs might have been reared.

DINOSAUR MYSTERIES
Mary Elting and Ann Goodman
Platt, 1980
Full-color illustrations by Susan Swan
[i, j] 64 pages

The authors encourage youngsters to hypothesize: here's what we have, here's how some scientists interpret it, what do you think? Their dramatic reenactment of dinosaur life will hold readers' interest and stimulate creative problem solving.

☞ Have students pretend they're reporters on an expedition and fossils have been discovered. Ask them to write (and tape for broadcast) a TV or radio newsflash describing the find, how big the dinosaur may have been, its diet, and whatever else can be surmised from the evidence. Have them also sketch its picture.

A FIELD GUIDE TO DINOSAURS
David Lambert and the Diagram Group
Avon (both), 1983
B/w illustrations and photographs
[i, j] 256 pages

Do you want to go on a dinosaur hunt? Let's go . . . and don't forget the "first complete guide to every dinosaur known." Precise scale and life-size illustrations (including silhouettes) show dinosaur forms, fossils, and habitats, the people who discovered them, and how the fossilized remains are displayed.

☞ Brainstorm a word list about dinosaurs and their era for boys and girls to convert into original word finds, riddles (see *Funny Side Up* [Scholastic]), codes, other word puzzlers, and funny cartoon strips. Let Joseph Rosenbloom's *The Funniest Dinosaur Book Ever!* (Sterling) set a jolly mood.

DINOSAURS OF NORTH AMERICA
Helen Roney Sattler
Lothrop, 1981
B/w illustrations by Anthony Rao
[i, j] 160 pages

This land is our land, this land was dinosaur land—sixty-five million or more years ago! Kids will discover which dinosaurs may have played in their backyards when they read that more than eighty kinds of dinosaurs lived here long ago. The author explains that this continent was once part of the single land mass when dinosaurs first appeared. By the time they disappeared, the one continent had divided into many.

☞ Introduce children to preschooler Patrick and his dinosaur-wise older brother, Hank, in two delightful blends of saurian fact and fancy: Donald and Carol Carrick's *Patrick's Dinosaurs* (both, Clarion) and *What Happened to Patrick's Dinosaurs?* (Clarion).

THE ILLUSTRATED DINOSAUR DICTIONARY
Helen Roney Sattler
Lothrop, 1983
Color and b/w illustrations by Anthony Rao and Christopher Santoro
[i, j] 316 pages

This outstanding reference has entries for more than 300 kinds of dinosaurs. The author describes what is known about their physical characteristics, where the fossils were found, and what they were. She also describes the animals sometimes mistaken for dinosaurs, lists by location where fossils were unearthed, and defines related terminology.

MACMILLAN BOOK OF DINOSAURS AND OTHER PREHISTORIC CREATURES
Mary Elting
Macmillan (both), 1984
Full-color illustrations by John Hamberger
[i, j] 80 pages

In her immensely interesting account of the changing earth and its creatures (Precambrian through the Quaternary periods), the author shares anecdotes about noted scientists, the fossils they studied, and the theories they developed.

☞ With a roll of adding machine tape, have youngsters construct a time line that stretches from the Precambrian to the Quaternary periods: measure one centimeter for every million years.

PTEROSAURS, THE FLYING REPTILES
Helen Roney Sattler
Lothrop, 1985
Full-color illustrations by Christopher Santoro
[i, j] 48 pages

Pterosaurs were contemporaries of dinosaurs. They had fur or long hair, and may have been warm-blooded, but they weren't mammals; they flew, but weren't birds; they weren't reptiles either, though they had reptilian skulls and teeth. Mrs. Sattler tells us what scientists have discovered and deduced since the first pterosaur fossil was unearthed in 1831. Breathtaking illustrations.

AUKS, ROCKS AND THE ODD DINOSAUR
Peggy Thomson
Crowell, 1985
B/w photographs
[i, j] 128 pages

This is a fascinating behind-the-scenes peek at exhibit preparations in the Smithsonian Museum of Natural History. When they read about the guesses and compromises scientists made to reconstruct the pterosaur Quetzalcoatlus, children will begin to appreciate that they can't always believe their eyes—even when looking at something in the Smithsonian.

Divorce

Teachers are ever on the alert for the causes of a child's continued inattention or changing level of performance. After the obvious inquiries about vision, hearing, and general health fail to uncover a cause for unusual behavior, a call home frequently reveals family stress. In many cases, that stress is caused by a recent or an impending divorce.

Divorce is a difficult subject to avoid: one or more children in virtually every classroom come from homes touched by this trauma. An understanding teacher can assist a child through the difficult transition divorce always represents.

The following books will help you open discussion at home or in school to show children that they are not at fault, that they are still loved and can, in time, adjust to a new family arrangement.

WHAT'S GOING TO HAPPEN TO ME?
WHEN PARENTS SEPARATE OR DIVORCE
Eda LeShan
Four Winds (both), 1978
B/w illustrations by Richard Cuffari
[i] 144 pages

Mrs. LeShan speaks directly to youngsters whose parents' divorce is imminent. She acknowledges the sadness, confusion, and shame that can accompany it, discusses individual and family counseling, and probes the difficult questions of money, custody, and new relationships.

THE KIDS' BOOK OF DIVORCE
Eric Rofes, ed.
Stephen Greene, 1981
B/w illustrations
[i, j] 124 pages

This book is the result of a two-year project, during which twenty eleven- to fourteen-year-olds in the editor's elementary school class interviewed experts, conducted research, discussed, wrote, and illustrated their book. It covers the causes, mechanics, and consequences of divorce, reviews a typical separation agreement, and probes relationships with siblings and friends.

HOW IT FEELS WHEN PARENTS DIVORCE
Jill Krementz
Knopf, 1984
B/w photographs by the author
[i, j] 115 pages

Ms. Krementz presents each child's story in his/her own words, edited from extensive, candid conversations, and she provides sensitive photographs of the children and their parents. The candor with which the nineteen seven- to sixteen-year-olds speak of important personal feelings will touch the emotions of all readers.

DIVORCE IS A GROWN UP PROBLEM
Janet Sinberg
Avon, 1978 (paperback only)
B/w illustrations by Nancy Gray
[p] 48 pages

This paperback, designed for reading aloud, is for a parent working together with a young child to resolve the ravages of divorce. The few words on each page, "spoken" by a preschooler, express his apprehensions caused by divorce and repeat the loving counsel offered by both mother and father. The book is prefaced by sound advice for parents and concludes with a list of other books for parents and children. (The fluffy-haired preschooler could be a boy or a girl.)

TALKING ABOUT DIVORCE AND SEPARATION
Earl A. Grollman
Beacon, 1975 (paperback only)
B/w illustrations by Alison Cann
[p] 112 pages

Written to be shared by parent and child, the first half of this book is a series of captioned sketches that depict a small child experiencing the breakup of his parents' marriage and their separation. A parents' guide follows, which covers children's psychological reactions to parental stress and separation. Rabbi Grollman is one of the experts consulted by Mr. Rofes's children (see *The Kids' Book of Divorce*).

WHEN YOUR PARENTS DIVORCE
William V. Arnold
Westminster, 1980
[j] 118 pages

Writing especially for teenagers and young adults, the author, a Presbyterian minister, divides his book into three sections, "Feelings," "Thoughts," and "Actions." He carefully distinguishes between emotional and rational reactions to discomforting events. His sensitive treatment of this difficult topic was influenced by extensive counseling with divorced parents and their children.

☞ The books above will guide you in helping children with this sensitive subject. To explore the subject further, however, I recommend Joanne E. Bernstein's *Books to Help Children Cope with Separation and Loss* (Bowker). In her annotated bibliography, Ms. Bernstein discusses the relative merits of 633 books, both fiction and nonfiction, on the subjects of death, divorce, separation, desertion, illness, and the consequences of war.

DINOSAURS DIVORCE
Laurene Krasny Brown and Marc Brown
Atlantic, 1986
Color illustrations by the authors
[p, i] 32 pages

This superb "guide for changing families" balances wise, straightforward truths about divorce and its impact upon the child reader with humorous dinosaur drawings to illustrate each point.

Dogs

"Carol is a very withdrawn girl. . . . She prefers to sit alone instead of engaging in any sort of free-time activity with her peers. Her only conversation lately has been about her new pup."

Carol's teacher (a teacher of disturbed children and one of my home study students) jumped at the chance the new pet offered to "involve and bring [Carol] positive attention." She gave the third-grader a photoessay on puppies as a guide and asked her to report to the class on the best ways to care for a new pup—with hers at hand to show everyone.

At home or at school, a book and a pet can ease a shy child's path to peers.

SUPERPUPPY
Jill and D. Manus Pinkwater
Clarion (both), 1976
[i, j] 208 pages

This guide on how to choose, raise, and train the best possible dog includes a five-part test for picking a puppy, information about a dog owner's responsibilities, and hints for finding lost dogs. The authors recommend children read about different breeds to determine mutual compatibility. They stress, however, that whether any dog is good or bad is more a matter of how it's been bred, chosen, raised, and trained.

☞ Take children to the local animal shelter to help them appreciate why all books in this section stress spaying or neutering pet dogs and cats. Preface the visit with Caroline Arnold's and Richard Hewett's photoessay *Pets Without Homes* (Clarion). It shows how the shelters obtain stray dogs, care for, and pair them with people.

TAKING CARE OF YOUR DOG
Joyce Pope
Watts, 1987

DOGS AND PUPPIES
Rose Hill
Usborne (both), 1982
Full-color illustrations
[i] 32 pages; 24 pages

Both abundantly illustrated books for kids about to acquire canine companions offer sound advice on choosing a healthy pup, housing, training, and keeping it fit. Both also point out the costs and responsibilities that accompany the new family member.

☞ Introduce youngsters to Alexandra Day's almost wordless picture book *Good Dog, Carl* (Green Tiger). The crème de la crème of canine babysitters, Carl delivers day care with a difference.

UNDERSTANDING DOGS
Su Swallow
Usborne (both), 1978
Full-color illustrations
[i] 32 pages

The focus is on the nature of adult dogs—their physical and social characteristics and their care and training as pets and workers.

A DOG'S BODY
Joanna Cole
Morrow, 1986
B/w photographs by Jim and Ann Monteith
[i] 48 pages

Youngsters will appreciate the beauty and efficiency of a dog's body after reading this information-packed photoessay. It clearly and effectively focuses on canine development and body language.

☞ Ask youngsters to visit the supermarket, list the dog foods they find, the ways they are packaged, and the amount of space they are given relative to other pet foods and human food. Have students compare respective ingredients, prices, packages, and advertising copy of the dog food. Then ask a veterinarian to visit the classroom and discuss the care of small pets. During the question/answer time, ask what a healthy diet is for dogs of varying ages. What conclusions can be drawn from what students learned from the vet and what they learned from the food they found on the shelves?

DOGS: ALL ABOUT THEM
Alvin and Virginia Silverstein
Lothrop, 1986
B/w photographs
[i] 256 pages

Extensive research and knowledge have been distilled into a relaxed, very readable, storylike account of *Canis familiaris*. In addition to writing about the evolution, breeds, characteristics, and wild relatives of dogs, the authors also discuss dogs in sports and science. Considerable detail, a bibliography, and a thorough index make this a noteworthy addition to any school or dog-lover's library.

☞ Mix mutts with mathematics: conduct a Canine Count. Have youngsters take a poll of their classmates' pet population. What percentage are dogs? Purebred? Mixed breed? Are your class pets representative of the school as a whole? What pets did your pupils' parents and grandparents have? Which generation had/ has more dogs? Why?

A PUPPY IS BORN
Heiderose Fischer-Nagel
Putnam, 1985
Full-color photographs by Andreas Fischer-Nagel
[p, i] 40 pages

The color photographs of Max, Missy, and their familiy are so vivid I'm tempted to pet the page each time I read the book! The coauthors introduce sire and dam, then simply show and tell how their offspring arrive and develop from birth to ready-for-adoption puppyhood.

☞ Max, Missy, and family are purebred wirehaired dachshunds. Suggest youngsters find the name and address of a local dog breeder in the phone book. Have them write to ask if she could visit and discuss her dogs—perhaps bring one to class and point out its championship features.

GREFF: THE STORY OF A GUIDE DOG
Patricia Curtis
Lodestar, 1982
B/w photographs by Mary Bloom
[i] 64 pages

CONNIE'S NEW EYES
Bernard Wolf
Lippincott, 1976
B/w photographs by author
[i, j] 96 pages

In Ms. Curtis's book, youngsters will learn how a dog (in this instance a Labrador retriever) is trained from puppyhood to become a guide dog for the blind. Mr. Wolf follows golden retriever Blythe from her training days to adulthood as Connie's guide dog. He also provides a moving view of Connie's first year as a teacher of handicapped children and the additional challenges she faces as a blind person.

SHEEP DOG
George Ancona
Lothrop, 1985
B/w photographs by the author
[i, j] 64 pages

MAGGIE, A SHEEP DOG
Dorothy Hinshaw Patent
Dodd, 1986
B/w photographs by William Muñoz
[i] 48 pages

Big, floppy-eared dogs with rounded heads and placid natures have watched over European and Mideastern sheep for thousands of years. Mr. Ancona explains why these dogs are effective guards and how a pair of biologists are encouraging American ranchers to use them. Dr. Patent details one Hungarian sheep dog's year among her sheep in Montana.

SLED DOGS
Brigid Casey and Wendy Haugh
Dodd, 1983
B/w photographs and illustrations
[i, j] 80 pages

This is a fascinating history of malamutes, Siberian huskies, and other intrepid dogs bred for life and work in the Arctic. It reveals how the animals' stamina helped explorers reach the North and South poles; how their intelligence and courage have saved many lives (their 600-mile run to deliver diphtheria serum to weather-isolated Nome in 1925, for example); and how dog sleds are returning as a form of transportation.

Endangered Species

Scores of millions of buffalo once roamed most of the North American continent. By 1871, when Frédéric-Auguste Bartholdi first visited America, there were no buffalo east of the central plains. When the sculptor's Statue of Liberty was dedicated two decades later, fewer than 500 of North America's only native cattle remained—anywhere. Through the concerted effort of conservationists, however, and in time for Liberty's centennial celebration, our continent's largest land mammal was saved from going the way of the dodo. More than 80,000 now grace our land.

BUFFALO
Dorothy Hinshaw Patent
Holiday House, 1986
B/w photographs by William Muñoz
[i] 73 pages

Essay and photos interestingly detail a year in the life of an American bison today.

☞ The buffalo was a source of food, clothing, and shelter for Native Americans of the Great Plains. Their mythology reflects the respect, appreciation, and admiration with which they treated the animal. Link youngsters to Paul Goble's stunning *Buffalo Woman* (Bradbury), an enchanting reweaving of similar legends from more than eight tribes, including the Crow, Wichita, and Cheyenne.

ENDANGERED ANIMALS
John Bonnett Wexo
Wildlife, 1983 (paperback only)
Full-color illustrations
[i] 18 pages

Nine dramatic double-page spreads include views of animals not yet on scientists' Endangered Species List, those that are extinct, and those that have been saved from extinction. Art and words stress the interdependence of all living things. The author concludes with suggestions for children who would like to help endangered wildlife

DAISY ROTHSCHILD: THE GIRAFFE THAT LIVES WITH ME
Betty Leslie-Melville
Doubleday, 1987
Full-color photographs
[i] 42 pages

This delightful "biography" of one of the fewer than 150 extant Rothschild giraffes will help youngsters appreciate that people can make a difference. Not all of us have a yard large enough to accommodate a giraffe or two, but it's nice to meet the Melvilles, who do—and to see how they did it.

☞ Link your youngsters to Barbara Ford's and Stephen Ross's *Wildlife Rescue* (Whitman) to discover how children and adults in the Big Rapids, Michigan, area help care for injured and orphaned wildlife. A veterinarian, the Humane Society, or the State Wildlife Office can put you in touch with similar local organizations.

SAVING THE PEREGRINE FALCONS
Caroline Arnold
Carolrhoda, 1985
Full-color photographs by Richard R. Hewett
[i] 48 pages

Thanks to scientists, peregrine falcons no longer face total extinction. The author describes how thin-shelled eggs (caused by insecticide in the parents' systems) are taken from nests, hatched, and the chicks fed and eventually returned to roosts in the wild or high above city streets in skyscrapers.

☞ Mention hacking to children of the electronic age and they're likely to think *computers*. Link kids to Paula Hendrich's *Saving America's Birds* (Lothrop) and they'll learn that hacking is a falconer's term for teaching captive birds to hunt and kill food in the wild. Young readers will also meet people who devote their lives to the preservation of peregrine falcons and other birds of prey.

AS DEAD AS A DODO
Peter Mayle
Godine, 1982
Full-color illustrations by Shawn Rice
[i, j] 32 pages

Portly dodos waddle across the endpapers of this beautifully designed book about sixteen vanished species. The magnificent paintings and wry words, brief and to the point, will leave neither you nor your youngsters indifferent to the plight of these creatures or those nearing extinction.

PLANTS IN DANGER
Edward R. Ricciuti
Harper, 1979
B/w illustrations by Ann Zwinger
[j] 96 pages

The facts may be about a decade old, but the message is timeless: it is as important to preserve plant species as any others. The thoughtless decimation of the dodo and the passenger pigeon, the near-destruction of the buffalo, and the creation of animal sanctuaries have their floral counterparts.

Farm Life

THE FARM BOOK
E. Boyd Smith
Houghton, 1982
Color illustrations by the author
[i] 64 pages

Travel back in time to 1910, when this book was originally published. The lovely artwork accurately portrays turn-of-the-century farm life and invites comparison with modern farming. The story of the birth and rebirth of his book (it's in the introduction) is a fascinating glimpse into children's literature.

THE PRICE OF FREE LAND
Treva Adams Strait
Lippincott, 1979
B/w photographs
[i] 96 pages

In 1914, 160 acres of "free land" cost $24 cash and three years of incredibly hard work. These reminiscences of growing up on a homestead farm in western Nebraska are good for reading aloud or alone.

JOEL: GROWING UP A FARM MAN
Patricia Demuth
Dodd, 1982
B/w photographs by Jack Demuth
[i, j] 96 pages

The author and photographer moved to a nearby farm and shadowed Joel Holland for a year to produce this fascinating photoessay. Joel was thirteen at the time and head of a hog operation that grossed over $40,000 a year on his father's Illinois farm.

☞ You can't talk farms, of course, without visiting the farm of farms. Link kids to Tracey Campbell Pearson's merry version of *Old MacDonald Had a Farm* (Dial) for a view of a blissfully bucolic couple carrying on sunup-to-sundown chores. When they've finished her version, let them write their own and change the old man's locale—in a zoo, perhaps, with a "roar roar" here and a "screech screech" there.

MACHINES ON A FARM
Hope Irvin Marston
Dodd, 1982
B/w photographs by the author
[p, i] 26 pages

Well-chosen photographs and descriptive commentary put more than
twenty-five pieces of modern farm equipment in your lap for a close-
up of the machines and their uses.

BABY FARM ANIMALS
Merrill Windsor
National Geographic, 1984
Full-color photographs
[p] 34 pages

This is a lovely collection of mothers and their kids, calves, chicks, lambs, goslings, foals, and piglets—at home

CHICKEN AND EGG
Christine Back and Jens Olesen
Silver Burdett, 1986
Full-color photographs by Bo Jarner and b/w illustrations
[p, i] 25 pages

INSIDE AN EGG
Sylvia Johnson
Lerner, 1982
Color photographs by Kiyoshi Shimizu
[i, j] 48 pages

A DUCKLING IS BORN
Hans-Heinrich Isenbart
Putnam, 1981
Full-color photographs by Othmar Baumli
[p, i, j] 40 pages

The first book, addressed to primary-graders, is an excellent introduction for readers of any age. Full-page photographs alternate with pages of text and illustrations that explain the development of a chick from a tiny spot on the yoke to a hatchling. The second includes the additional details older students will understand. The third, a drake's tale, provides a complete picture: courtship, mating, egg-laying, growth inside the egg, hatching, and the whole family out for a swim.

☞ Fill egg baskets, or cover a bulletin board with as many pictures as youngsters can draw of different hatchlings popping out of shells or sacs. Link your artists to Ruth Heller's *Chickens Aren't the Only Ones* (Grosset) for an introduction to the wide world of oviparous creatures.

Fire Fighting

Use the beginning-of-the-school-year fire drill to introduce or review recommended behavior during different kinds of emergencies in school and at home. One of the best ways is to have children role-play. For example, if you keep a play or disconnected phone handy, they can practice-dial the local emergency number, state the emergency, and give the address until the procedure becomes automatic. (The practice paid off for me when my home caught fire!)

FIRE FIGHTERS
Ray Broekel
Children's (both), 1981
Full-color photographs
[p] 48 pages

This introduction for very young readers has a brief but informative text by a writer who does not talk down to his intended audience.

FIRE! FIRE!
Gail Gibbons
Crowell (both) 1984
Full-color illustrations by the author
[p] 40 pages

Young readers will learn how blazes are battled in city apartments, on country farms, in forests, and on the waterfront. Included are helpful fire-prevention tips and rules of behavior you'll find highly useful for role-playing activities.

☞ With *Fire! Fire!* as a guide, have children make a "Fire Prevention Checklist" for home inspection. They can make certain, for example, that electrical outlets aren't overcrowded or electrical cords dangerously old or frayed. Teachers can put a "Fire Check Receipt" on the bottom of each child's list. After the house inspection, the youngster can bring the parent-signed receipt to school and leave the list itself at home for reference.

A DAY IN THE LIFE OF A FIREFIGHTER
Betsy Smith
Troll (both), 1981
Full-color photographs by Catherine Noren
[i] 32 pages

Follow a "truckie," a member of a ladder company, whose fifteen-hour day begins at 6:00 P.M.

> ☞ As you read about fire prevention, ask children to create an alphabet of fire-fighter–related items. When they've finished, see how their list compares with Jean Johnson's nonsexist *Firefighters: A to Z* (Walker).

FIREHOUSE
Bernard Wolf
Morrow, 1983
B/w photographs by the author
[j] 96 pages

Fire fighting is dirty, life-threatening, and plain hard work, as this perceptive photoessay shows. Readers will marvel at and be thankful for the dedicated people who accept the fire fighter's awesome responsibilities.

FIRE TRUCKS
Hope Irvin Marston
Dodd, 1984

BUILDING A FIRE TRUCK
Jerry Bushey
Carolrhoda, 1981
B/w photographs by the authors
[i] 64 pages; 32 pages

Pair these books to show children a variety of specialized fire-fighting equipment (one of which can pump eight thousand gallons of water a minute!) and how the trucks are made, many with ⅛" steel (twice as thick as that on a car).

☞ Wrap up your fire-prevention unit by having one group of children create two-minute skits on fire prevention and emergency behavior they can dramatize for other classes—how to stop, drop, and roll, for example. Have another group write and illustrate a coloring book on the same subjects. After the first group has performed, the second can distribute the coloring book to reinforce the message.

Food—Growing at Home

Offer children the chance to share the fruit of their labors—literally: let them plant seeds in the spring for a salad the whole family will savor this summer. While they munch their first fresh-from-the-garden goodies, have your gardeners brainstorm the activities that produced them. Transcribe that list down the side of a chart you've headed math, reading, science, and other areas of the curriculum. Let your youngsters color in the boxes: "Math" and "measure distance between plants," for example, or "Reading" and "follow directions from seed packet or book." The colorfully completed chart will help them appreciate that "school" subjects aren't only for schoolwork, but part of the "real" world.

IN MY GARDEN
Helen Oeschli
Macmillan, 1985
Full-color illustrations by Kelly Oeschli
[p] 32 pages

In this excellent guide for youngsters farming on a simple scale, detailed illustrations accompany clear directions for preparing soil, planting seeds/seedlings, and cultivating easy-to-grow vegetables. Together they make process and product perfectly appetizing.

GROWING THINGS
Angela Wilkes
Usborne, 1984 (paperback only)
Full-color illustrations by John Shackell
[p] 14 pages

Little gardeners "demonstrate" the step-by-step instructions and practical tips for growing flowers, trees, herbs, and vegetables inside and out, in text and lively illustrations.

BOOK OF VEGETABLES
Harriet L. Sobol and Patricia Agre
Full-color and b/w photographs by Patricia Agre
[i] 48 pages

This first-rate look at the commonplace from an uncommon angle shows each plant in blossom and at harvest time. The book is a must-see for youngsters far from the farming crowd, and a fine preview for youngsters about to plant their own vegetables.

POTATOES
Sylvia Johnson
Lerner, 1984
Full-color photographs by Masaharu Suzuki
[i] 48 pages

BEAN AND PLANT
Christine Back
Silver Burdett, 1986
Full-color photographs by Barrie Watts
[p] 25 pages

Though the first book is addressed to middle-graders and the second to primary-graders, the photography makes both appropriate for all ages.

☞ If there's room and students live close enough (or you've a willing principal or maintenance person) to water them during the summer, plant pumpkins and sunflowers in the spring. The children who plant them can harvest them in the fall. If they then set aside a few seeds for other children to sow the following spring, they'll keep alive the cycle they started. Just the way toddler Jamie does in Jeanne Titherington's simple yet stunning *Pumpkin Pumpkin* (Greenwillow)—an aesthetic delight for readers of all ages.

Food—Nutrition

Fact-filled posters, coloring books, and attractively designed brochures are useful tools. Especially those from the dairy councils and other food commodity boards and commissions. I've used them many times in the past. Their ready availability at low (or no) cost makes them particularly attractive. They'll brighten walls and, when linked to good nonfiction books, sharpen critical thinking skills.

When you send for these and other "freebies," however, please remember that they are *not* a source of unbiased information. Their primary purpose is to stimulate sales of the commodities they represent. While they forthrightly present the benefits of their sponsoring organization, they seldom offer a balanced view. Insist children weigh information from many sources before accepting any one at face value.

Use commercially sponsored materials to teach good eating habits. But use them also to teach children to take everything they read with a grain of salt. Remember, there's no such thing as a free lunch.

YOU AND YOUR FOOD
Judy Tatchell and Dilys Wells
Usborne (both), 1986
Full-color illustrations
[i, j] 48 pages

In a deft blend of illustrations and text, the authors discuss food allergies and provide important tips on buying, preparing, and safely storing fresh foods. They also offer facts about calories, vitamins, and basic nutrition.

☞ Accentuate the positive, but don't eliminate the negative. During the same few weeks youngsters cut out pictures, make up grocery lists, plan menus, and read about or otherwise concentrate on recommended foods and their ingredients, have them establish a Junk Food Hall of Shame: a collection of junk food wrappers pinned on the bulletin board.

When they've identified the half-dozen least nutritious foods, suggest girls and boys make and send an "Empty Cup Award" to their manufacturers. Include a rationale for the "honor" and suggestions for improving the product. The maker of any nutritious snack discovered during the search deserves a class-made gold medal and a note of appreciation, of course.

VITAMINS: WHAT THEY ARE, WHAT THEY DO
JUNK FOOD: WHAT IT IS, WHAT IT DOES
Judith S. Seixas
Greenwillow, 1986; 1984
B/w illustrations by Tom Huffman
[p, i] 56 pages; 48 pages

Though these books are designed for primary-graders, older readers will find them excellent starting points. In the first book, the author introduces the thirteen known vitamins, six basic food groups, and conditions under which some people need vitamin supplements. In the second, she discusses the harmful effects of excessive salt, sugar, and fat. She describes a well-balanced diet and includes an eight-question junk food quiz.

HOW DID WE FIND OUT ABOUT VITAMINS?
Isaac Asimov
Walker, 1974
B/w illustrations by David Wool
[i] 64 pages

In his inimitable easy-to-read-and-understand style, Dr. Asimov introduces the scientists and their research on the structure and role of vitamins.

FAST-FOOD GUIDE
Michael F. Jacobson and Sarah Fritschner
Workman, 1968
[j, adult] 228 pages

An essential ingredient whenever the topic is good-for-you food, this paperback reveals the nutritional value of items at fifteen fast-food chains—from Arby's to Wendy's. Readers will discover what they really swallow at the eateries: fifteen teaspoons of fat, for example, in a Burger King Double Beef Whopper with Cheese. (Show your children fifteen teaspoons of fat. Yuck!) Fast food and junk food are synonymous, more often than not.

The fast-food industry is here to stay, however, so wherever possible, the authors tell how to choose relatively healthy meals from overall nutritionally meager pickings. They survey the history of fast foods, review healthy diets for children and adults, and also suggest ways to improve fast foods.

☞ A Fast-Food Eating Guide, in the form of an 18 x 24" poster, lists calories, fat and sodium content, and nutritional values of chain-eatery food. Write to Center for Science in the Public Interest (CSPI), 1501 16th St. N.W., Washington, D.C. 20036 for information on how to get it.

GOOD FOR ME!
Marilyn Burns
Little (both), 1978
B/w illustrations by Sandy Clifford
[i, j] 128 pages

The interesting origins of margarine (Napoleon III needed a cheap butter for his army, navy, and poor people) and Eskimo Pies (a youngster couldn't decide between a candy bar and ice cream so a store owner combined them) are among the many anecdotes in this "food" book of the excellent "Brown Paper School" series.

FOOD, NUTRITION, AND YOU
Linda Peavy and Ursula Smith
Scribner's, 1982
[j] 192 pages

Historical anecdotes enliven food facts for teenagers: Dr. Beaumont's experiments on the man with the hole in his stomach, Lavoisier's invention of calories, Roger Bannister's running of the first under-four-minute mile, the discoveries of vitamins, and more. The last quarter of the book is devoted to the nutritional needs of adolescents.

MAMMALS AND THEIR MILK
Lucia Anderson
Dodd, 1985
Full-color illustrations by Jennifer Dewey
[i, j] 48 pages

If you ask where milk comes from, chances are children will shout "Cows!" Yet reindeer share their milk in Norway and Finland, yaks in Nepal, and water buffalo, llamas, camels, and mares in their native countries. The author reveals these and other ordinary facts with extraordinary vitality. She also includes easy-to-conduct experiments to help children learn even more about milk, firsthand.

THE MILK MAKERS
Gail Gibbons
Macmillan (both), 1985
Full-color illustrations by the author
[p, i] 32 pages

MILK
Donald Carrick
Greenwillow, 1985
Full-color illustrations by the author
[p] 24 pages

The author/artists introduce children to milk as it moves from cow to consumer.

☞ Use Ms. Gibbons's and Mr. Carrick's books as an introduction to art as well as milk and its production. Gather together other books by the same authors to help children familiarize themselves with each author's style. Have them point out the similarities and differences.

DAIRY FARMING
Geoffrey Patterson
Deutsch, 1984
Full-color illustrations by the author
[i, j] 32 pages

The absorbing text and detailed drawings beautifully illuminate specialized equipment and the means of milk delivery—from milkmaids and animal skins in the days of the New Stone Age, to modern milking machines and glass bottles.

☞ Ask your boys and girls to jot down as many milk-related items as they can in ten minutes. If milk bottles, straws, Tollhouse cookies, Kellogg's Corn Flakes, or variations thereof are on their lists, you can read aloud their stories from *Steven Caney's Invention Book* (see page 204). When ice cream is mentioned, turn to Marilyn Burns's *Good for Me!* (see above).

MILK: THE FIGHT FOR PURITY
James Cross Giblin
Crowell, 1986
B/w photographs
[i, j] 128 pages

After you've read this account of the struggle to keep it uncontaminated from cow to consumer, you'll appreciate what a luxury fresh milk is—yours for the asking just about anywhere you go. The more than 150-year battle has produced clean dairies, well-fed cattle, pasteurization, and refrigerated trucks—just a few of today's industry's givens.

Grandparents

We live in California and my son's grandparents live in Massachusetts. Such geographical gaps between the two generations are common in our peripatetic society. Don and I kept our parents up to date with David's progress from infancy through toddlerhood by creating nonfiction photoessays. We'd snap shots of ordinary and special occasions, write a descriptive narrative, and at the end of the year forward another "Year in the Life of David" back East.

School-age youngsters can narrow the gap and enrich the relationship between themselves and their grandparents (whether they're near or far) with special-edition, autobiographical photoessays. Set them loose on the project with pencil, paper, camera, and any of the photo-essays I've recommended as models.

GRANDPARENTS: A SPECIAL KIND OF LOVE
Eda LeShan
Macmillan, 1984
B/w illustrations by Tricia Taggart
[i] 112 pages

A simple, straightforward, sympathetic guide to understanding people that focuses upon the child/grandparent relationship. Mrs. LeShan explains why grandparents are not always comfortable to be with and provides advice for turning painful situations into pleasant ones.

☞ Help children appreciate the differences between growing up today and "yesterday." With tape recorder in hand (or via casettes or letters exchanged through the mail), suggest they interview their parents' parents about their school, home, and recreational activities. The recordings or letters will provide insight into the way it was and become treasured keepsakes for family archives.

When I Grew Up Long Ago (Lippincott) is an excellent model for the activity. Alvin Schwartz traveled around the country, recorded what people told him about being young at the turn of the century, and grouped their answers according to topics such as school days, working, and family outings.

CHILDTIMES: A THREE-GENERATION MEMOIR
Eloise Greenfield
Crowell, 1979
B/w illustrations by Jerry Pinkney and photographs
[i, j] 160 pages

We can better appreciate what shaped us and our world when we know about our ancesters and their childhood experiences. The three-generation memoir noted author Eloise Greenfield, her mother, and her grandmother have written is an eloquent reflection on growing up black in America and a memorable book for all children.

GRANDMOTHER CAME FROM DWORITZ
Ethel Vineberg
Tundra, 1987 (paperback only)
B/w illustrations by Rita Briansky
[i, j] 44 pages

The author, a "link between the old country and the new," vividly re-creates the days of her grandmother's and mother's youth in Russia, their marriages (the grandmother's arranged by her parents and their rabbi), and their emigration from oppression to freedom.

☞ Like Ms. Vineberg's grandmother, my grandmother came from Russia, her marriage was arranged, and the ceremony was a traditional one. Ask youngsters to learn how their grandparents or parents met and what their weddings were like. Expand the activity into a multicultural unit that begins with comparisons of wedding customs around the world.

Use Jon Mayled's *Marriage Customs* (Silver) to introduce the traditional ceremonies of seven different religious groups.

TALES OF A GAMBLING GRANDMA
Dayal Kaur Khalsa
Clarkson Potter, 1986
Full-color illustrations by the author
[p, i] 32 pages

The author/artist recalls vignettes of her grandmother (who had played poker to support her family) and their times together in Queens, New York. They reflect the humor, understanding, and respect unique be-tween "grandgenerations." If you don't have a child or grandchild with whom to share the story and pictures, read it for the one you once were. It's a special book.

☞ Have youngsters take a poll of their classmates' grandparents' birthplaces and present homes, locate the sites on a map or globe, make a chart of the data, and discuss what they discovered: which grandparent traveled the farthest, for example.

HOW DOES IT FEEL TO BE OLD?
Norma Farber
Creative Arts, 1979
Two-color illustrations by Trina Schart Hyman
[i, j] 32 pages

With touching warmth and wit, Ms. Farber poetically portrays the pleasures and pains of old age: independence somewhat restrained by loneliness, for instance, and memories and feelings that remain young in bodies that don't. Ms. Hyman's perceptive drawings of grandmother and granddaughter sharing past and present are moving. (My husband cried when he read it.)

☞ Have youngsters ask an older person how it feels to be old. When my students have asked parents or neighbor senior citizens that question, almost every answer noted the loss of agility or the ability to read small print. On the next special or no-special occasion, suggest boys and girls provide senior friends or relatives a service to alleviate that loss. They could volunteer to read the newspaper, magazines, or a story aloud for ten to fifteen minutes each day, for example; take books back and forth to the library once a week; or dust very low, very high, or otherwise hard-to-reach nooks and crannies.

Guinea Pigs, Rabbits, Hamsters

Animate youngsters' activities. Create a Creature Corner—perhaps a Hamster Haven, Guinea Pig Gulch, or Rabbit Rookery. Small mammals make marvelous subjects for writing, math, science, and art projects. Children can read, write stories, create poetry, put on puppet plays, paint pictures, sing songs, and poll peers for opinions about them. Best of all, the furry four-leggers are there for warmth, loving, and companionship when needed.

TAKING CARE OF YOUR GUINEA PIG
Joyce Pope
Watts, 1986
Full-color photographs
[p, i] 32 pages

Ms. Pope's "Taking Care of Your . . ." series is the best I've found for youngsters who are, or are about to be, pet owners. In this book, as in the others, she offers practical advice on selecting healthy pets and discusses the different breeds. She neatly balances the pleasure of a pet's company with the responsibility of keeping it housed and healthy. Best of all, however, she respects the intelligence of her young audience and writes without condescension. Some other titles in the series focus on cats, dogs, hamsters, and rabbits. Also gerbils, the gentle and prolific little creatures not allowed in my home state of California.

SMALL PETS
Rose Hill
Usborne (both), 1982
Full-color illustrations
[p] 24 pages

Children will be attracted to the wealth of detailed illustrations and simple text on the physical characteristics and general behavior of rabbits, guinea pigs, other rodents, and parakeets.

MAKING FRIENDS WITH GUINEA PIGS
DIARY OF A RABBIT
Lilo Hess
Scribner's, 1983; 1982
B/w photographs by the author
[i] each 48 pages

The first photoessay concerns three little guinea pigs and how one became a young girl's pet, another a laboratory animal, and the third a prize-winning show pig. In the second, readers watch a lop-eared rabbit grow from birth to motherhood and, en route, win best-of-group in a rabbit show.

☞ Let *Rabbits, Rabbits* (Harper), Aileen Fisher's poetic musings about cottontails, snowshoe hares, jackrabbits, and others of their kind inspire youngsters' poetry about their pets.

RABBITS AND HARES
Colleen Stanley Bare
Dodd, 1983
B/w photographs by the author
[i, j] 80 pages

Did you know that cottontails are rabbits, jackrabbits are hares, and neither are rodents? In a light, conversational style, the author discloses these and other facts as well as information about many breeds of domestic rabbits.

☞ Ms. Bare's book begins with a review of rabbits and hares in literature. Use it to inspire a month-long "Rabbit Reading Roundup." Center such rabbit-related activities as reading, writing, dramatizing, and drawing in a hutch children can build out of an empty refrigerator carton. Fill it with as many books as they can find and stuffed or other toy rabbits, if a real one in a cage isn't available.

Since Peter Rabbit will undoubtedly hop into the hutch in one form or another, make sure Judy Taylor's *That Naughty*

Rabbit (Warne) is around. You can read aloud excerpts about and show young readers pictures of the woman who created *The Tale of Peter Rabbit* (Warne) and other facets of the immortal rabbit's past.

HAMSTER
Barrie Watts
Silver Burdett, 1986
B/w illustrations by Helen Senior and full-color photographs
[p, i] 26 pages

A simple text and striking close-ups allow young readers to follow the development of a hamster from birth to maturity with ease. Occasional line drawings highlight details. This is one of the excellent "Stopwatch" series, in which children can see each stage in the development of a plant or an animal.

INSIDE THE BURROW: THE LIFE OF THE GOLDEN HAMSTER
Heiderose Fischer-Nagel
Carolrhoda, 1986
Full-color photographs by Andreas Fischer-Nagel
[i, j] 48 pages

The two biologists transferred a pair of pet hamsters into a burrow specially fitted on one side with glass to observe and photograph them in their very-close-to-native habitat. The hamsters did what hamsters do and readers now have an extraordinary view of what is naturally hidden below ground: nest building, birthing, and litter raising. A flowing text describes, explains, and enriches it all.

☞ Transform a list of animal dwellings into a "Home Sweet Home" guessing-game book. Ask children to draw two pictures; the first of an animal and the second of its home. Under the animal they'll write "Where do I live?" and under the home, its name. A hamster, a fox, and a snail, for example, would be paired with a burrow, a den, and a shell. Alternate animal and abode and collate the picture pairs into an original guessing-game book kids can share with siblings and friends.

Holidays

Every day, somewhere in the world, someone is celebrating something: a religious holiday, secular festival, anniversary, sporting event, birthday, or some such occasion. Let youngsters pick their birthday or another date out of a hat, refer to appropriate pages in either of the first two books in this section, and individually or in groups use the event(s) noted as the focus of a special project. Elephant Round-up Day in Surin, Thailand, on November 16, for example, might prompt an original poem, drawing, song, elephant investigation, or preparation of a meal with youngsters *Cooking the Thai Way* (Lerner).

BOOK OF HOLIDAYS AROUND THE WORLD
Alice van Straalen
Dutton, 1986
Full-color photographs and illustrations
[i, j] 192 pages

AMAZING DAYS
Randy Harelson
Workman, 1979 (paperback only)
B/w illustrations
[i] 256 pages

In a beautiful 6½ x 8½″ book that will grace any desk top or coffee table, Ms. van Straalen identifies one or two special events per day, including children's literature events worth noting. The illustrations (many from classic children's books) and photographs will delight browsers. Ms. Harelson's 8½ x 11″ paperback is filled with 365 one-a-day, date-related puzzles, jokes, codes, craft ideas, recipes, and other activities tied to historical or contemporary events.

☞ So that many youngsters can use *Amazing Days* at the same time, separate, laminate, three-hole-punch, and put its pages into a three-ring binder. Children can then "borrow" the pages during free time, pick any activity that particularly interests them, and earn extra credit.

LET'S CELEBRATE
Caroline Parry
Kids Can (both), 1987
B/w illustrations
[i] 256 pages

Ms. Parry arranged her review of Canadians' ethnic holidays and festivals by season and enlivened them with historical and contemporary anecdotes, folklore, art activities, poetry, and recipes. Most of the events are those celebrated in the United States and aren't noted in the books above. Those not on our calendars are worth discovering.

☞ Although Hanukkah and Christmas occur near each other annually, there is no historical or religious reason to connect them. Because their proximity often confuses children, link kids to the following books to help them understand the significance and customs of these very different holidays.

A PICTURE BOOK OF HANUKKAH
David A. Adler
Holiday House, 1982
Three-color illustrations by Linda Heller
[p] 32 pages

In short, simple sentences, the author retells the 2,000-year-old story of the destruction of the first temple in Jerusalem, the Maccabees' revolt against the oppressive Greeks, and the miracle of a minute quantity of oil burning for eight days. Stylized illustrations depict the violence of the conflict without the horror.

THE HANUKKAH BOOK
Marilyn Burns
Four Winds, 1981
B/w illustrations by Martha Weston
[i] 128 pages

Beginning with the history of the holiday, the author proceeds to describe and explain the candle-lighting ceremony and other traditions—providing songs, recipes, and directions for appropriate toys and gifts. Ms. Burns explores whether Jews observe Christmas traditions: she provides testimony from Jewish youngsters on the variety of ways their families treat the matter. Since this sensitive topic inevitably arises each December, her book is a valuable resource.

CHRISTMAS TIME
Gail Gibbons
Holiday House (both), 1982
Full-color illustrations by the author
[p] 32 pages

With brightly hued illustrations and clear, unadorned prose, the author/illustrator conveys the warmth and joy of a three-generation family celebrating the holiday. I especially like Grandma and Grandpa embracing under the mistletoe. This is one of Ms. Gibbons's fine holiday series for preschool/primary-graders, which includes *Valentine's Day* and *Thanksgiving Day* (both Holiday House).

☞ Open youngsters' eyes to *The Truth About Santa Claus* (Crowell). James Giblin traces the history of the jolly gentleman—an amalgam of fact and fancy that begins over 1,600 years ago with the real Saint Nicholas.

THE ALL-AROUND CHRISTMAS BOOK
Margery Cuyler
Holt (both), 1982
B/w illustrations by Corbet Jones
[i] 96 pages

The author delves into the origins of Christmas rituals and explains how celebratory customs vary around the world. She provides detailed instructions for children to make Christmas foods and decorations, and ends with suggestions for holiday games.

☞ "When I was born," Trina Schart Hyman once explained, "the faeries gave me two gifts...a need to translate life into pictures...and a vivid imagination." Youngsters can enjoy those faeries' gifts when you share Ms. Hyman's exquisite setting of Dylan Thomas's *A Child's Christmas in Wales* (Holiday House). To translate Mr. Thomas's "life" when young, Ms. Hyman visited his home, researched the toys and costumes of his childhood, and entered his world. That her imagination captured its vitality is evident in every one of her magically vivid scenes. Her drawings to his words are music to our eyes.

HOLIDAY TREATS
Esther Hautzig
Macmillan, 1983
B/w illustrations by Yaroslava
[i] 93 pages

Brief descriptions of the holidays precede easy-to-follow recipes that span sixteen festive occasions from January to December and include special cakes for Mother's and Father's Day, Hamantashen for Purim, and Sweet Easter Bread.

WITCHES, PUMPKINS, AND GRINNING GHOSTS:
THE STORY OF THE HALLOWEEN SYMBOLS
Edna Barth
Clarion (both), 1972
Orange-and-black illustrations by Ursula Arndt
[i] 96 pages

Ms. Barth discusses the history of witches and their mystique, ghosts, jack-o'-lanterns, foods, and other paraphernalia and practices associated with October 31. Her book is one in a series about holidays in which she reveals the origins of related symbols and customs.

MEET THE WITCHES
Georgess McHargue
Lippincott, 1984
B/w illustrations
[i] 128 pages

This fascinating, well-researched discussion of the multicultural evolution of witches (and witch hunters), from the primitive to the contemporary, includes a bit of Shakespeare and retellings of old witch tales—in the spirit of things.

ALL ABOUT GHOSTS
Christopher Maynard
Usborne, 1977
Full-color illustrations and photographs
[i] 32 pages

A colorful exposé of a variety of ghosts—haunting spirits, phantom ships, demon dogs, and the like—explaining how many have been shown to be the result of trickery or misunderstood natural phenomena. Among the illustrations are three ghosts' photographs (considered untampered by experts). Don't read this on a spooky night!

☞ Halloween is the time for singing of Slithery Slitches, droning about Dreary Dreezes, and sneezing like Sneezysnoozers—all of whom can be found in Jack Prelutsky's *The Baby Uggs Are Hatching* (Greenwillow). Only David Greenberg's *Slugs* (Little) are grosser. Your children will relish them all.

HALLOWEEN
Joyce K. Kessel
Carolrhoda, 1980
Orange-and-black illustrations by Nancy L. Carlson
[p] 48 pages

Such holiday customs as Jack-o'-lanterns, trick-or-treating, and bobbing for apples are explained in a simple, well-written book for beginning readers. It is one of the excellent "On My Own" holiday series, which includes *Martin Luther King Day* and *Squanto and the First Thanksgiving.*

☞ Link elementary-graders to Burton and Rita Marks's *The Spook Book* (Lothrop) if they need demonic disguises, monstrous makeup, or terror-iffic treats. They'll find simple directions for making costumes, decorations, and refreshments, and for eerily entertaining fellow spooksters with ghoulish games.

DRAW 50 MONSTERS, CREEPS, SUPERHEROES, DEMONS, DRAGONS, NERDS, DIRTS, GHOULS, GIANTS, VAMPIRES, AND ZOMBIES
Lee J. Ames
Doubleday (both), 1983
B/w illustrations by the author
[i] 64 pages

ED EMBERLEY'S BIG ORANGE DRAWING BOOK
Ed Emberley
Little (both), 1980
Orange-and-black illustrations by the author
[i] 96 pages

With step-by-step instructions from both artists, girls and boys will have a devilishly good time drawing Halloween-appropriate characters.

Horses

More than 250 different types of horses have lived on earth since the first horse appeared over 50 million years ago. Of those extant, only zebras, wild asses, and Mongolian wild horses (Przewalski horses) are true wild horses; their anatomy and behavior have not been changed by selective breeding and training.

A FIRST LOOK AT HORSES
Millicent E. Selsam and Joyce Hunt
Walker, 1981
B/w illustrations by Harriett Springer
[p] 32 pages

is one of the excellent "First Look at . . ." series for primary-graders that helps them observe the distinct characteristics that differentiate the members of a species, one from the other—here, horses.

A HORSE'S BODY
Joanna Cole
Morrow, 1981
B/w photographs by Jerome Wexler
[p, i, j] 48 pages

What tiptoes through life? A horse, of course, as youngsters will soon learn from this intriguing blend of information and sharply focused images.

BIRTH OF A FOAL
Hans-Heinrich Isenbart
Carolrhoda, 1986
Color photographs by Thomas David
[i, j] 48 pages

You are there—at the birth of a foal. Close-up photographs show its first few hesitant steps. The book also includes drawings that detail foal fetal development and birth and a glossary of terms.

HAROLD ROTH'S BIG BOOK OF HORSES
Margo Lundell
Grosset, 1987
Full-color photographs by Harold Roth
[p, i] 48 pages

This 8½ x 11″ introduction includes portraits of nine breeds, views of a day in the life of a ten-year-old girl and her pony, and single-page glimpses of horses and riders at the races, chasing hounds, in the circus, and on patrol.

☞ Keep *The Illustrated Marguerite Henry* handy for youngsters who've read *Justin Morgan Had a Horse, King of the Wind, Brighty of Grand Canyon,* or any other of Ms. Henry's marvelous horse stories. It introduces children to her illustrators and explains how she worked with them. And if anyone is about to or has read her *Misty of Chincoteague,* then you must show them the real Misty in *A Pictorial Life Story of Misty.* (All books Macmillan.)

QUARTER HORSES
Dorothy Hinshaw Patent
Holiday House, 1985
B/w photographs by William Muñoz
[i] 96 pages

This is a history of the world's most popular equines, the ones that working cowboys favor. They have a natural talent for controlling livestock, are strong enough to pull against roped, struggling calves, and can sprint from a standstill to stop straying cattle. (Dr. Patent has also written *Arabian Horses, Thoroughbred Horses, Draft Horses,* and *Horses of America.*)

MUSTANGS: WILD HORSES OF THE AMERICAN WEST
Jay Featherly
Carolrhoda, 1986
Full-color photographs by the author
[i, j] 48 pages

Dramatic close-ups and an insightful narrative relate the physical and behavioral characteristics that allowed descendants of the Spanish Conquistadors' horses to survive as wild horses in the American West.

☞ Savor with children the songs poets sing of horses. Share Lee Bennett Hopkins's anthology *My Mane Catches the Wind* (Harcourt), illustrated by Sam Savitt.

Mr. Savitt's drawings were inspired by the poets. Experiment: Cover the words and have youngsters create their own poems to Mr. Savitt's illustrations. Have them compare the similarities and differences between the mood of their poetry and that of their classmates. Uncover the words and make the same comparisons with the original. What they notice and discuss will provide a valuable lesson in the variety of interpretations possible among artists.

ONE HORSE, ONE HUNDRED MILES, ONE DAY: THE STORY OF THE TEVIS CUP ENDURANCE RIDE
Sam Savitt
Dodd, 1981
B/w illustrations by the author
[i, j] 96 pages

Every year hundreds of riders (they can be as young as twelve) test the stamina of their horses and themselves by entering the unparalleled Tevis Cup Endurance Race. Words and drawings describe the rugged course, once used by Wells Fargo Express Riders when they carried mail between nearby mining camps, and the precautions taken to ensure the safety of horse and rider.

BEHIND THE SCENES AT THE HORSE HOSPITAL
Fern Brown
Whitman, 1981
Color photographs by Roger Ruhlin
[i, j] 48 pages

The treatment of Ginger's cancer, Amara's ripped tendon, and Butterscotch's colic add touches of drama to information about large animal medical care. Ms. Brown answers questions about starting a veterinary career. Medical terms are carefully explained as they appear and are summarized in a comprehensive glossary.

TRY THESE ON FOR SIZE, MELODY!
Karen O'Connor
Dodd, 1983
B/w illustrations by Douglas K. Emry
[p, i] 48 pages

Bare-hoofed is fine for horses in the wild, but once they are domesticated, shoes are necessary. As readers watch the step-by-step process by which Melody is shod, they'll learn about the peculiarities of horses' hoofs and how a farrier shoes them.

India

India is a fascinating amalgam of places, people, and beliefs, rich and varied, although it is only one-third the size of the United States.

INDIA: AN ANCIENT LAND, A NEW NATION
Amita Vohra Sarin
Dillon, 1985
Full-color and b/w photographs
[i] 176 pages

This inviting book opens with a quick tour of the country and moves on to its people—about seven and a quarter million—and their beliefs. The author describes native food, festivals, family life, education, and art.

☞ Introduce primary-graders to India with two engaging stories-based-on-fact: *The First Rains* and *The Festival* (both Lerner). Peter Bonnici created the central character, Arjuna, from memories of his Bombay childhood. When I read these stories aloud, they remind children of their similar experiences.

WE LIVE IN INDIA
Veenu Sandal
Bookwright, 1984
Full-color photographs
[i] 64 pages

Twenty-eight people of all ages talk about their professions and beliefs. The two-page interviews provide a fascinating view of Indians from all levels of society, including the wealthy and poor, skilled and unskilled, working and retired, students and teachers.

☞ Introduce youngsters to two views of family life after they've met the individuals in Veenu Sandal's book (above). P. O. Jacobsen's and P. S. Kirstensen's *A Family in India* (Bookwright) is about the Kaushiks, whose lives are little different from those of their forebears, who tilled the same land. The weavers in

Tony Tigwell's *A Family in India* (Lerner) live near the Ganges River.

Remind children that these families are not typical of the country as a whole, but of only two segments. With the books as models, have your youngsters write a "Family in . . ." book, with their families as the subject.

I AM A HINDU
I AM A SIKH
I AM A MUSLIM
Manju Aggarwal
Watts, 1985
Full-color photographs
[i] each 32 pages

About 80 percent of India's population is Hindu, 2 percent is Sikh, and India is home to the second-largest Muslim community in the world. In each of these books (three of a series), a young person describes his/her heritage, places of worship, holy books, holidays, and traditional clothing. The author elaborates upon each child's comments and adds religious calendars, a glossary, and an index.

☞ Flavor your children's imaginations with Indian myths and legends. Slip a Ravi Shankar cassette into the player and read aloud excerpts from Madhur Jaffrey's *Seasons of Splendor* (Atheneum and Puffin). Make certain that you also share the introductions to these beautifully told tales. The author shares memories of her childhood and the circumstances in which she first heard them. Michael Foreman's illustrations are as delightful to the eyes as the stories are to the ears.

And since you can best capture the "flavor" of a country by sampling its food, sample recipes from Vijay Madavan's *Cooking the Indian Way* (Lerner). Teachers can use them to inspire youngsters to share samples of their traditional foods. If parents contribute easy-to-make recipes, youngsters can put together a round-the-world cookbook, prefacing the recipes with information about the country of origin.

THE MUSLIM WORLD
Richard Tames
Silver Burdett, 1982
THE HINDU WORLD
Patricia Bahree
Silver Burdett, 1982
Full-color photographs
[i] each 48 pages

Each of these volumes (two of a series) explores the origins and development of the religion, expounds upon its philosophy, and describes how it is integrated into everyday life.

☞ Share George Ancona's *Dancing Is* (Dutton). This photoessay on people of all ages and cultures expressing joy through dance contains a four-page, sixteen-picture sequence of a classic Indian dance captioned with the story the dancer is "telling." Use the book as an invitation to students or their parents to teach one of their traditional folk dances to the class. The class can practice it for presentation to the whole school. Some of the best assemblies are the ones children dance through.

Insects

More than a million species of insects (perhaps 200,000 insects for every person) constitute three-fourths of the world animal population. With more than a thousand different species in any backyard, children can embark upon intriguing entomological investigations. How many insects can your children find in their own backyards?

BUGS
Nancy Winslow Parker and Joan Richards Wright
Greenwillow, 1987
Full-color illustrations by Nancy Winslow Parker
[i, p] 40 pages

Merriam-Webster's *Ninth New Collegiate Dictionary* defines a bug as "an insect or other creeping or crawling invertebrate." Sixteen creepy-crawlies—including a flea, a louse, and a slug—infest the pages of this outstanding introduction to the creatures. A funny riddle and a large, clear illustration accompany each description. The authors conclude with a chart listing specific characteristics of the 16 profiled and information on the growth of bugs in general.

☞ *When It Comes to Bugs* (Harper), Aileen Fisher likes crawlers and creepers, flyers and leapers. And young children will like the eighteen poems in her delightful collection.

BACKYARD INSECTS
Millicent E. Selsam and Ronald Goor
Four Winds, 1983
Full-color photographs by Ronald Goor
[p] 40 pages

The authors explain how common garden insects are camouflaged by their color and shape. The photographs will help youngsters find and identify 20 of them.

WHERE DO THEY GO? INSECTS IN WINTER
Millicent E. Selsam
Four Winds, 1982
Full-color illustrations by Arabelle Wheatley
[i] 32 pages

Ms. Selsam explains why insect hunters may not find many subjects for study if it's cold outside. Detailed drawings illustrate the winter whereabouts of such creatures as flies, mosquitoes, crickets, and ants.

AN INSECT'S BODY
Joanna Cole
Morrow, 1984
B/w photographs by Jerome Wexler and Raymond A. Mendez
[i, j] 48 pages

The insect under inspection is a cricket. Close-up photographs and line drawings lay bare the inner workings and outer appearance in a manner that will fascinate all readers—aspiring entomologist or casual browser.

GIANTS OF SMALLER WORLDS:
DRAWN IN THEIR NATURAL SIZES
Joyce Audy dos Santos
Dodd, 1983
Full-color illustrations by the author
[i] 48 pages

When children place their hands by the vivid illustrations they'll get a "feel" for the Goliath beetle, mammoth cicada, and other arthropods. The life-size, life-colored illustrations are matched by an equally compelling discussion of the physical characteristics and habitats of these insects and the relationship between body construction and relative size.

LADYBUG
Barrie Watts
Silver Burdett, 1987
Full-color photographs and b/w illustrations
[p] 25 pages

LIFE OF THE LADYBUG
Heiderose Fischer-Nagel
Carolrhoda, 1986
Full-color photographs by Andreas Fischer-Nagel
[i] 48 pages

About 230 of the 4,000 species of ladybug extant live in the United States and Europe. Youngsters will enjoy learning more about the spotted beauties in these well-designed books. They are sterling representatives of two excellent nature series that feature close-up photographs and all-age appropriate texts. The Silver Burdett series is simply simpler and concludes with uncaptioned photos, so that very young readers can retell what they've learned in their own words.

DO ANIMALS DREAM? CHILDREN'S QUESTIONS ABOUT ANIMALS
MOST OFTEN ASKED OF THE NATURAL HISTORY MUSEUM
Joyce Pope
Two- and full-color illustrations by Richard Orr and Michael Woods

WHY DO THE SEASONS CHANGE?
QUESTIONS ON NATURE'S RHYTHMS AND CYCLES
ANSWERED BY THE NATURAL HISTORY MUSEUM
Dr. Phillip Whitfield and Joyce Pope
Viking Kestrel 1986; 1987
Two- and full-color illustrations
[i, j] each 96 pages

Why do bees make honey? How does a wasp sting? How long does a cicada take to grow up? Why do mosquitoes hum? These and other questions are among those most often asked at the Natural History Museum in London, where Joyce Pope works in the Zoology Department. The clearly written answers enhanced by first-rate illustrations will satisfy youngsters' initial inquiries about natural history and send them scurrying for more books and additional details.

Inventions and Inventors

Look in your garage, ask friends and neighbors, or visit small repair shops for nonfunctioning, nonrepairable, or otherwise unwanted small household appliances and mechanical gadgets—cameras, locks, tape recorders, and the like. Deposit them in a box labeled Homeware Hospital, along with screwdrivers, pliers, and a wrench or two and let resident "interns" operate to see what makes them "tick."

HOW THINGS WORK
Neil Ardley
Wanderer, 1984
Full-color photographs and illustrations
[i] 127 pages

Keep handy this colorfully illustrated book of almost 300 questions and answers about things mechanical (including those items noted above). They'll provide further insight into the workings of the appliances youngsters "dissect" and others that surround us.

THINGS AT HOME
Eliot Humberstone
Usborne (both), 1981
Full-color illustrations
[p] 32 pages

Illustrated, beneath-the-surface descriptions clearly reveal the structure of telephones, vacuum cleaners, refrigerators, and other things around the house.

☞ I've found *Things at Home* (above) and others in the Usborne "Finding Out . . ." series particular favorites with children learning English as a second language. It encourages dialogue between them and their English-as-a-first-language buddies. Other titles in the series include *Things That Go* and *Things Outdoors.*

SMALL INVENTIONS THAT MAKE A BIG DIFFERENCE
Donald J. Crump, ed.
National Geographic, 1984
Full-color photographs and illustrations
[i] 104 pages

Here are histories of the kitchen stove, ready-made clothes, traffic lights, and other everyday items we don't think twice about. This enticingly designed book also discusses young contemporary inventors and their ingenious contrivances.

☞ An assortment of little wheels, springs, tongue depressors, toothpicks, paper clips, thumbtacks, cotton swabs, and assorted similar paraphernalia make a perfect "inventor's kit." Keep one handy for a day your child just can't find anything to read or do. Once a year, I'd prepare identically filled brown bags to give my youngsters just before a long weekend or week-long seasonal break in the school year. To heighten the challenge, I required that everything in the kit had to be used.

SHOES FOR EVERYONE: A STORY ABOUT JAN MATZELIGER
Barbara Mitchell
Carolrhoda, 1986
B/w illustrations by Hetty Mitchell
[i] 64 pages

Individually sized shoes weren't available until the middle of the nineteenth century—and relatively few people could afford them, even then. In 1883, Jan Ernst Matzeliger patented the shoe-lasting machine that revolutionized the industry. This compelling story recounts the black inventor's dedication, perseverance, and eventual success, despite severe hardships.

STEVEN CANEY'S INVENTION BOOK
Steven Caney
Workman, 1985 (paperback only)
B/w photographs and illustrations
[i] 208 pages

In addition to giving fascinating facts behind thirty-five American inventions, such as Band-Aids, toothpaste, and straws, the author discusses

how to set up a workshop, get a patent, create a name for, package, and market an item.

GUESS AGAIN: MORE WEIRD AND WACKY INVENTIONS
Jim Murphy
Bradbury, 1986
B/w photographs and illustrations
[i, j] 96 pages

Youngsters (and you) will be challenged to identify the purpose of the inane inventions in this collection. Right answers are tantalizingly elusive even with illustrations and clues.

THE WORLD ALMANAC BOOK OF INVENTIONS
Valerie-Anne Giscard d'Estaing
World Almanac, 1985
B/w photographs
[i] 361 pages

This is an 8½ x 11″ compendium of the histories of more than 2,000 inventions (with index), divided into fourteen categories. This translation (yes, she is related to the former French president) begins with the wheel and ends with the world's largest telescope.

☞ The *World Almanac*... (above) contains a treasure trove for trivia buffs, the wherewithal for hours of fascinating browsing during Sustained Silent Reading time, interesting read-alouds during the few minutes before the bell rings, or inspiration for research projects.

Japan

COMMODORE PERRY IN THE LAND OF THE SHOGUN
Rhoda Blumberg
Lothrop, 1985
B/w illustrations
[i] 128 pages

Your youngsters might believe they have no interest in nineteenth-century Japan, but that will quickly change as they are drawn into the pages of Rhoda Blumberg's book. The United States wanted to trade with Japan, but as Perry was to learn, the Japanese would proceed cautiously, treating the "evil men" from the West with great suspicion.

In a remarkable piece of eminently readable yet scholarly research, Ms. Blumberg introduces the history, people, and customs of a Japan long isolated from the rest of the world. Her book is chock-full of facts presented in a clear narrative form, backed up by appendices, annotated source notes, bibliography, and a detailed index. The generous assortment of drawings lets readers see how the events were recorded from a Japanese viewpoint.

JAPAN FROM SHOGUN TO SONY, 1543–1984
John R. Roberson
Atheneum, 1985
B/w illustrations
[i] 208 pages

Mr. Roberson's book tells about Commodore Perry's visit, too. But it also relates the visit by Portuguese traders 200 years earlier, and covers Japanese history to the present. The author methodically describes how Japan evolved from many independent, samurai-defended territories to today's unified society—and one of the world's greatest economic entities.

WE LIVE IN JAPAN
Kazuhide Kawamata
Bookwright, 1984
Full-color photographs

A FAMILY IN JAPAN
Peter Jacobsen and Preben Kristensen
Bookwright, 1985
Full-color photographs
[i] 64 pages; 32 pages

Twentieth-century Japanese speak for themselves in these two enlightening photoessays. In the first, Mr. Kawamata asked twenty-six people from a cross section of the population—from schoolgirl to school-teacher, Buddhist priest to politician, and cook to Kabuki actor—to describe their backgrounds, occupations, and goals.

Mr. Jacobsen and Mr. Kristensen focus on Hisao Fujii and his family. They begin at the Mitsubishi factory in Okazaki, two hours by "bullet train" from Tokyo, where Mr. Fujii works. During the interview, Mr. Fujii discusses the responsibilities of each family member, the clearly defined roles of husband and wife, and the importance of raising children to be "self-sufficient, independent people."

☞ The study of Japan would be incomplete without time set aside for *Easy Origami* (Viking). Dokuihtei Nakano's clear and easy-to-follow instructions are for fun-to-make finger puppets, a jumping frog, a walking dog, and other figures for hang-from-the-ceiling mobiles or miniature stabiles.

COOKING THE JAPANESE WAY
Reiko Weston
Lerner, 1983
Full-color photographs
[i] 48 pages

For a real "taste" of Japan, let your children try restaurateur Reiko Weston's recipes. She explains that Japanese meals are planned around contrasts in flavor and cooking style. Ms. Weston describes the special ingredients in Japanese food and offers children simple recipes from which they can create a typical menu. She explains how to use chopsticks, how to set a Japanese table, and how to pronounce the Japanese terms.

Lasers

Lasers light up our lives. They scan bar codes at supermarket and library checkout counters, transmit telephone messages, and align tunnels, bridges, and high-rise buildings. They track and analyze dust clouds, set skies aglow at outdoor concerts, and create three-dimensional images on credit cards. And in the hands of doctors, they help heal.

LIGHT AND LASERS
Kathryn Whyman
Gloucester, 1986
Full-color photographs
[i] 32 pages

In this fine introduction to the subject, the author helps children understand how lasers work with simple, clearly illustrated, easily replicated experiments. They demonstrate, among other things, how light travels, bends, and splits. The photographs depict how these characteristics are reflected in nature and used in science.

LASERS
Charles De Vere
Gloucester, 1984
Full-color illustrations
[i] 40 pages

Clearly labeled diagrams and annotated illustrations nicely clarify a simplified explanation of lasers. The design, layout, and amount of text in this book provide a useful introduction for older, less scientifically inclined students as well as for intermediate-grade children.

LASERS: WHAT THEY CAN DO AND HOW THEY WORK
Lynn Myring and Maurice Kimmitt
Usborne (both), 1986
Full-color and b/w illustrations
[i, j] 48 pages

The excellent integration of captioned illustrations, labeled diagrams, animated and cut-away drawings, and small blocks of strategically placed text makes this one of the most effective introductions to what lasers are and how they work.

LASERS
William Burroughs
Warwick, 1982
Full-color photographs and illustrations
[j] 64 pages

The most comprehensive of the laser books I've listed, this provides a solid foundation in the principles and uses of Light Amplification by Stimulated Emission of Radiation. It is particularly appropriate for gifted science students and teachers who, like me, have little science background.

FIBER OPTICS: BRIGHT NEW WAYS TO COMMUNICATE
Charlene W. Billings
Dodd, 1986
Full-color photographs and illustrations
[i] 64 pages

Fiber optics is the transmission of laser light through flexible glass threads. The technology allows four and a half pounds of optical fiber to carry the same number of messages as 16,000 + pounds of copper wire, doctors to look inside the body without surgery, and the 2,700 pages of Webster's Unabridged Dictionary to flow between computers in six seconds.

Marine Life

SEA CREATURES DO AMAZING THINGS
Arthur Myers
Random House, 1981
Two-color illustrations by Jean Day Zallinger
[i] 72 pages

Among the sixteen denizens of the deep described her are octopi, "the joker(s)" that change color and shape to fool enemies; the horseshoe crab, a "crab that's not a crab" (it's more closely related to spiders and scorpions); and jellyfish, the "water balloons."

MYSTERIES & MARVELS OF OCEAN LIFE
Rick Morris
Usborne (both), 1983
Full-color illustrations
[i] 32 pages

Colorful illustrations, amusing cartoons, and succinct text offer young-sters eye- and mind-appealing views of the unusual behavior and habitats of marine life. Fifteen two-page "chapters" focus on particular characteristics, such as defense mechanisms and camouflage.

AMAZING CREATURES OF THE SEA
Howard F. Robinson, ed.
National Wildlife Federation, 1987
Full-color photographs
[i, j] 96 pages

Stunning photographs of fish, invertebrates, and sea mammals and reptiles fill this book for readers and browsers of all ages.

HOW TO HIDE AN OCTOPUS
Ruth Heller
Grosset, 1985
Full-color illustrations by the author
[p] 32 pages

Camouflage is a way of life for animals that "disappear" when predators approach. In light verse and lovely colors, the author/artist distinctly delineates eight sea creatures' ability to be there one moment and gone the next.

☞ If a trip to the beach is in the offing, link children to *A First Look at Seashells* (Walker). Millicent E. Selsam and Joyce Hunt help very young readers hone their powers of observation with an eye-opening introduction to the differences and similarities among and between univalves and bivalves.

WHERE THE WAVES BREAK:
LIFE AT THE EDGE OF THE SEA
Anita Malnig
Carolrhoda, 1985
Full-color photographs
[i] 48 pages

When won't you find comets in orbit around the sun, trivia as obscure facts, and cucumbers in your salad? When they are, respectively, a starfish whose body and arms are regenerated from one broken-off arm, a small Gulf of California snail, and a sea cucumber. They and other enchanting views of life at the edge of the sea appear in this next-best-thing to visiting tide pools in person.

WHAT'S FOR LUNCH? THE EATING HABITS OF SEASHORE CREATURES
Sam and Beryl Epstein
Macmillan, 1985
B/w illustrations by Walter Gaffney-Kessel
[i] 48 pages

The Epsteins focus on the eating habits of twenty "fliers, swimmers, water pumpers, crawlers and burrowers" at the beach—from seagulls to worms. It's nutritious fodder for student reports.

☞ Children planning dioramas of underwater life can become familiar with the marine flora and fauna details as they color Anthony D'Attilio's *Seashore Life Coloring Book* (Dover). The same illustrations, in color, are on the book's covers as a guide.

NIGHT DIVE
Ann McGovern
Macmillan, 1984
Full-color photographs by Martin and Jim Scheiner
[i] 64 pages

In the guise of a twelve-year-old making her first two night dives, the author describes the necessary scuba gear and procedures for the descent. Youngsters joining her lantern-lit underwater adventure will see many fish arrayed in their nighttime colors.

NIGHT OF GHOSTS AND HERMITS: NOCTURNAL LIFE ON THE SEASHORE
Mary Stolz
Harcourt, 1985
B/w illustrations by Susan Gallagher
[i] 48 pages

With supreme skill, Ms. Stolz weaves a spellbinding tale of nocturnal seashore life. She describes the interactions of animals in their quest for food and housing; she ingeniously relates human/animal cross currents; and she recognizes that special child who knows exactly who he is and what he will be (in this instance a nine-year-old marine biologist).

A DAY IN THE LIFE OF A MARINE BIOLOGIST
William Jaspersohn
Little, 1982
B/w photographs by the author
[i, j] 96 pages

Catfish can smell, taste, and sense water vibrations and electric fields that other fish produce. Why do they need so many sense organs? Young readers will discover how scientists find answers to that question and others when they follow Dr. Arthur Humes as he teaches, conducts a field trip to a salt marsh, and continues his own research—he's discovered some 400 new species of copepod (crustaceans) over the last thirty years.

Math and Counting

Make much ado about nothing!

The zero is one of the world's greatest inventions. Created about A.D. 600 by the Hindus, it derives from their symbol *sunya* ("empty") and makes numbers easy to represent and mathematical operations easier to perform. Our Hindu-Arabic numeral system is predicated upon its existence, yet it is absent from most books about counting. When "nothing" is missing, say *something* to your children.

THE MOST AMAZING HIDE-AND-SEEK COUNTING BOOK
Robert Crowther
Viking, 1981
Full-color illustrations and pop-ups by the author
[p] 14 pages

The author/artist's illustration of zero-equals-empty is graphic: slide a tab on the blank title page and uncover title, author, and copyright data—in the shape of a zero! Clever pop-up fare illustrates delightful things to count from one to one hundred.

THE FIRST BOOK OF NUMBERS
Angela Wilkes and Claudia Zeff
Usborne, 1982
Full-color illustrations by Stephen Cartwright
[p] 40 pages

More than a counting book, this humorously illustrated book introduces children to such mathematical concepts as sets, sequence, measurement, shapes, size, and a world without numbers. Throughout, young readers are challenged to solve problems and puzzles.

HOW MUCH IS A MILLION?
David M. Schwartz
Lothrop, 1985; Scholastic, 1986
Full-color illustrations by Steven Kellogg
[p, i] 40 pages

This brilliant book is filled with millions, billions, and trillions of things, all marvelously enlivened by exuberant illustrations. On the last few pages, the author explains the mathematical manipulations by which he arrived at his comparisons.

☞ Children love to recite big numbers, particularly when they're more than a million. Just how much is a million or more, though, is difficult to visualize. You could have kids collect something to find out firsthand—a million pop-top rings, perhaps. (That took one school two years!)

Let Mr. Schwartz's enthusiasm for numbers and their relativity inspire your youngsters. In "How Minute Is a Minute" or "How Small Is a Second," for instance, they can figure out the distance light, animals, and other objects can travel in sixty seconds or one-sixtieth of a minute.

ANNO'S MYSTERIOUS MULTIPLYING JAR
Mitsumasa and Masaichiro Anno
Philomel, 1983 (paperback only)
Full-color illustrations by Mitsumasa Anno
[p, i, j] 48 pages

Coauthors collaborate to explain factorials, the numerical relationships represented mathematically by an exclamation point: 4! for example, means $4 \times 3 \times 2 \times 1$. Here, they illustrate 10! with a story in which there are ten jars in each of nine boxes in each of eight cupboards and so on down the line to the one island upon which everything rests—for a total of 3,628,800 jars.

☞ *Anno's Mysterious Multiplying Jar* (see above) contains an afterword that explains how factorials are used to compute other permutations—the variations possible when a given number of desks are rearranged, for example. When your youngsters next ask for new seating arrangements in class or at the dinner table, share the contents of Anno's jar and together figure out how many times you could grant their request without repeating yourself.

ANNO'S HAT TRICKS
Mitsumasa Anno and Akihiro Nozaki
Philomel, 1985
Illustrations by Mitsumasa Anno
[i] 44 pages

To illustrate the challenge—and pleasure—of deductive reasoning or, mathematically speaking, binary logic, author and mathematician have collaborated on a guessing game in which Shadowchild (the reader) is given an "if" and must deduce the "then." The puzzles range from relatively simple problems of determining who is wearing either of two hats to the more complex ones involving five hats. Gather together a child and an assortment of hats, share the book, and enjoy the game.

THE I HATE MATHEMATICS! BOOK
Marilyn Burns
Little (both), 1975
B/w illustrations by Martha Hairston
[i, j] 128 pages

Share this if children are having trouble with multiplication tables or double-digit division, or simply can't "get" fractions—when they're beginning to think that if that's all there is to math, they hate it. The author's creative ideas—playing "step on the crack in the sidewalk," for example, or determining how many different triple-decker-cone combinations they could buy at the local ice-cream parlor—help them see that there is more to mathematics than arithmetic.

Children who *do* like math will enjoy the book, too.

☞ Your children may never say "I hate math!" if you remember the acronym *MATH* and ask Mitsumasa Anno To Help you show them the subject is more than just numbers. Alone or in collaboration, he has written and illustrated outstanding books that help learners of all ages visualize basic mathematical concepts. Anno's illustrations are so interestingly detailed they have a magical quality—it seems as though something new has been added each time you look. Some titles are *Anno's Counting Book*, *Anno's Counting House*, and *Anno's Math Games* (all Philomel).

NUMBER ART: THIRTEEN 1 2 3'S FROM AROUND THE WORLD
Leonard Everett Fisher
Four Winds, 1982
Blue-and-white illustrations by the author
[i, j] 64 pages

Thirteen notation systems from around the world, including Arabic, Greek, Mayan, Roman, and Tibetan, have been strikingly drawn by the artist/author. He's displayed each sign with its numerical value and accompanied each system with a full-page scratchboard illustration and brief background of its origins. Art and history form a pleasurable blend of the aesthetic and intellectual.

☞ In the book above, Mr. Fisher provides phonetic respellings of numerical signs, as does Jim Haskins in his series for elementary grade children: *Count Your Way Through China,* . . . *Russia,* . . .*Japan,* and . . . *the Arab World* (Carolrhoda). They don't agree, however, on the pronunciation of words in two languages they both discuss: Chinese and Arabic.

Which is right? Is the other wrong? Introduce children to someone who can speak the language of the notation system or any culture you may be discussing in any subject area. Let them hear the language as well as see it. They will better appreciate that, as in American English, respellings can reflect regional dialects and frequently there is no "right" or "wrong."

AHA! INSIGHT
AHA! GOTCHA
Martin Gardner
Freeman, 1978; 1982
[j, adult] 180 pages; 164 pages

A teacher introduced me to these. She'd bought them at a conference on gifted children and said she'd never seen anything capture the imagination of her son the way these had.

The first explains how to tackle problems in nontraditional ways and includes exercises to help readers avoid making false assumptions. The second introduces such paradoxes as

A: Sentence B is false.
B: Sentence A is true.

and demonstrates their value in the development of mathematical theory.

Both books were written with a light touch, contain generous lists of references, and, though not written specifically for children, will intrigue and delight young people who enjoy mental gymnastics.

Medieval Days

Slay the dragons of ennui! Establish "Knights of the ———— Table" orders, filling in the blank with different types of books: biography, history, or nature, for example (even fiction, she says with a slight smile). For each book finished during your "Bookland" festival, let children make a bulletin board display of miniature shields. On each shield, they can put the book's title, author, and illustrator and an illustration of the most fascinating fact they learned. Crown the King and Queen of Bookland during a schoolwide assembly to honor the youngsters who have read the most.

CRUSADERS, AZTECS AND SAMURAI
Anne Millard
Usborne (both), 1978

KNIGHTS AND CASTLES
Judy Hindley
Usborne (both), 1976
Full-color illustrations
[i, j] each 32 pages

The first book explores the Dark and Middle ages in Europe, the rise of Islam, and life in China and Japan. The second book focuses upon Europe about A.D. 1240, when the Crusades were beginning to affect life in towns and villages.

LIVING IN CASTLE TIMES
Robyn Gee
Usborne (both), 1982
Full-color illustrations
[i] 24 pages

One of a "First History" series of primarily annotated illustrations, this book shows how two children spend their time at home, in school, and at activities that prepare them for adulthood: nine-year-old Thomas as a wool trader working for his uncle, and twelve-year-old Alice as a lord's lady.

☞ Alice, in the book above, was engaged before she became a teenager. Link youngsters to Joe Lasker's beautifully illustrated *Merry Ever After* (Puffin) for more details on how marriages were arranged and celebrated during medieval days.

What other similarities and differences do your children note between their lives and those of the youngsters in the Middle Ages? Given the chance, would they change places and go back in time? What one contemporary invention do they think would most benefit people living in "castle times"?

KNIGHTS
Deirdre Headon
Schocken, 1982
B/w and full-color illustrations by Julek Heller
[j] 192 pages

In this excellent integration of romance and research, the tales of eleven legendary heroes (among them Arthur, El Cid, and Lohengrin) are nicely balanced by facts about knighthood, including the mystique and religious significance of the sword and the training of knights. Ms. Headon's truths demolish literature's chivalrous "white-knight-in-shining-armor" image as effectively as Russell Freedman's do movies' gun-toting image of *Cowboys of the Wild West.*

☞ With Lynn Edelman Schnurnberger's *Kings, Queens, Knights and Jesters* (Harper), making medieval costumes is as easy as drawing a circle or a *T.* Life-size, the costumes can be worn for original plays or the Awards Ceremony suggested above. Made in miniature, they can adorn puppets, dolls, or characters in a diorama.

QUEEN ELEANOR, INDEPENDENT SPIRIT OF THE MEDIEVAL WORLD: A BIOGRAPHY OF ELEANOR OF AQUITAINE
Polly Schoyer Brooks
Lippincott, 1983
[, j] 160 pages

This is an absorbing biography of the twelfth-century queen of France and England.

☞ Link youngsters to Doris Faber's *Margaret Thatcher* (Viking and Puffin) so that they can compare Eleanor with a contemporary strong-willed, independent leader.

A MEDIEVAL FEAST
Aliki
Crowell, 1983; Trophy, 1986
Full-color illustrations by the author
[, j] 32 pages

When a fourteenth-century monarch announced that he and his en-tourage would drop in for a visit, the lord and lady of the manor needed weeks to get ready for the royal house call.

☞ How do your children's families prepare for a big feast—a Thanksgiving meal, Passover Seder, Christmas dinner, or other special occasion? How would they get ready to host the president of the United States if he were to stop by for dinner?

CATHEDRAL: THE STORY OF ITS CONSTRUCTION
David Macaulay
Houghton (both), 1973
B/w illustrations by the author
[i, j] 80 pages

The author-artist describes how craftsmen cooperated for eighty-six years on the construction of a cathedral. The details, which dramatize its growth with striking perspectives, are accurate, though the building is imaginary.

☞ Mr. Macaulay constructed his fictional *Cathedral* around the framework of facts. Have children compare details in the build-ing of his Chutreaux with those in Percy Watson's factual photoessay *Building the Medieval Cathedrals* (Lerner).

THE STORY OF A CASTLE
John S. Goodall
McElderry/Macmillan, 1986
Full-color illustrations by the author
[p, i, j] 60 pages

This wordless picture book uses alternate full- and half-page illustra-tions to depict eight hundred years in the life of a castle, from birth as a Norman fortress to old age as a contemporary tourist highlight.

☞ Chances are a local printer will be very happy to give you odds and ends of card stock and selvages. With Huck Scarry's *Looking into the Middle Ages* (Harper) as a model, challenge youngsters to use the stock to construct their own medieval pop-up books. Set aside a place for the project so that they can work on it during free time over many weeks.

Mummies

What do King Tutankhamun, a baby mammoth, and John Paul Jones have in common? They all became mummies: professional embalmers preserved the king, nature preserved the mammoth (it froze and became encased in ice), and friends preserved the naval hero (they immersed his body in alcohol). Any well-preserved body is called a mummy, though most people think *Egypt* as soon as they hear the term. The tales mummies tell aren't only of ancient Egypt.

TALES MUMMIES TELL
Patricia Lauber
Crowell, 1985
B/w photographs
[i,j] 128 pages

The author skillfully reveals what scientists have discovered about ancient life from well-preserved animal and human remains found around the world. This book will hold readers spellbound. It did me.

MUMMIES MADE IN EGYPT
Aliki
Crowell, 1979; Trophy, 1985
Full-color illustrations by the author
[i] 32 pages

This is the best book for young readers I've seen on the ancient Egyptians' belief in life after death, and how they prepared the body and tomb. Many of Aliki's colorful illustrations were adapted from paintings and sculptures found in Egyptian tombs.

PHARAOHS AND PYRAMIDS
Tony Allan
Usborne (both), 1977
Full-color illustrations
[i] 32 pages

A typical wealthy landowner and his household are shown as they farm, feast, fight, and generally fare during the New Kingdom, Egypt's most prosperous and powerful period. Blocks of text, superimposed onto the illustrations, pull readers into the action-packed scenes.

☞ Link your children to a story ancient Egyptian children may have heard, *The Prince Who Knew His Fate* (Philomel), as recorded by an Egyptian scribe more than 3,000 years ago. Lise Manniche translated the scribe's writing, set it against a background of her own paintings based upon ancient artwork, and copied the original hieroglyphs as decoration along the bottom of each page.

IN SEARCH OF TUTANKHAMUN
Piero Ventura and Gian Paolo Ceserani
Silver Burdett (both), 1985
Full-color illustrations by Piero Ventura
[i] 48 pages

On November 26, 1922, British archaeologist Howard Carter discovered the treaure-filled antechamber of the boy-king's tomb after a five-year quest for the burial site. This book will whet young readers' appetites for more information about ancient Egypt.

☞ The book above is part of a series incipient archaeologists will adore. Two other titles are *In Search of Ancient Crete* and *In Search of Troy.*

HIEROGLYPHS: THE WRITING OF ANCIENT EGYPT
Norma Jean Katan
Atheneum, 1981
B/w photographs and illustrations
[i] 96 pages

Ms. Katan does a superb job of explaining the origins of the signs, the letters or sounds some of them represent, how they are read, and the status of the scribes who wrote them.

☞ Let youngsters copy the signs that correspond to the letters or sounds of their names, carve them in Styrofoam, and create a stamp they can then use to identify their papers.

ANCIENT EGYPT
Rosalie and Antony E. David
Warwick, 1985
Full-color illustrations and full-color and b/w photographs
[i] 40 pages

The authors' expertise makes ancient Egypt come alive. They demonstrate how historical "facts" are often only interpretations of the available evidence. Among the indisputable items they share is the origin of the word *mummy* (it has nothing whatever to do with bodies). Look for the flies!

GODS AND PHARAOHS FROM EGYPTIAN MYTHOLOGY
Geraldine Harris
Schocken, 1983
Full-color illustrations by David O'Connor
and b/w line drawings by John Sibbick
[i, j] 132 pages

Enticing double-page paintings will attract readers to these twenty-six myths and legends of ancient Egypt. The stories are interspersed with chapters that describe the land and culture of the people who created them. An oversize volume (8½ x 11"), it is one of a series that includes *Spirits, Heroes and Hunters from North American Indian Mythology* and *Dragons, Gods and Spirits from Chinese Mythology*.

Music

When I grew up, we sang every day in school. Follow-the-bouncing ball sing-alongs were shown every weekend at the movies. And no

Sunday drive was complete without family sing-togethers and occasional solos from my dad. (Not even Nelson Eddy could match his "Let Me Call You Sweetheart.") Singing was and remains an integral part of my life in school and at home. We sang around the piano as my son was growing up and, whether children or adults, my students and I always sing together.

Sing with your children: around the keyboard or campfire, in the car or school bus, during class or family sing-alongs, for special occasions or at take-a-break time. Anytime there's music in the air (or could be). Wherever.

EYE WINKER, TOM TINKER, CHIN CHOPPER
Tom Glazer
Doubleday, 1973 (paperback only)
B/w illustrations by Ron Himler
[p] 64 pages

Add this to Mr. Glazer's *Do Your Ears Hang Low?* and *Music for Ones and Twos* (both Doubleday), and you'll have an invaluable repository of musical merriment for preschoolers: the finger play, acting out, and silly songs all children should have in their repertoires.

☞ Link Marc Brown's fourteen *Hand Rhymes* (Dutton) for very young children to those you'll find in the books above. Mr. Brown's humorous illustrations (inset with black-and-white line drawings to illustrate the action motion by motion) are as delightful as the rhymes.

SHARON, LOIS AND BRAM'S MOTHER GOOSE SONGS,
FINGER RHYMES, TICKLING VERSES, GAMES AND MORE
Sharon, Lois, and Bram
Atlantic (both), 1986
Full-color illustrations by Mary A. Kovalski
[p, i] 92 pages

A jauntily illustrated selection of choice songs, finger rhymes, verses, games, and other marvelous rhythmic pleasantries, which include "Pop! Goes the Weasel," "Fine Plump Peas in a Pea Pod Pressed," and "Star

Light, Star Bright." It's just right for change-of-pace activities on the spur of the moment.

SINGING BEE! A COLLECTION OF
FAVORITE CHILDREN'S SONGS
Jane Hart
Lothrop, 1982
B/w and full-color illustrations by Anita Lobel
[p] 160 pages

"Hush Little Baby," "Polly Put the Kettle On," and "Here We Go Round the Mulberry Bush" are among the 125 songs in a collection of songs that are a significant part of our American musical heritage. The merry illustrations are as marvelous to see as the lullabies, nursery rhymes, and rounds are to sing.

GO IN AND OUT THE WINDOW:
AN ILLUSTRATED SONGBOOK FOR CHILDREN
Metropolitan Museum of Art
Holt, 1987
Full-color illustrations
[all ages] 144 pages

Each of the sixty-one songs in this collection, from finger-twisting "Eensy Weensy Spider" through the serene "We Gather Together" is paired with a beautiful reproduction of a painting or print from the Metropolitan Museum of Art in New York. Melodies and piano accompaniments are within the grasp of first-year piano students.

☞ Have you had a school songfest or sing-along lately? They're great fun and they help establish and maintain a warm camaraderie. And if you don't have a school song, suggest your youngsters create one by rewriting the lyrics to a lively tune. Many years ago, our sixth-graders changed the lyrics from "Hey, Look Me Over" to "Hey, We're from Whisman," and our get-togethers were never the same. There's nothing like a school song to end an assembly on a spirited note—or keep kids humming merrily as they step-in-time back to their classes!

WEE SING AND PLAY
Pamela Con Beall and Susan Hagen Nipp
Price, 1983 (paperback only), with cassette
B/w illustrations by Nancy Klein
[p] 64 pages

Keep these or any of the "Wee Sing" cassettes and booklets on the shelf or in your backpack or the car glove compartment, where they'll be ready for the next trip. They have songs and rhymes to brighten any day at home or away. The best part is that the taped music is pitched just right for children's voices.

☞ Keep a supply of spoons, pop-top chains, jar covers, and cans filled with rice, beans, or small pebbles for impromptu rhythm sections to accompany your favorite songs. If you turn to Tom Walther's *Make Mine Music* (Little), you'll find easy-to-follow directions for building other instruments, among them a thumb piano, tubular glockenspiel, and simple flute. And if your children would like to *be* the instruments, try his supercolossal musical band.

THE WHEELS ON THE BUS
Maryann Kovalski
Little, 1987
Full-color illustrations by the author
[p] 32 pages

Words and melody to this funny favorite complement a joyously illustrated picture book grandparents, parents, and young children will giggle over together. The humorous story portrays a brother and sister shopping with their grandmother. The trio becomes so engrossed in singing the silly song while they wait for the bus home, they miss it!

OLD MacDONALD HAD A FARM
Tracey Campbell Pearson
Dial (both), 1984
Full-color illustrations by the author
[p, i] 32 pages

This merry version of the old favorite depicts a blissfully bucolic couple carrying on sunup-to-sundown chores among and within a sporadically unpastoral flock.

☞ When you next sing about Old MacDonald, change his profession. Put him in a zoo with a "roar roar" here and a "screech screech" there, a bakery with a "sift sift" here and a "mix mix" there, or a track meet with a "sprint sprint" here and a "jump jump" there.

THE GREAT ROUNDS SONGBOOK
Esther L. Nelson
Sterling, 1985 (paperback only)
B/w illustrations by Joyce Behr
[p, i] 96 pages

Rounds are the easiest way to introduce children to the pleasures of singing in harmony. Among the more than one hundred here are the oldest extant, "Summer Is A-coming In," the tongue-twisting "My Dame Hath a Lame, Tame, Crane," rounds in French, German, Spanish, Latin, Hebrew, and Moroccan, and "There Once Was an Icthyosaurus," without which no dinosaur unit is complete.

WALK TOGETHER CHILDREN:
BLACK AMERICAN SPIRITUALS
Ashley Bryan, compiler
Aladdin, 1981
B/w illustrations by the compiler
[all ages] 64 pages

Out of the horrors of black slavery came the haunting beauty of the black American spiritual, the unique religious songs of an uprooted, transplanted people. These selections from the myriad musical creations of black Africans in America include "Swing Low, Sweet Chariot," "Let Us Break Bread Together," and "Jacob's Ladder." Mr. Bryan's vibrant woodcuts reflect the integrity, warmth, and emotional intensity of the people who produced this unparalleled form of expression.

Pandas

One of the first things children will notice as they read about giant pandas is how little we know about them. Some scientists, for example, believe they are related to bears, some believe them closer to raccoons, and yet others put them in a class by themselves. Much of what we do know, however, including how and what they eat and how far they roam in their native habitat, was discovered only within the past decade by Project Panda Watch (PPW). PPW is a joint undertaking between scientists from the Chinese government and the World Wildlife Fund.

PROJECT PANDA WATCH
Miriam Schlein
Atheneum, 1984
B/w illustrations by Robert Shetterly
[i] 96 pages

In addition to explaining the way in which the project scientists go about their research, the author discusses panda history, their introduction to the Western world, and how great are the problems in keeping the species extant. Perhaps only 1,000 remain.

THE GIANT PANDA
Jin Xuqi and Markus Kappeler
Putnam, 1986
Full-color photographs
[i, j] 48 pages

This account of the giant panda's life cycle, its habitat, and efforts to preserve the species reflects the most recent findings of Chinese zoologists. The photographs, also from China, include scenes of pandas at home in their bamboo forests and close-ups of a captive panda and her cub from its birth through its first year.

☞ John Bonnett Wexo's *Giant Pandas* (Wildlife) is as dramatically informative as his *Bears* (see review on page 105). Suggest children note the similarities and differences between the two animals by comparing details from both books.

You can also help youngsters appreciate the role of scientific consultants and other specialists if you point out and discuss the people acknowledged on the back cover of *Giant Pandas*. You'll find that some of the Project Panda Watch scientists (see above) advised Mr. Wexo.

PANDA
Susan Bonners
Delacorte, 1978
Full-color illustrations by the author
[p, i] 32 pages

The watercolor paintings provide an almost palpable portrait: the snow seems cold and crunchy, the panda's coat furry and warm. Against this vivid backdrop, the author/artist tells of a panda, her cub, the cub's growth to motherhood, and the mountain forest in which they live. Though addressed to young children, it is an exquisite book for all readers.

☞ Let youngsters create their own pandas in a variety of mediums: watercolor, poster paints, ripped construction paper, and masks (see *Paper Masks and Puppets*).

Plants

Ask children to make a list of carnivores and chances are they'll name only animals. There are, however, almost 450 species of meat-eating plants, many of which "dine" on insects. Open youngsters' eyes to the beauty and the variety of plants.

CARNIVOROUS PLANTS
Cynthia Overbeck
Lerner, 1982
Full-color photographs by Kiyoshi Shimizu
[i] 48 pages

These plants survive in nutrient-poor soil by attracting, trapping, and digesting small animals—sources of nitrogen and other essential elements ordinarily unavailable in such a habitat. Vivid photographs provide stunning views of the predators: Venus's-flytrap, butterwort, sundew, and pitcher plant, for example.

PITCHER PLANTS: THE ELEGANT INSECT TRAPS
Carol Lerner
Morrow, 1983
Full-color and b/w photographs by the author
[i] 64 pages

The author describes eight species that grow only in North America. Her exquisite drawings reveal how these plants have adapted to their environment.

SECRETS OF THE VENUS'S FLY TRAP
Jerome Wexler
Dodd, 1981
B/w photographs by the author
[i] 64 pages

"I ask questions and study most anything that catches my fancy," Mr. Wexler once told me. "I select a subject . . . then study it, using a camera as my notebook." Invite your children to peek into Mr. Wexler's "notebook." They'll share his excitement as he satisfies his curiosity, asking questions, experimenting, and finding answers about the food, structure, propagation, and care of this insectivorous plant.

☞ One of the most beautiful flowers you can add to a child's garden of books is Arnold and Anita Lobel's *The Rose in My Garden* (Greenwillow; Scholastic). In this-is-the-house-that-Jack-built fashion, Mr. Lobel's rhyme begins with a single flower and blossoms into a bustling bouquet. Ms. Lobel's glorious pictures capture the colorful display and the creatures cavorting within.

THE LORE AND LEGENDS OF FLOWERS
Robert L. Crowell
Crowell, 1982
Full-color illustrations by Anne Ophelia Dowden
[j] 88 pages

The rose in the Lobels' garden (above) seems to be a cabbage rose, one of the four species from which all garden roses (except special hybrids) are descended. If so, the Romans brought its ancestors to Europe before it arrived in America, and Pliny wrote in his nature encyclopedia that it had as many as a hundred petals—hence the Latin name, *Rosa centifolia*. Mr. Crowell's book will help children learn about the rose and nine other flowering plants that have had a more prominent role in history than anyone might have imagined.

THE REASON FOR A FLOWER
PLANTS THAT NEVER EVER BLOOM
Ruth Heller
Grosset, 1983; 1984
Full-color illustrations by the author
[p] each 48 pages

With brilliant full-page drawings, the author/artist describes flowers that produce the seeds that grow the plants that become our food, animal fodder, and the fabric from which we manufacture many things. And the plants that never flower, but are as beautiful. Youngsters will be attracted to the brilliantly colored, full-page drawings in both books.

SEEDS: POP, STICK, GLIDE
Patricia Lauber
Crown (both), 1981
B/w photographs by Jerome Wexler

HOW SEEDS TRAVEL
Cynthia Overbeck
Lerner, 1982
Full-color photographs by Shabo Hani
[i] 64 pages; 48 pages

If the seeds of flowering plants fell to the ground around the parent plant, there'd be no room for them to grow. How do they leave "home"? They stick to animal fur and people's clothing, travel in the wind and water, or scatter themselves. The authors write about the travel methods of more than twenty plants, one of which is the wild oat.

☞ When I visited the photographer Jerome Wexler (see above), he plucked a wild oat seed from a dried plant, dipped it in water, and set it in my hand. The seed is shaped like a wedge, with barbs and a long tail. Within a few minutes, the tail began twisting and turning. I have since fascinated my students with the same procedure. You can find wild oat among the dried plants in most florist shops: get some, wet it, and watch it move.

YOUR FIRST GARDEN BOOK
Marc Brown
Little, 1981 (paperback only)
Full-color illustrations by the author
[p] 48 pages

EAT THE FRUIT, PLANT THE SEED
Millicent E. Selsam
Morrow, 1980
Full-color and b/w photographs by Jerome Wexler
[i] 48 pages

Children will enjoy following Mr. Brown's directions for making a flying monster plant (birdseed in a sponge), planting potatoes in a bucket, or getting a start on Halloween by planting pumpkin seeds in the spring. (One year, my sixth-graders had a wonderful time carving the pumpkins they'd planted as fifth-graders.) Ms. Selsam shows how to grow such plants as avocado, citrus, and kiwi fruit.

CACTUS, THE ALL-AMERICAN-PLANT
Anita Holmes
Four Winds, 1982
B/w illustrations by Joyce Ann Powzyk
[j] 192 pages

CACTUS
Cynthia Overbeck
Lerner, 1982
Color photographs by Shabo Hani
[i, j] 48 pages

Ms. Holmes focuses on Sonoran cacti and the animals who cohabit their ecological niche. She includes cactus recipes and suggestions for raising the plant. Ms. Overbeck details the parts of a cactus and describes how it has adapted to an arid environment.

☞ Make the Three Bean Plus One Salad from Ms. Holmes's book and see if your children can guess that the "one" is cactus!

President's Day

Milton Meltzer and Russell Freedman, gifted authors whose meticulous research and skilled writing vivify the past, have each presented young readers with a fine biography of legendary presidents. Both books reveal the men as they were, not the symbols they have become. Both belong in the hands of young readers in time for President's Day.

GEORGE WASHINGTON AND THE BIRTH OF OUR NATION
Milton Meltzer
Watts, 1986
B/w photographs and illustrations
[i] 176 pages

In this unvarnished view, the author recounts the virtues we have come to expect in a Washington biography, but he points out weaknesses, too. Readers learn of Washington's intolerance, impulsiveness, and vulnerability, as well as his vision, energy, and leadership in peace and war.

IF YOU GREW UP WITH GEORGE WASHINGTON
Ruth Belov Gross
Scholastic, 1982 (paperback only)
Two-color illustrations by Jack Kent
[i] 64 pages

In colonial times, you might leave mail at the nearest tavern in the hope that someone would pick it up, pass it on, and eventually deliver it; you could use tobacco as a substitute for money; and everybody could have enough food, although wealthy people had more variety.

☞ Link the book above to *George Washington's Breakfast* (Coward). Interweaving fact and fiction, Jean Fritz tells the story of a young boy who wants to learn what our first president ate in the morning. With humor and insight, she imbues the search for facts with the excitement of a mystery.

IF YOU GREW UP WITH ABRAHAM LINCOLN
Ann McGovern
Scholastic, 1985 (paperback only)
Two-color illustrations by Brinton Turkle
[i] 64 pages

As a child on the frontier, you would go to school two or three months a year—if a teacher was nearby; you'd practice writing with a stick in the dirt, since paper was too expensive to use for practice; and because it was the law, you'd give your dad whatever money you earned until you turned 21 years old.

☞ Have children write an "If You Grew Up with ———" and fill in the blank with today's president. After they've written out the facts that parallel those in the books above—the food, games, symbols, et cetera—have them consider the differences. Would they rate themselves more or less fortunate today? Why?

LINCOLN: A PHOTO-BIOGRAPHY
Russell Freedman
Clarion, 1987
B/w photographs and prints
[i] 160 pages

A choice assortment of archival prints and photographs enhance this warm portrait. In the chapter entitled "This Dreadful War," for example, a series of photos from 1861–65 graphically illustrate how quickly the war-beleagured president aged. This Newbery Award winner, enriched by a superb design, provides pleasure as much aesthetic as intellectual.

☞ In *The Abraham Lincoln Joke Book* (Scholastic, paperback only), Beatrice Schenk de Regniers has collected more than sixty of the funny stories and jokes Abraham Lincoln enjoyed and inspired. Among them are amusing anecdotes recalled by his friends and acquaintances, jokes from his favorite joke book—Joe Miller's, apocryphal stories, and bits of humor he made up himself.

TRUE STORIES ABOUT ABRAHAM LINCOLN
Ruth Belov Gross
Scholastic, 1973 (paperback only)
B/w illustrations by Charles Turzak
[p] 48 pages

These one-to-a-page stories trace Lincoln's life. Anecdotal "chapters," for all their brevity, provide a "feel" for the fellow. The illustrations are striking woodcuts and the type is set in a muted red. It is a gem for young readers.

THE DEATH OF LINCOLN: A PICTURE HISTORY OF THE ASSASSINATION
Leroy Hayman
Scholastic, 1968 (paperback only)
B/w photographs and prints
[i] 128 pages

In this chronicle of the assassination and the events that surrounded it, the author sets the scene with General Lee's surrender to General Grant at Appomattox. He describes the president's last day, and what we know of the comings and goings of the assassin and his co-conspirators, their apprehension, trial, and execution. And he cites interesting parallels between Lincoln and John F. Kennedy in his conclusion.

☞ The inexpensive paperbacks (above) will enrich youngsters' personal libraries. Order multiple copies as rewards for work well done or any other behavior worth calling attention to.

Robots

Ask youngsters how many robots (that aren't toys) they have at home. They'll probably say none, until they understand that machines automatically performing some of the actions of people—electric dishwashers, washing machines, and clock radios, for example—are considered robots.

GET READY FOR ROBOTS
Patricia Lauber
Crowell, 1987
Full-color illustrations by True Kelley
[p] 32 pages

Young readers will read about the many kinds of robots that exist today, those that are yet to be developed, and the tedious or dangerous tasks they are designed to take over.

ROBOTICS
Tony Potter and Ivor Guild
Usborne (both), 1983
Full-color and b/w illustrations
[i] 48 pages

Addressing what robots can do and how they work, the authors' eighteen double-page, self-contained "chapters" are superbly detailed with vivid drawings and diagrams. Notwithstanding some anglicisms and the British components listed in directions for building a microrobot, this will fascinate readers.

☞ Let boys and girls design three-dimensional robots out of paper sacks and cardboard boxes or draw pictures of ones that will do the tasks children least like to do. Link more mechanically

inclined youngsters to Steven Lindblom's *How to Build a Robot* (Crowell) for a look at what it takes to create a computer-controlled robot.

ROBOTS
Hilary Henson
Warwick, 1982
Full-color and b/w illustrations
[i, j] 80 pages

Sustaining interest throughout this lavishly illustrated book, the author recounts the history of mechanical marvels in fact and fiction. She explains contemporary and future robotics and describes a robot's brain—the computer.

WORKING ROBOTS
Fred D'Ignazio
Lodestar, 1982
[j] 160 pages

The older student who wishes more detail will find information on working robots, here defined as those having "senses" and under computer control. Mr. D'Ignazio's comprehensive discussion and suggested class projects include robot languages and the impact of robots on society.

Rocks

UNDERSTANDING AND COLLECTING ROCKS AND FOSSILS
Martyn Bramwell
Usborne, 1983
Full-color illustrations
[i] 32 pages

A superb guide for incipient rock hounds. Drawings and text help children learn how to find, identify, and collect common rocks, minerals, and fossils. The author includes suggestions for growing crystals, modeling earth folds, and examining stone-faced buildings for minerals and fossils.

☞ One of the most impressive rock events of the last decade took place May 18, 1980, when Mount Saint Helens erupted. The blast created a "stone wind" of steam and rocks that traveled at speeds up to 200 miles an hour, leveling 150 square miles of country-side—a real rocky horror show! Patricia Lauber's *Volcano: The Eruption and Healing of Mount Saint Helens* (Bradbury) vividly describes the destruction of the mountain and its "healing"—the marvelous return of life to the burned earth.

ALBUM OF ROCKS AND MINERALS
Tom McGowen
Rand, 1981; Checkerboard, 1987
Full-color and b/w illustrations by Rod Ruth
[i] 64 pages

The narrative, as entertaining as any fictional tale, recounts how twenty-two different rocks and minerals were formed and how people put them to use. For instance, halite left behind when ancient seas evap-orated is used to season our food and is more commonly called salt; cinnabar, when heated, releases the "liquid" you'll find in thermom-eters and silent light switches—it's called mercury.

ROCKS AND MINERALS
George S. Fichter
Random House, 1982
Full-color illustrations by Patricia Wynne
[i] 96 pages

This pocket- or backpack-size Audubon Society Beginner Guide (3 x 4″) contains succinct descriptions of over seventy-five rocks and min-erals and an index for easy reference. In addition to providing the realistic illustrations, the artist has color-coded the page corners to facilitate identification of specimens.

HOW TO DIG A HOLE TO THE OTHER SIDE OF THE WORLD
Faith McNulty
Harper, 1979
Full-color illustrations by Marc Simont
[p] 32 pages

Is the earth solid rock beneath the topsoil? What would you find if you started digging and didn't stop? The question isn't trivial: Enrico Fermi used to ask physicists similar questions during doctoral exams. This entertaining blend of fact and fancy enlightens young readers about the earth's composition, from topsoil to a white-hot, solid iron core about 4,000 miles down.

☞ Your youngsters will enjoy being part of the magical Ms. Frizzle's class when they take a trip in *The Magic School Bus, Inside the Earth* (Scholastic). Joanna Cole's wonderful sense of humor and enthusiasm wrap basic scientific facts with humor in an exciting, imaginative, eye-opening way.

ROCK CLIMBING IS FOR ME
Tom Hyden and Tim Anderson
Lerner, 1984
B/w photographs
[i] 48 pages

Rocks are as fascinating to scale as to study. Shelly Hyden explains— with the help of photographs on every page—how she learned the sport, mastering its terms, its special equipment, and, most important, its safety procedures to the point where she could comfortably climb a 60-foot cliff.

MOUNTAIN CLIMBING
Jim Hargrove and S. M. Johnson
Lerner, 1983
Full-color photographs
[i] 48 pages

The authors detail the special techniques, equipment, and problems that face mountaineers, concluding with exciting stories of the conquest of the Matterhorn, Annapurna, and Mount Everest.

Science Experiments

GEE WIZ! HOW TO MIX ART AND SCIENCE OR
THE ART OF THINKING SCIENTIFICALLY
Linda Allison and David Katz
Little (both), 1983
B/w illustrations by Linda Allison
[i] 128 pages

Youngsters will learn "how to mix art and science" when they experiment with liquid chromatography to create colorful bookmarks or wall hangings, or when they probe the properties of immiscible liquids to design marbled endpapers or book covers. The underlying scientific principles for each project are clearly explained and the authors inspire creative thinking by asking questions along the way.

☞ If you need a soundly based, well-designed series of experiments to develop positive attitudes toward science and the scientific method, get Herb Strongin's *Science on a Shoestring* (Addison). It's an easy-to-follow, inexpensive-to-implement, student-centered, hands-on program. It contains step-by-step instructions, with explanations, for more than fifty investigations coded for K–7th grade, requirements for readily available and low-cost materials, and suggestions for encouraging additional experimentation at home.

MESSING AROUND WITH BAKING CHEMISTRY
Bernie Zubrowski
Little (both), 1981
B/w illustrations
[i] 64 pages

While they're in the kitchen (or a baking center you've set up in your classroom), give your children this book. They'll learn about the rise and fall of bread and cake batter as these experiments with baking soda, baking powder, and yeast reveal each ingredient's peculiar properties.

KITCHEN CHEMISTRY: SCIENCE EXPERIMENTS TO DO AT HOME
Robert Gardner
Messner, 1982
B/w illustrations
[i] 128 pages

Mr. Gardner groups his practical experiments according to where they can be performed—at the sink, refrigerator, stove, counter, and all around the kitchen.

☞ Assign some of the above experiments as homework and let the whole family become intrigued by the investigations of its resident junior scientist.

AMAZING AIR
Henry Smith
Lothrop (both), 1983
Full-color illustrations

LIQUID MAGIC
Philip Watson
Lothrop, 1983 (paperback only)
Full-color illustrations
[i] each 48 pages

Two of a series of four that will tempt children to experiment. They contain a list of supplies; a review of laboratory procedure *with appropriate warnings;* simple, easy-to-follow instructions; and an explanation of the experiment's outcome. *Light Fantastic* and *Super Motion* complete the quartet.

SO YOU WANT TO DO A SCIENCE PROJECT!
Joel Beller
Arco, 1982
B/w photographs
[i] 160 pages

The author, a science educator and former science fair judge, will inspire youngsters with his excellent advice on picking a topic, meeting teacher requirements (for classroom project), judge reactions (for science fair entry), and display requirements. He provides examples of successful projects and explains how to do effective library research, and when and how to seek help.

INTRODUCTION TO CHEMISTRY
Jane Chisholm and Mary Johnson
Usborne (both), 1984
Full-color illustrations
[i] 48 pages

This is an excellent place to begin understanding the basic ideas of chemistry. The text, which ranges from atoms and molecules through chemical reactions to organic compounds, is set within and around colorful illustrations, charts, and diagrams that imaginatively amplify and clarify each concept.

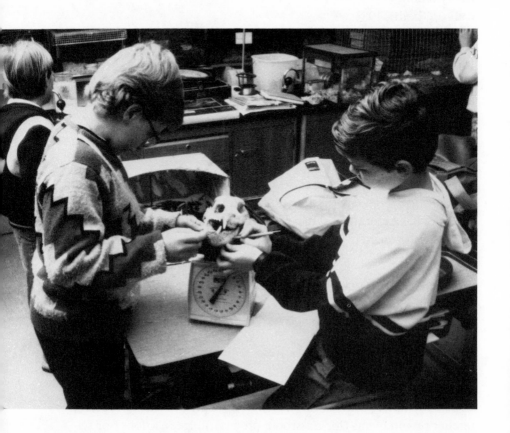

CHEMISTRY EXPERIMENTS
Mary Johnson
Usborne (both), 1981
Full-color illustrations
[i] 64 pages

A teacher in one of my summer classes borrowed this, and her fifth-grade son picked it up, exclaimed "I can do these!' and became so engrossed in the experiments he didn't want to let her return it! He'd discovered that Mary Johnson's safe and simple projects to do at home are just that.

CHEMICALLY ACTIVE! EXPERIMENTS YOU CAN DO AT HOME
Vicki Cobb
Lippincott, 1985
B/w illustrations by Theo Cobb
[i] 160 pages

Ms. Cobb has refined the art of writing science books for children. Her experiments work; they're practical and instructive (with all necessary warnings noticeably noted); her writing is upbeat and understandable; she stimulates as much curiosity as she satisfies; and she conveys an excitement and contagious enthusiasm about science (in this instance, chemistry) experiments kids can do at home.

THE CHEMIST WHO LOST HIS HEAD:
THE STORY OF ANTOINE LAVOISIER
Vivian Grey
Coward, 1982
B/w illustrations
[i] 128 pages

In the middle of the eighteenth century, chemistry was a disorganized mixture of truth and superstition. Antoine Lavoisier revolutionized the infant science when, among other accomplishments, he demonstrated the importance of conducting and describing experiments with accurate measurements, founded the metric system, and discovered the role of oxygen (which he named) in combustion. Unfortunately, his business interests incurred the wrath of French Revolutionaries and he was guillotined.

THE SECRET LIFE OF SCHOOL SUPPLIES
Vicki Cobb
Lippincott, 1981
B/w illustrations by Bill Morrison
[i] 96 pages

What do your children imagine school would be like if there were no paper and pencil, pen and ink, erasers, or glue? How do they think those items came to be? It's easy to assume they've always existed, but, as Vicki Cobb reveals, they haven't and their "stories" are very interesting. Ms. Cobb describes how these everyday materials are made and she provides formulas so that young scientists can make their own school supplies. Ms. Cobb's other exposés are *The Secret Life of Hardware* and *The Secret Life of Cosmetics* (both Lippincott).

☞ When the eye and visual perception, math and geometric figures, or art and perspective are on your agenda, combine the three and focus on optical illusions. Youngsters will enjoy drawing stationary lines that wiggle, converging lines that are parallel, and ovals that aren't as they discover why they can't—and oftentimes mustn't—believe everything they see.

THE OPTICAL ILLUSION BOOK
Seymour Simon
Morrow (both), 1984
B/w illustrations by Constance Ftera
[i] 80 pages

Mr. Simon clarifies the physiology of sight and tells how experience, contrast, and color affect our perception with illustrations, including those of Escher and Vasarély.

☞ Youngsters can make their own optical illusions by following the simple instructions, which conclude Arlene and Joseph Baum's imaginative *Opt: An Illusionary Tale* (Viking Kestrel).

EYE FOOLED YOU
Roy Doty
Collier, 1983 (paperback only)
B/w illustrations by the author
[i] 48 pages

More than one hundred optical illusions are included, as well as directions for experimenting with afterimages and making a zoetrope.

🕮☞ Cut apart Mr. Doty's inexpensive book and use it in a learning center or as a bulletin board display. The lively illustrations and directions for activities will inspire boys and girls to experiment on their own.

ROUND TRIP
Ann Jonas
Greenwillow, 1983
B/w illustrations by the author
[p, i] 32 pages

Read forward or backward, right-side-up or upside-down—the images ingeniously demonstrate that what you see depends upon how you look at it.

Sharks and Whales

Sharks rival dinosaurs on kids' Awesome Animals lists. And whales, the giants of the sea, run close. Wrap a great white or humpback around your school wall. Instead of the temporary murals that adorn the classroom or hallway bulletin boards during an investigation of these fascinating sea creatures, let children permanently preserve sharks and whales by painting them on the outside walls, where the community-at-large can enjoy them for many years.

SHARKS
WHALES
John Bonnett Wexo
Wildlife, 1983
Full-color photographs and illustrations
[p, i, j] each 20 pages

These dramatic blends of text and illustrations highlight each creature's characteristics. The author explains why sharks are different from other fish and supreme sea predators and he dispels myths about their danger to people. *Whales* contains fascinating views of the animal's musculature and skeletal structure and a splendid four-page centerfold showing twenty-seven of the sea mammals and a scuba diver—drawn to scale.

SEA WORLD BOOK OF SHARKS
SEA WORLD BOOK OF WHALES
Eve Bunting
Harcourt (both), 1979; 1980
Full-color photographs
[i, j] 80 pages; 96 pages

Ms. Bunting, a noted author of fiction, writes with the dramatic flair of a gifted storyteller. Readers attracted by the abundant photographs in both books will soon find themselves hooked on her anecdote-laden, fact-filled chapters. Her book on whales contains the story of Gigi, the only gray whale captured, studied, and returned to the sea by scientists.

☞ Some people say whales sing songs. Tony Johnston maintains they are counting. Let your little ones visit beneath the waves and count along with the majestic humpback whales Ed Young painted for Mr. Johnston's lyrical counting book, *Whale Song* (Putnam). Borrow a recording of whale songs from the library to provide background music to count by.

SHARKS: THE SUPER FISH
WHALES: THE NOMADS OF THE SEA
Helen Roney Sattler
Lothrop, 1986; 1987
B/w illustrations by Jean Day Zallinger
[i, j] 96 pages; 128 pages

Chances are, children will find information about any whale or shark species under discussion in these books. Their illustrated glossaries are cross-referenced and include each animal's scientific name, diet, and habitat. Excellent read-aloud chapters, liberally laced by drawings, present what scientists have discovered and surmise about the creatures.

☞ Link kids to Ann McGovern's *Shark Lady* (Four Winds) for an introduction to Dr. Eugenie Clark and her early research in shark-infested waters.

SEVENGILL: THE SHARK AND ME
Don C. Reed
Knopf, 1986; Scholastic, 1987
B/w illustrations by Pamela F. Johnson
[i] 144 pages

For many years, the diver/author scrubbed the tanks that housed the sharks at Marine World/Africa USA, near San Francisco. He recounts those experiences and the profound effect of one female sevengill upon his life. The opening chapter describes a sevengill's birth. It's an eye-opener! Read it aloud.

HUNGRY, HUNGRY SHARKS: A STEP TWO BOOK
Joanna Cole
Random House, 1986 (paperback only)
Full-color illustrations by Patricia Wynne
[p] 48 pages

This especially-for-beginning-readers nonfiction book is exactly what such a book should be: intelligently written for intelligent readers, information-packed, and well illustrated. Irresistible.

☞ Mention *shark* and many people will think *Jaws* and the teeth they hold. For good reason: razor-sharp shark teeth never stop growing! A tiger shark, for example, may form, use, and lose 12,000 teeth in five years. Youngsters will sink their teeth into a "Dentures with a Difference" project when you link them to Patricia Lauber's *What Big Teeth You Have!* (Crowell). Your "dental technicians" can extract information from it, shark books, and other references to create a bulletin board, mobile, card game, or board game illustrated with teeth of many shapes, their purpose (chewing, biting, gnawing, etc.), and the animals that grow them.

WHALE WATCHER'S HANDBOOK
Erich Hoyt
Doubleday, 1984
B/w photographs and drawings
[i, j] 208 pages

This book succinctly identifies seventy-seven species (one-to-a-page) by distinguishing features. The data are accompanied by photographs which show the whale as whale watchers see it (feeding, spouting, breaching) and/or diagrams which clearly define unique tail, fin, and head shapes.

☞ On October 10, 1987, a forty-five-foot-long, forty-ton humpback whale entered San Francisco Bay. Read aloud Wendy Tokuda's and Richard Hall's brightly illustrated account of *Humphrey, the Lost Whale* (Heian) and his twenty-six-day, 128-mile round trip up the Sacramento River.

A POD OF GRAY WHALES
François Gohier
Blake, 1988 (paperback only)
Full-color photographs
[i, j] 40 pages

Striking, often full-page photographs of the whale believed to be the oldest of all living whale species illustrate each page in this exciting 8 x 11" paperback. Scenes include close-ups of the unique species of barnacle and lice that live on the gray's skin.

☞ Have youngsters hold hands until they form a line as long as the longest whale or shark. Let them mark out and draw its life-size image on the playground hardtop. Link them to David Peters's *Giants of Land, Sea and Air* (Knopf), where they'll find dramatic paintings of the largest sharks and whales drawn to a scale of 1 inch = 22½ inches. The largest of all are set on gatefold pages to further dramatize their gigantic proportions. Each spread includes a jogging or snorkeling man and woman for relative size. Be forewarned! This impressive book is hard to put down.

Snakes

SNAKES
John Bonnett Wexo
Wildlife, 1981 (paperback only)
Full-color illustrations and photographs
[p, i] 20 pages

The emerald-green snake staring out from the cover is hypnotic: once they see it, youngsters will have to look inside. And when they do, they'll discover beneath-the-skin views of snakes, and different species' means of locomotion, diets, and behavior patterns. The author also details the different ways that large-fanged, rear-fanged, and front-fanged snakes inject their poisonous venom and lists ways of avoiding bites.

A SNAKE'S BODY
Joanna Cole
Morrow, 1981
B/w and color photographs by Jerome Wexler
[i] 48 pages

This is a splendid collaboration in which clear close-ups vividly enhance a description of snakes' anatomy. A word of caution is due, however.

Some youngsters (and adults) may be upset by the rather long sequence of a python killing and eating a chick.

☞ Link your youngsters to Lisa Grillone's and Joseph Gennaro's *Small Worlds Close Up* (Crown) for marvelous micrographs—pictures taken with a scanning electron microscope—which clearly show the similarities and differences in the scales and the hills and valleys on the smooth skin of a timber rattlesnake—magnified 9,000 times. They'll also find a striking picture of the snake's fang, 40 times larger than life.

POISONOUS SNAKES
Seymour Simon
Four Winds, 1981
B/w illustrations by William R. Downey
[i] 74 pages

Mr. Simon has nicely balanced his informative book between describing the threat of poisonous snakes in some parts of the world (15–20,000 people in India are killed by them each year) and the extremely small risk they represent to Americans (more people are killed by lightning than snakes in the United States). His book will not frighten children as they learn about the habits and habitats of cobras, sea snakes, true vipers, and pit vipers.

Space and Astronomy

Every astronomy book in this section is out of date. Every astronomy book in any bibliography is out of date. Thanks to information-gathering devices such as Voyager 2, knowledge of our universe is expanding astronomically. Publishers are hard pressed to keep up with it. That does not mean, however, that the books I've recommended are obsolete.

On the contrary. Astronomy, space exploration, and every other subject dramatically affected by ongoing research help you impress upon youngsters the importance of noting copyright dates, consulting a multitude of reference sources (at least three!), and, most important, appreciating that what we "know" today may change tomorrow.

THE SKY IS FULL OF STARS
Franklyn M. Branley
Crowell, 1981
Full-color illustrations by Felicia Bond
[p] 40 pages

Young readers will discover where and when to look for the brightest stars and constellations. They'll also find easy-to-follow directions for a tin can constellation projector.

LOOK TO THE NIGHT SKY
Seymour Simon
Viking, 1977; Puffin, 1979
B/w illustrations and star charts
[i] 96 pages

The Big Dipper is the reference point in this stargazing guide to constellations throughout the four seasons. Star charts and specific advice for buying and using a telescope are included.

☞ At bedtime, share Karla Kuskin's *A Space Story* (Harper) with a little one you know. It's a trip through our solar system via the gentle story of an inquisitive little boy who wonders if anyone lives on the stars.

THE CONSTELLATIONS
Roy A. Gallant
Four Winds, 1979
B/w illustrations
[i, j] 224 pages

The heroes of ancient myths and legends people our skies as constellations. Mr. Gallant describes forty-four of them, discusses their mythic origins, and explains how to locate them.

☞ Read aloud Native American star myths retold by Jean Guard Montore and Ray A. Williamson in *They Dance in the Sky* (Houghton) and animal star tales and myths as retold by Alison Lurie in *The Heavenly Zoo* (Farrar).

THE MOON
Seymour Simon
Four Winds, 1984
B/w photographs
[p, i] 32 pages

A simply written, descriptive text introduces the moon with close-up shots of it and of Apollo astronauts exploring its surface. The superb photos will attract readers of all ages.

FLYING TO THE MOON AND OTHER STRANGE PLACES
Michael Collins
Farrar, 1976
[i, j] 192 pages

On February 20, 1969, Michael Collins was command pilot on the spacecraft *Columbia* as it circled the moon. This first-person account of his early flying experience, his training to become an astronaut, and his subsequent Gemini 10 and 11 flights is an absorbing view of a noteworthy American. His unique skills also include fine writing.

☞ Have youngsters find out where their parents were during the 1969 moon landing. Send some students to the library to photocopy 1969 headlines, ads for clothing, cars, records, TV programs, and other signs of the 1969 times to set the historic event in perspective.

FIRST TRAVEL GUIDE TO THE MOON: WHAT TO PACK, HOW TO GO, AND WHAT TO SEE WHEN YOU GET THERE
Rhoda Blumberg
Four Winds, 1980
B/w illustrations by Roy Doty
[i] 96 pages

The subtitle says it all!

THE PLANETS IN OUR SOLAR SYSTEM
Franklyn M. Branley
Crowell, 1981
B/w photographs and full-color illustrations by Don Madden
[p] 32 pages

This simple yet substantive introduction includes instructions for two models: one to show planets' relative sizes, and the other, their relative distances from the sun.

☞ If one wall is too small to show the planets in relation to the sun, try going up one wall, across the ceiling, and down the other wall.

IS THERE LIFE IN OUTER SPACE?
Franklyn M. Branley
Crowell, 1984; Trophy, 1986
Full-color illustrations by Don Madden and b/w photographs
[p] 32 pages

Witty drawings illustrate this explanation of ideas and misconceptions about life on other planets. The author also conjectures upon what life might be like elsewhere in the galaxy, though there is no scientific evidence that any exists.

> ☞ Use *Is There Life* . . . to familiarize children with other planets' environments. Have them describe, in words and pictures, the physical attributes of life forms that could live there without special equipment. How would those other-planet beings have to prepare for a vacation on earth? What special equipment would their space suits need, where would they live, and what would concern them the most?

JUPITER
Seymour Simon
Morrow, 1985
Full-color photographs
[p, i, j] 32 pages

One of an outstanding series of oversize books (10 x 10″) aimed at introducing primary-graders to celestial bodies. The clear writing and computer-generated photographs and drawings, however, make them superb resources for readers of any age. Other titles include *The Sun, The Stars, Mars,* and *Uranus.*

VOYAGE OF THE RUSLAN: THE FIRST MANNED EXPLORATION OF MARS
Joshua Stoff
Atheneum, 1986
B/w illustrations by the author
[j] 96 pages

This nicely integrated tale of fact and not-improbable fancy is an "account" of the first manned exploration of Mars by Russian cosmonauts in the mid-1990s. It is based upon data available from American and Soviet space research and development.

☞ Ask boys and girls to design a flag for Mars and a postage stamp for the first letter mailed from there. Have them adapt earth habitats and vehicles to the environmental peculiarities of the planet.

TO SPACE AND BACK
Sally Ride and Susan Okie
Lothrop, 1986
Full-color photographs
[i, j] 96 pages

A veteran of two trips into space presents an astronaut's-eye view of events in and around the space shuttle from launch to landing. Her warm first-person narrative will captivate readers of all ages as they view earth from orbit and learn about life in zero gravity.

☞ What would life be like in the zero gravity of space? After youngsters have read how astronauts cope, have them redesign activities to accommodate weightlessness. How would they eat, play baseball, or get back and forth to school?

NOVA SPACE EXPLORER'S GUIDE:
WHERE TO GO AND WHAT TO SEE
Richard Maurer
Clarkson N. Potter, 1985
Full-color and b/w photographs
[i, j]

Expand youngsters' horizons with this superlative guide to where to go and what to see when outward bound. The author's conversational descriptions of the moon, the planets, and their natural satellites will fire the imagination of all readers.

☞ Since Sputnik went into orbit in 1959, Soviet cosmonauts have logged more than twice the flight time of American astronauts.

Because most American-published children's books focus primarily on NASA's work, share the October 1986 *National Geographic* magazine to help youngsters appreciate how dramatic is the progress of "Soviets in Space."

FINDING OUT ABOUT ROCKETS AND SPACEFLIGHT
Lynn Myring
Usborne, 1982
Full-color illustrations
[p, i] 72 pages

This attractive introduction provides beginning facts to very young readers and older reluctant ones. The style and format will attract both.

DRAWING SPACESHIPS AND OTHER SPACECRAFT
Don Bolognese
Watts, 1982
B/w illustrations by the author
[i, j] 64 pages

Clearly illustrating each step, the author/artist offers young artists excellent suggestions on how to achieve three-dimensional effects when sketching space vehicles and crews.

SATELLITES & SPACE STATIONS
Moira Butterfield
Usborne, 1985
Full-color illustrations
[i, j] 48 pages

This is the best-illustrated description I've seen of American and Soviet satellites and space stations. Ms. Butterfield reviews current and projected uses—from simple relay stations to sophisticated science labs, permanent factory sites, and wayside stops for space travelers.

SPACE CHALLENGER
Jim Haskins and Kathleen Benson
Carolrhoda, 1984
B/w and full-color photographs
[i, j] 56 pages

Guion S. Bluford ignored high school counselors, who suggested he learn a mechanical trade. He entered college, earned his wings in the Air Force ROTC, went on to earn a Ph.D. in aerospace engineering, and in 1983 became the first black American in space.

CHRISTA McAULIFFE
Charlene Billings
Enslow, 1986
[i, j] 64 pages

This warm portrait highlights the qualities that led to Ms. McAuliffe's entrance into the teacher-in-space program. It also offers youngsters insight into how astronauts train and prepare for work on the shuttle. In her final chapter, the author discusses the country's reaction to the Challenger tragedy and Christa's legacy.

NATIONAL GEOGRAPHIC PICTURE ATLAS OF OUR UNIVERSE
Roy A. Gallant
National Geographic, 1986
Full-color photographs, drawings, diagrams, maps, and charts
[p, i, j] 284 pages

This belongs in every elementary and junior high school library and the home of seriously star-struck youngsters. The oversize (11 x 11"), lavishly illustrated book covers a broad spectrum, from a 4,000-year-old Egyptian sun myth to the shuttle disaster and life in space settlements.

☞ Stop! Don't throw out those empty plastic bottles. Give them to your children along with *The Inter-Planetary Toy Book* (Macmillan) and a few other easy-to-get supplies author J. Alan Williams recommends. Step back and watch. A space city will appear with shampoo speedsters and all-terrain cola cargo carriers staffed with little green people on runabouts and bionic beasties. Encourage your kids to become author/actors after they've built their city and bring everything to life with fact and fancy-filled dramatizations of space travel.

ASTRONOMY ENCYCLOPEDIA
Frances M. Clapham and Ron Taylor, eds.
Rand McNally, 1984
Full-color and b/w photographs, illustrations, diagrams
[i, j] 144 pages

Perfect for a home reference library: the breadth of coverage of this simply written text makes this the best general book on astronomy and space exploration I've found in the $10 price range. A variety of enhancing photographs, an 11-page dictionary of terms, and an index complete the package.

Trains

TRAINS
Byron Barton
Crowell, 1986
Full-color illustrations by the author
[p] 32 pages

The author-artist's boldly outlined, brightly colored drawings are perfect for preschoolers. His spare commentary is just enough to introduce them to trains and what they carry. The companion books *Boats, Airplanes,* and *Trucks* are similarly appropriate for petite perusers, and sized at 7 x 6″, are just right for little hands.

TRAINS
Gail Gibbons
Holiday House, 1987
Full-color illustrations by the author
[p] 32 pages

Though simply written for primary-graders, this picture book provides considerable detail about passenger and freight trains and the wide variety of cargo they carry.

☞ Have your children locate a local model railroad club (if not listed in the Yellow Pages, model toy store owners know how to reach them) and phone for permission to visit when the trains are in action. Read aloud excerpts from Ron Hollander's history of the Lionel Electric Train Company, *All Aboard* (Workman). Then turn to Harvey Weiss's *How to Run a Railroad* (Crowell) for just about everything you need to know to enjoy model trains and construct their "habitats."

THE BIG BOOK OF REAL TRAINS
Walter Retan
Grosset, 1987
Full-color illustrations by Richard Courtney
[p, i] 48 pages

This 9 x 12 ″ book explores the evolution of rail travel from horse-drawn carts to bullet trains. It also presents nine types of freight cars, an explanation of freight yard operations, and a view of passenger service that includes rapid transit systems.

☞ You can help children appreciate that all progress is relative. When talking trains, for instance, point out that the locomotives that carried new immigrants forward reversed the fortunes of Native Americans. American Indians were helpless against the railroad's intrusion and decimation of their homelands. They lost the war, but on August 8, 1867, they did win one battle: Cheyennes derailed a Union Pacific freight train. Paul Goble's *Death of the Iron Horse* (Bradbury) is loosely based upon that incident and it's a bit of history worth sharing. Read aloud his beautifully illustrated retelling of a futile but courageous act.

TRAIN WHISTLES
Helen Roney Sattler
Lothrop, 1985
Full-color illustrations by Giulio Maestro
[p] 32 pages

When an engineer blows the whistle, perk up your ears! Two longs, a short, and a long and watch out!—the train is approaching a crossing. Two shorts and it's off again. Ms. Sattler's explanations will help young children understand what train toots tell.

**TRAIN TALK: GUIDE TO LIGHTS,
HAND SIGNALS AND WHISTLES**
Roger Yepson
Pantheon, 1983
B/w illustrations
[i, j] 96 pages

In addition to using whistles, railroad people communicate with markings, hand signals, lights, and other codes. This fine guide clears away the mystery of the many languages of railroading and its special terms.

☞ When talking trains, share Chris Van Allsberg's *The Polar Express* (Houghton). Though it's about a Christmas train ride, it's an any-season classic for all children.

ABOARD A STEAM LOCOMOTIVE
Huck Scarry
Prentice, 1987
B/w illustrations by the author
[i, j] 68 pages

Satisfying a childhood dream, the author-artist tracked down coal-fired steam engines in the U.S. and Europe. His drawings illustrate, more clearly than photographs, the locomotives' ingenious mechanisms, as well as steam-train development from James Watt's 1769 original to its heyday earlier in this century.

Besides train buffs naturally attracted to the title, incipient and seasoned artists, engineers, writers, inventors, historians, and others will be held spellbound by Mr. Scarry's sketchbook-journal. A book for all reasons, it reflects the intelligence, insatiable curiosity, and sense of the aesthetic I wish every child could experience and be influenced by.

☞ Take children back in time and show them what riding the rails was like when steam trains were *the* way to travel. Share E. Boyd Smith's *The Railroad Book* (Houghton), originally published more than seventy years ago. Suggest youngsters interview parents or grandparents for their memories of train trips.

Trucks

TRUCK
Donald Crews
Greenwillow, 1980; Puffin, 1985
Full-color illustrations by the author
[p] 32 pages

With bright-yellow horns perched atop the cab, exhaust pipe puffing diesel fumes, and boldly painted white-on-red letters, a truck transports tricycles from pickup to delivery without a hitch. Stylized graphics reduce the highway, its travelers, and surroundings to their simplest forms.

☞ Joe Mathieu takes very young readers behind the scenes of a delivery like the one portrayed above. Crisply detailed illustrations in his *Big Joe's Trailer Truck* (Random House, 1974) trace loads from dispatcher's office to final delivery.

TRUCKS
Byron Barton
Crowell, 1986

TRUCKS
Gail Gibbons
Harper, 1981; Trophy, 1985
Full-color illustrations by the author
[p] 32 pages

Mr. Barton's simple, bold graphics and Ms. Gibbons's detailed, fine-line drawings nicely complement one another. Both will excite youngsters about the vehicles that push, pull, lift, load, dump, drag, and deliver just about everything and anything.

TRUCKS OF EVERY SORT
Ken Robbins
Crown (both) 1981
B/w photographs by the author
[p, i] 48 pages

Readers will find intriguing front, side, and close-up views of eighteen multi-wheelers. They begin with a funnel-shaped, trap-doored, conveyor-belted truck that delivers potatoes and end with an elevator platform truck that transports furniture.

☞ In the introduction to his book, Mr. Robbins recalls counting the different kinds of products trucks carried by his home one day. During an outing or ride anywhere, see if your youngsters can collect an alphabetful of items on the trucks that pass by.

MONSTER TRUCKS AND OTHER
GIANT MACHINES ON WHEELS
Jerry Bushey
Carolrhoda, 1985
Full-color photographs
[p, i] 32 pages

One of the dozen giants that will elicit gasps from young fantastic-fact fans is a 335,000-pound, 53-foot-long front-end loader with tires that are almost 12 feet tall and cost $45,000 each.

Wolves, Coyotes, and Foxes

Wolves play an important role in the balance of nature and merit respect and admiration, not the fear or destruction encouraged by classic children's tales. Help children fix the "big, bad wolf" firmly in fiction's realm. Open their eyes to the facts: healthy, wild wolves pose no danger to humans and are extremely afraid of us.

WOLVES
John Bonnett Wexo
Wildlife, 1984 (paperback only)
Full-color photographs and illustrations
[i] 20 pages

Wolves are among the best animal parents in the world. They usually live in close family groups within a clearly established, purposeful hierarchy, cooperatively hunting and rearing their young. These and other truths about the intelligent creatures, as well as their physical and social attributes, are clearly delineated.

THE WOLF PACK: TRACKING WOLVES IN THE WILD
Sylvia A. Johnson and Alice Aamodt
Lerner (both), 1985
Full-color photographs
[i, j] 96 pages

With smoothly flowing text, highlighted by vivid photographs, the coauthors elaborate upon wolves and their packs' structure, growth, and change. The last chapter focuses on the methods scientists use to track and study wolves in the wild and in captive packs. One of those scientists is wolf biologist Dr. L. David Mech, the subject of Laurence Pringle's *Wolfman* (below).

WOLFMAN: EXPLORING THE WORLD OF WOLVES
Laurence Pringle
Scribner's, 1983
B/w photographs
[i, j] 80 pages

Much of what little we know about wolf ecology was discovered because of projects Dr. L. David Mech designed, conducted, or supervised. This book introduces the man children will probably read about whenever the subject is wolves. (He's the first person Mr. Wexo thanked in his book on wolves; see above.) It will open young readers' eyes to scientific research in the field, a process that takes years of dedicated perseverance.

WONDERS OF COYOTES
Sigmund A. Lavine
Dodd, 1984
B/w photographs and illustrations
[i, j] 80 pages

Among other subjects, the author describes the coyote's history (they're found only on the North American continent), physical characteristics (probably the most musical land mammal, with a howling range of at least two octaves), diet (almost anything animal or vegetable), and ecological niche (they control small rodent populations).

TWO COYOTES
Carol Carrick
Clarion, 1982
Full-color illustrations by Donald Carrick
[p, i] 32 pages

This picture book is a realistic portrayal of a pregnant female and her mate as they struggle to survive the winter in the New England wild.

☞ Have youngsters compare (in fact and fiction) the wolf to the coyote, its closest wild relative in North America. They'll find the contrasts fascinating. The wolf has become an endangered species, for example, while the coyote has increased its range. And, unlike those of the wolf, most coyote tales reflect its real intelligence and amazing adaptability. Suggest children also read John Bierhorst's *Doctor Coyote* (Macmillan), a retelling of tales created by Aztec storytellers around Aesop's fables, which Spaniards brought them four hundred years ago.

WATCHING FOXES
Jim Arnosky
Lothrop, 1985
Full-color illustrations by the author
[p] 24 pages

Captivating drawings reveal the playfulness of a litter of red foxes the author/artist observed scampering in front of their den one spring.

ON THE TRAIL OF THE FOX
Claudia Schnieper
Carolrhoda, 1986
Full-color photographs by Felix Labhardt
[i, j] 48 pages

The photographer and writer focus on a vixen, her pups (they're also called kits, cubs, or whelps), and their growth to maturity. Foxes are so difficult to track, there is much yet to learn about them. These shots would have been almost impossible to get if not made through a sliding hatch in the back of a man-made den on a game preserve.

☞ What could be better than *Fox Went Out on a Chilly Night* (Doubleday) when watching or on the trail of foxes? Use Peter Spier's wonderfully illustrated version. The melody is included, for a class or family sing-along around the piano. Tejima's bold woodcuts in *Fox's Dream* (Philomel) set a different mood for a fox out on a chilly night. Link it to Mr. Spier's.

REYNARD: THE STORY OF A FOX RETURNED TO THE WILD
Alice Mills Leighner
B/w photographs by the author
[p, i] 48 pages

This is the true story of Reynard, a red fox pup, who was found by the side of a highway, raised by wildlife volunteers, and released when he was old enough to care for himself, wild and free.

Wordless Picture Books

These are the books that invite conversation—a major ingredient in the recipe for good readers. Conversation between you and your children and your children and themselves! I loved to overhear David "reading" aloud as he turned the pages and repeated what I'd said when we looked at books together. When you peruse these pages, talk with your youngsters. Have them name the characters, create dialogue, provide background, and invent incidents that aren't illustrated: ask them what took place before the story began and after it ended or between the scenes depicted. Talk about the sequence of events: what came first? And then what? Read the book from back to front and have youngsters recall what happened in reverse. Discuss sensations: the smells (burning toast in *Sunshine*), the sounds (swings clanking in the wind in *Peter Spier's Rain*), and the textures (painted feet in *Hanimals*) you'd both experience if you were inside the images the artist drew.

PETER SPIER'S RAIN
Peter Spier
Doubleday (both), 1982
Full-color illustrations by the author
[p, i] 40 pages

A booted, slickered, and umbrellaed brother and sister sloshingly explore their neighborhood in the rain. As the downpour increases, they run home, take a hot bath, play with their toys, scramble into bed, and awaken to a bright, sunny morning.

☞ Show youngsters how to create the feeling of a rainstorm at whim. Lead the way and have them follow as you 1) rub the palms of your hands together to start the wind rustling in the leaves, 2) snap your fingers slowly, then quickly, to bring on the rain drops, 3) slap your thighs with increasing speed to strengthen and increase the downpour, 4) stamp your feet to add thunder to the downpour, then 5) slowly reverse the procedure to end the rain and return to the quiet of sunny skies.

PETER SPIER'S CHRISTMAS!
Peter Spier
Doubleday, 1983
Full-color illustrations by the author
[p, i] 40 pages

Follow a family of five as they prepare for, enjoy, and clean up after Christmas Day. Mr. Spier portrays a crisp, snowy New England December, the festive seasonal spirit, and family warmth.

☞ Take Peter Spier's *Dreams* (Doubleday) along on your next picnic. After you and your children see what the youngsters in his pictures saw when they looked up at the clouds, stretch out on the grass with your little ones and let your imagination reshape the puffs of white above your heads.

SUNSHINE
Jan Ormerod
Lothrop, 1981, 1982; Puffin, 1984

MOONLIGHT
Jan Ormerod
Lothrop, 1982; Puffin, 1984
Full-color illustrations by the author
[p] each 32 pages

Whether tinted with the rich hues of morning sun or cool ones of night lights, Ms. Ormerod's images reflect the warmth and security of a loving family. These are for sharing anytime of day. In the first, a preschooler awakens before her parents, breakfasts with Dad, dresses herself, and leaves for nursery school with Mom. In the second, unable to sleep after the bedtime story and requisite glass of water, she reads with her mom in the living room until everyone is tired enough to retire for the night.

☞ In each of their books, Ms. Ormerod and Mr. Spier varied both the size of their illustrations and the page design. Discuss how that affects the "telling" of the story. Let your children experiment with these design techniques when they put together written reports or write their own books.

ANNO'S JOURNEY
Mitsumasa Anno
Philomel (both), 1981
Full-color illustrations by the author
[i, j] 48 pages

Armchair travelers who follow the blue-capped fellow on his many sojourns—there are three others, *Anno's Britain, Anno's U.S.A.,* and *Anno's Italy* (all Philomel)—will come upon people, places, and creatures, real and imaginary, where they least expect them. Cinderella, behind the Fountain of Trevi in Rome, for example, and the Giant, Jack, and their magic hen at Stonehenge. One youngster told me reading this was like playing hide-and-seek.

IN MY GARDEN
Ermanno Cristini and Luigi Puricelli
Picture Book Studio (both), 1985
Full-color illustrations by the authors
[p] 28 pages

Tour a backyard and discover the world as beetles in the begonias might view it—from ground level. In a similar fashion, youngsters can walk *In the Pond* and *In the Woods* (Picture Book) and meet marsh life at, above, and below the water line, and the forest at ground level. All three books are marvelous jumping-off places for flights of fact and fancy from unusual perspectives.

☞ In the style of *In My Garden,* suggest your children draw a picture of their room as seen by a bug in the rug or a fly on the wall.

HANIMALS
Mario Mariolti
Green Tiger, 1982 (paperback only)
Full-color photographs by Roberto Marchiori
[all ages] 40 pages

With a little bit of paint and a great deal of imagination, the author ingeniously transformed his arms and hands into a menagerie of ducks, elephants, octopuses, and other creatures. In *Humages* and *Humands* (also Green Tiger), his face and feet also become "canvas" for ingenious images.

☞ When children have finished reading about creatures of their choice, have them share what they've learned via a Hanimal act. A youngster who's finished *Daisy Rothschild* (Doubleday), for example, can transform an arm into the giraffe and explain how she came to live with author Betty Leslie-Melville.

Words

Before students enter the room, I write "Brain Bracers" on the board to stump them—a petite puzzle, tongue twister, regular riddle, or clever conundrum—anything to challenge children as they charge into class. The daily dares quickly involve kids, set a good mood, and often keep them and their friends purposefully engaged in spare moments the rest of the day.

A CHILD'S ALMANAC OF WORDS AT PLAY
Willard Espy
Crown (both), 1982
B/w illustrations by Bruce Cayard
[i] 256 pages

Here is a leap year's worth of just about every kind of imaginative configuration of words and letters: puns, palindromes, puzzles, anagrams, nonsense poems, spoonerisms, limericks, and more, arranged one per day.

BUSY BUZZING BUMBLEBEES
Alvin Schwartz
Harper (both), 1982
Illustrations by Kathie Abrams
[i] 64 pages

Hand these tongue tanglers to your kids and observe as they become breathless while unabashedly and unabatedly bellowing, bantering about, or otherwise broadcasting their own carefully crafted, terrifically tantalizing tongue twisters. Phew!

WORDWORKS: WHY THE ALPHABET
IS A KID'S BEST FRIEND
Cathryn Berger Kaye
Little (both), 1985
B/w illustrations by Martha Weston
[i] 128 pages

Excellent activities in this "Brown Paper School" book keep children enthusiastically engaged in learning about, playing around with, and using words at home and in school.

☞ Herbert Kohl's 298-page *A Book of Puzzlements* (Schocken, both) is a superb resource for "play and invention with language." Parents will find a wealth of fun and games with words that can begin when children are learning the alphabet and last into adulthood. Teachers will cherish it as an invaluable source of language arts activities.

EASY AS PIE: A GUESSING GAME OF SAYINGS
Marcia and Michael Folsom
Clarion (both), 1985
Full-color illustrations by Jack Kent
[p] 64 pages

The Folsom's alphabetized collection of sayings is designed as a game: readers must turn the page to see the last word of each phrase, so they've time to guess what it will be. The humorous illustrations are as right as rain.

QUICK AS A CRICKET
Audrey Wood
Child's Play, 1982
Full-color illustrations by Don Wood
[p] 32 pages

JAFTA
Hugh Lewin
Carolrhoda, 1981
Brown-and-black illustrations by Lisa Kopper
[p] 24 pages

Two boys compare themselves to the creatures they most resemble. Ms. Wood's youngster sees himself, for example, as small as an ant and as large as a whale. Jafta likens himself to animals native to his African homeland.

☞ With the books in the above trio as models, have youngsters collect favorite phrases from parents, grandparents, or neighbors and create modern sayings of their own. Ask them to decide what creatures they most resemble when cranky, crafty, curious, creative, or acting out any other characteristic.

EIGHT ATE: A FEAST OF HOMONYM RIDDLES
Marvin Terban
Clarion (both), 1982
Illustrations by Giulio Maestro
[p] 64 pages

HINK PINK BOOK
Marilyn Burns
Little, 1981
B/w illustrations by Martha Weston
[i] 48 pages

What's an obese feline, an unhappy father, and a riddle answered by two rhyming, single-syllable words? A fat cat, a sad dad, and a hink pink (or homonym riddle), respectively. Enjoy.

WHAT'S A FRANK FRANK?
TOO HOT TO HOOT: FUNNY PALINDROME RIDDLES
Marvin Terban
Clarion (both), 1984; 1985
Two-color illustrations by Giulio Maestro
[i] both 64 pages

In *What's a Frank Frank?* readers consider such homograph puzzlers as a "swell swell," "sole sole," and "meal meal." In *Too Hot...*, they peruse palindromes—words or phrases that can be read forward and backward—from "mom" and "pop" to "No misses ordered roses, Simon" and "Marge lets Norah see Sharon's telegram."

☞ When they've created original homograph puzzlers or palindromes, let children pin them up on bulletin boards: one marked "PAPER with PAPER," the other "REPaPER."

TAKE MY WORD FOR IT
Vernon Pizer
Dodd, 1981
[i] 128 pages

Acrobat Jules Leotard wanted to attract attention and top billing, so he introduced the flying trapeze into the circus repertoire. Clad in a unique, skin-tight costume, he executed the world's first aerial somersault. Leotard and other figures, from Derrick to Diddler, are long gone but their names live on as eponyms, words derived from people's names. Readers will find some of them here.

MARMS IN THE MARMALADE
Diana Morley
Carolrhoda, 1984
Illustrations by Kathy Rogers
[p] 24 pages

PENguins don't write with pens, you won't find fur on a FURnace, nor are DENTists covered with dents—except in this book. Children of all ages will find the unusual view of words delightful.

☞ Use *Marms . . .* to combine etymology with creative writing. For example, after they discover that the word *dentist* derives from the French word for tooth, children can write a silly story that shows *dentist* "really" evolved from the impression, or dent, left in the first jaw from which a tooth was pulled. Or from all the teeth someone once found in a lion's den.

A CACHE OF JEWELS AND OTHER COLLECTIVE NOUNS
Ruth Heller
Putnam, 1987
Full-color illustrations by the author
[p] 48 pages

BEASTS BY THE BUNCHES
A. Mifflin Lowe
Doubleday, 1987
Full-color illustrations by Susan J. Harrison
[i] 48 pages

Enlarge your vocabulary with poetic introductions to things by the group. Ms. Heller's oversize picture book (about 10″ square) is perfect to hold up for a group of children to see. Mr. Lowe's warm and witty verses on knots of toads, parliaments of owls, and other such collections are for older readers.

FUNNY SIDE UP!
Mike Thaler
Scholastic, 1985 (paperback only)
B/w illustrations by the author
[p] 64 pages

Whet youngsters' appetite for and appreciation of witty wordplay with this pun-master's practical paperback on how to write riddles. His sure-fire formula will make kids voluntarily compile and syllabicate word lists and search through the dictionary, the thesaurus, and encyclopedias for new words and ideas to create riddles à la Thaler.

☞ Join Giulio Maestro for a *Riddle Romp* (Clarion) with *Razzle-Dazzle Riddles* (Clarion); *Paws* (Archway) a moment with *Oinkers Away!* or any of Mike Thaler's other books; fool around with Katy Hall's and Lisa Eisenberg's *Fishy Riddles* (Dial); savor Caroline Anne Levine's *Silly School Riddles* (Whitman); "space out" on Joanne E. Bernstein's and Paul Cohen's *Unidentified Flying Riddles* (Whitman) or howl over their *Happy Holiday Riddles to You* (Whitman); zero in on Joseph Rosenbloom's *Zaniest Riddle Book in the World* (Sterling); or enjoy *Unriddling* (Lippincott), Alvin Schwartz's puzzles from American folklore. To mention but a few of the funny books that have tickled my kids' ribs.

HOW TO WRITE A GREAT SCHOOL REPORT
HOW TO WRITE A TERM PAPER
Elizabeth James and Carol Barkin
Lothrop (both), 1983
[i] 80 pages
Lothrop (both), 1980
[j] 96 pages

These writing guides are a pleasure to read and learn by. Each contains sound advice with appropriate examples on choosing a topic, gathering and recording information, arranging notes, and constructing a unified paper. Best of all, the authors practice what they preach: their books are logically organized and convey information in a comfortable, easy-to-understand style.

SPELLING BEE SPELLER
Sam Chang
Hondale, 1984 (paperback only)
[i] 3 volumes, each 240 pages

The best children's self-study guide I've seen is in these three volumes. Each contains one hundred groups of ten words arranged in order of increasing difficulty. The phonetic respelling(s), definition, and sentence for each word in the group precede their correct spellings.

Zoos

UNDERSTANDING ZOO ANIMALS
Rosamund Kidman Cox
Usborne (both), 1980
Full-color illustrations and photographs
[p] 32 pages

Excellent suggestions on preparing for a visit to the zoo precede a group of projects children can conduct while there. The author also discusses such topics as special enclosures for wild animals and behind-the-scenes zoo activities.

A CHILDREN'S ZOO
Tana Hoban
Greenwillow, 1985; Mulberry, 1987
Full-color photographs by the author
[p] 24 pages

This beautifully designed book of eleven animal portraits is just right for a preschooler's book-souvenir of a trip to the zoo. On the last page, the author tells where each animal lives and what it eats.

ZOOS
Karen Jacobsen
Children's, 1982 (paperback only)
Full-color photographs
[p] 48 pages

There is a surprising amount of information in this brief text on the attributes and diets of zoo animals. Primary-graders learning basic research/reporting skills will find the table of contents, glossary, and index in this interesting book useful.

BLIZZARD AT THE ZOO
Roger Bahr
Lothrop, 1982
Full-color illustrations by Consuelo Joerns
[p] 32 pages

During one of the worst blizzards in American history, zookeepers in Buffalo, New York, had to rescue water birds from a fast-freezing lake, deliver food on toboggans and sleds, and lure polar bears away from the ice-encrusted moats to their more secure enclosures—in addition to their regular chores!

MAYBE YOU BELONG IN A ZOO!
ZOO AND AQUARIUM CAREERS
Karen O'Connor
Dodd, 1982
B/w photographs by Douglas K. Emry
[i] 160 pages

The author isn't poking fun at her readers. She has written a lively description of the responsibilities, educational requirements, and salary ranges for professional zoo employees, while recounting interesting experiences many of them shared with her.

CAREERS AT A ZOO
Mark Lerner
Lerner, 1980
Full-color photographs by Milton J. Blumenfeld
[p, i] 36 pages

Perfect for younger readers. Full-page photographs alternate with single-page descriptions for each of fifteen zoo jobs. A letter from the director of the Minnesota Zoological Gardens, in Apple Valley, Minnesota, where the photographs were taken, concludes the book and explains the modern zoo's emphasis on conservation and preservation of wildlife.

12

How to Use the Quick-Link Index

This index will make it easy for you to find books linked by subject matter—even when the subject is not obvious from the title. For example, take the title *Try These on for Size, Melody.* Would you guess that it was about shoeing a horse? Probably not. Yet, if you were interested in horses, the Quick-Link Index would bring you right to this book with a listing under HORSES.

Use the index creatively. Scan it and let serendipity work for you. If you are interested in FOOD and the index links you to *A Medieval Feast,* be prepared to branch out into hosting a meal fit for a king. When you can't recall the title of a book you remember reading about, try finding it in this Quick-Link Index—you'll save time, *and* you may trip over a related book of interest.

PRACTICAL, NOT SCHOLARLY

Because I know MULTICULTURAL is a subject of special interest to teachers and librarians, I've included it, but it isn't practical to cross-link to every possible term you might search for. This is not a scholar's index. It has been developed to suit my teacher's instincts and to satisfy the needs of parents and other educators working with children. You'll find it guides you into strange areas where you'll be presented with unexpected learning opportunities. It is meant to be practical—to make fast connections.

Some Quick-Link Index categories are particularly useful: BIOG-RAPHY and its cross-references leads to more than 50 books about real people; FICTION pulls together the five dozen non-nonfiction books that are scattered throughout *Eyeopeners!;* and SPORTS includes titles covering a variety of non-traditional activities. Sadly, space constraints have prevented me from listing many other wonderful books that deserve recommendations throughout the Guide.

HOW TO MAKE MORE LINKS

To find books you might otherwise miss, take advantage of the suggested "see also" cross-references. For instance, FOOD refers you to COOKING, MILK, and NUTRITION. DINOSAURS sends you to PREHIS-TORIC, a category which includes books about museum artifacts, crocodiles, and an unearthed village in the Orkney Islands. And HISTORY will lead you to alphabets, bicycles, cowboys, robots, and witches, among others—subjects of high interest to children.

Explore general categories as well as individual items within them. For example, when looking for books on HORSES, check ANIMALS and you'll discover *Farm Babies* and *Mammals and Their Milk.* In fact, the only books in the lengthy ANIMALS list are those without specific animal names in their titles. BEARS, CATS, DINOSAURS, DOGS, SNAKES, and other species have listings of their own.

To keep matters simple and to save space, there are few listings under BIOLOGY, ARCHEOLOGY, GEOLOGY, or other "ology" terms. Look instead under ANIMALS, PLANTS, MUMMIES, or ROCKS—the terms children are more likely to use.

SEARCHING FOR ACTIVITIES

Titles containing activities of a scientific nature are listed under SCI-ENCE EXPERIMENTS in the Quick-Link Index. Those titles coded with an asterisk (*) contain instructions for other activities, most of them of an arts and crafts nature. You may wish to scan the index for asterisks if you are confronted with restless children on a rainy day.

The Quick-Link Index

Notes

1. Speech at National Council of Teachers of English conference, Washington, D.C., November 1982.
2. Speech at Society of Children's Book Writers conference, Los Angeles, August 1981.
3. Leonard Wood, "Who Buys Children's Books?" *Publishers Weekly,* Feb. 26, 1988, p. 112.
4. *Children's Books: Awards & Prizes.* New York: The Children's Book Council, 1986, pp. 1–95.
5. Margery Fisher, *Matters of Fact: Aspects of Nonfiction for Children.* New York: Crowell, 1972. Jo Carr, *Beyond Fact: Nonfiction for Children and Young People.* Chicago: American Library Association, 1982.
6. Jim Trelease, *The Read-Aloud Handbook.* New York: Penguin, 1982; rev. ed., 1985.
7. *The Crises in California School Libraries.* Sacramento: California State Department of Education, 1987, p. 2.
8. *Foxfire,* vols. 1–9, Eliot Wigginton, ed. Rabun Gap, Ga.: Foxfire Press, 1972–86. Neighbors and relatives were interviewed by the students of Mr. Wigginton, an English teacher in Rabun Gap, about everything from midwifery to moonshining, candy pullin' to corn shucking.

9. The Children's Book Council, Inc., P.O. Box 706, 67 Irving Place, New York, NY 10276, Attn: *Features.* There is a one-time-only fee of $25.
10. Allan Ahlberg, *Please Mrs Butler.* London: Puffin UK, 1983.
11. "The Road from Home: The Story of an Armenian Girl," *The Horn Book,* vol. LVI, no. 1 (February 1980): 97–99.
12. *The Crises in California School Libraries.* Sacramento: California State Department of Education, 1987, p. 3.
13. "The Book," *Washington Post Book World,* vol. 9, no. 14 (December 30, 1979).
14. Susan Ohanian, *The Atlantic,* September 1987.

Bibliography

Appraisal: Science Books for Young People. Boston University School of Education and The New England Roundtable of Children's Literature. Boston, quarterly.

Bernstein, Joanne E. *Books to Help Children Cope with Separation and Loss,* 2nd ed. New York: Bowker, 1983.

Bulletin of the Center for Children's Books. University of Chicago Press, monthly except August.

Carr, Jo. *Beyond Fact: Nonfiction for Children and Young People.* Chicago: American Library Association, 1982.

Children's Books: Awards & Prizes. New York: The Children's Book Council, 1986.

Children's Choices. International Reading Association and Children's Book Council, Chicago, annual annotated listing.

The Crises in California School Libraries. Sacramento: California State Department of Education, 1987.

Fisher, Margery. *Matters of Fact: Aspects of Nonfiction for Children.* New York: Crowell, 1972.

The Five Owls. Minneapolis: The Five Owls, bimonthly.

Foxfire, vols. 1–9, Eliot Wigginton, ed. Rabun Gap, Ga.: Foxfire Press, 1972–86.

Friedberg, Joan Brest, June B. Mullins, and Adelaide Weir Sukiennik. *Accept Me as I Am: Best Books of Juvenile Nonfiction on Impairments and Disabilities.* New York: Bowker, 1985.

Graves, Ruth, ed. *The Reading Is Fundamental Guide to Encouraging Young Readers.* Garden City, N.Y.: Doubleday, 1987.

Hearne, Betsy. *Choosing Books for Children*. New York: Laurel, 1981.

The Horn Book. Boston: The Horn Book, bimonthly.

Huck, Charlotte. *Children's Literature in the Elementary School*. New York: Holt, Rinehart and Winston, 1987.

"Informational Books for Children," *The Lion and the Unicorn: A Critical Journal of Children's Literature*. Baltimore: John Hopkins University Press, vol. 6, 1982.

Kimmel, Margaret M., and Elizabeth Segal. *For Reading Out Loud! A Guide to Sharing Books with Children*. New York: Delacorte, 1983.

Kirkus Reviews. New York: The Kirkus Service, Inc., semi-monthly.

The Kobrin Letter: Concerning Children's Books about Real People, Places and Things. Palo Alto, Calif.: Dr. Beverly Kobrin, eight issues per year.

Kohl, Herbert. *On Teaching*. New York: Schocken, 1976.

Kohn, Rita, Catherine Hanley Lutholtz, and Dennis Kelly. *My Country 'Tis of Me: Helping Children Discover Citizenship Through Cultural Heritage*. Jefferson, N.C.: McFarland, 1988.

Larrick, Nancy. *A Parent's Guide to Children's Reading*. New York: Bantam, 1982.

LeShan, Eda. *The Conspiracy Against Childhood*. New York: Atheneum, 1980.

Lieberman, Jan. *TNT: Tips & Titles of Books: Grades K–8*. Santa Clara, Calif.: Santa Clara University, three issues per year.

The Museum of Science and Industry Basic List of Children's Science Books. Chicago: American Library Association, 1987.

Notable Children's Books. Chicago: Association for Library Service to Children, American Library Association, listed annually.

"Notable Children's Trade Books in the Field of Social Studies," *Social Education*. New York, National Council for the Social Studies and Children's Book Council, listed annually.

Outstanding Science Trade Books for Children. New York, National Science Teachers Association and Children's Book Council, listed annually.

Parents' Choice. Newton, Mass.: Parents' Choice Foundation, quarterly.

Parsons, Cynthia. *Seeds: Some Good Ways to Improve Our Schools*. Santa Barbara, Calif.: Woodbridge Press, 1985.

Publishers Weekly. New York: Bowker.

The Reading Teacher. Newark, Del.: International Reading Association, eight issues per year.

Rochman, Hazel. *Tales of Love and Terror: Booktalking the Classics, Old and New*. Chicago: American Library Association, 1987.

Roginsky, Jim. *Behind the Covers: Interviews with Authors and Illustrators of Books for Children and Young Adults*. Littleton, Colo.: Libraries Unlimited, 1985.

School Library Journal. New York: Bowker, Monthly.

Science Books and Films. Washington, D.C.: American Association for the Advancement of Science, five issues per year.

Smith, Frank. *Insult to Intelligence*. New York: Arbor House, 1986.

Trelease, Jim. *The Read-Aloud Handbook,* rev. ed. New York: Penguin, 1985.

The Web: Wonderfully Exciting Books. Columbus, Ohio: College of Education, Ohio State University, quarterly.

Index of Authors, Illustrators, and Book Titles